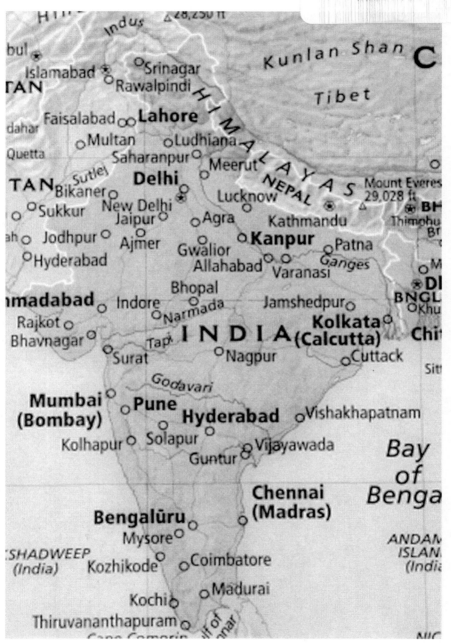

Bengalūru = Bangalore
Kochi= Cochin

For Ira
and
Josh, Rachael, Adam, Rachel, Aaron and Jordan

Contents

Acknowledgements

The seeds of this memoir were planted during my years as a graduate student at Spertus College in Chicago. I am especially thankful for the year I spent writing and rewriting my master's thesis under the watchful eye of Dr. Elliot Lefkovitz. After multiple rewrites, I learned that writing is a process with many twists and turns.

When I wrote a series of biographical essays on nineteenth- and twentieth-century American Jewish women, my desire to write became more pronounced. These articles were published in *Women Building Chicago 1790–1990: A Biographical Dictionary* (2001), *Jewish Women in America: An Historical Encyclopedia* (1997), and the Jewish Women's Archives online edition of *Jewish Women: A Comprehensive Encyclopedia*.

In the following years, ideas for different books—fiction and non-fiction, children's and adult—floated in and out of my consciousness. Although many of these topics held some promise, other commitments prevented me from pursuing my passion. Instead, I focused on a second passion—education. By studying at a graduate-level program at the University of Colorado at Boulder, I improved my teaching skills while continuing to enhance my writing. Dr. Ruben Donato, Dr. Brian Sevier, and Dr. Caroline McKinney encouraged my writing, while Dr. Diana Geisler made me keenly aware of how my Jewish background added a special layer to multicultural education.

My writing redemption occurred in an unexpected place: a trip to India and a blog that chronicled my unique adventure. My confidence was fueled by the positive comments I received from my American followers.

Using the blog as a starting point, along with e-mails, my private journal, my memories, and my family's recollections, I wrote *May This Be the Best Year of Your Life*. I realized that my story would resonate with individuals who contemplate living outside their comfort zones, and that my experiences could serve as a guide for others and a resource to help overcome challenges. This book is my way of sharing the lessons I learned, and taking others on my wild adventure.

The narrative provides my perspective on the events that occurred, while the dialogue is an abbreviated version of actual conversations that I had with numerous people. I tried my best to maintain the intent and integrity of the original conversations. In order to protect the privacy of the students in 5C, I have changed all of their names. Many of the adult names and some of the Indian institution names have also been modified.

Throughout this process, my husband, Ira, and my sons and their wives (Josh, Rachael, Adam, Rachel, Aaron, and Jordan) were by my side encouraging me to reach my goal. Each added a unique perspective to my story and acted as proofreaders at different points in time. Ira spent countless hours reading through most of my drafts, while Adam shared his editorial and writing expertise whenever possible. Josh and Rachael provided technical support for Indian-related matters. Jordan and Aaron assisted with social media. Without my family's patience and understanding, the completion of my memoir would not have been possible.

I received exceptional editorial assistance from Mike Zimmerman, Joe Kita, Eric Rinehimer, and Kimberly, an editor at CreateSpace. Mike read the first few chapters and provided some directions, while Joe identified my voice and the multiple threads I needed to weave together. Eric made me more aware of the mechanics of writing. Kimberly did the CreateSpace edit. I am grateful to Kim White and Wendy Kipfmiller O'Brien for designing a book cover for my website. Kim also created my original website. Jan Bear updated and revised my website after CreateSpace designed a new book cover.

A tremendous thank you goes to my prepublication reviewers, Rita Golden Gelman, Rabbi Bernard Gerson, Marsha Lee Berkman, Janet Ungless, Betsy Katz, and Abby Lerner who took time from their busy schedules to read my manuscript. The publication of my story would not be possible without the collective and dedicated effort of numerous people at CreateSpace. Working together, we created a new book cover, put the finishing touches on my manuscript, formatted the interior, and made marketing decisions.

My life was enriched by the places in India that I visited and the people I met. I am indebted to the students in 5C, who made me proud to be a teacher. The fall semester in that classroom confirmed a noteworthy passage from the Talmud: "Much I have learned from my teachers; even more from my friends; most of all from my students."

Deciding to Change Direction

1

"Josh, I need to get off the bus. Now!"

Maybe it's the tone in my voice, but Josh, my oldest son, gives in to my demands. We're somewhere near the outskirts of Delhi and the pain in my abdomen is close to unbearable. Nightfall is casting eerie shadows, but I can see a modern building with oversized windows and a large neon sign blinking "Haldiram's Restaurant." The minibus pulls off and parks in a rutted, debris-filled parking area.

Despite the gnawing pain, I jump out of my seat, bolt down the steps, and gallop through the parking lot with my husband, Ira, trailing. Inside, I race into the ladies' room and instinctively lean over the grubby toilet. I begin vomiting, keeping my head above the toilet as my internal temperature rises and my body shakes uncontrollably.

The relief that usually accompanies such a release is not on the horizon. I stagger back into the restaurant and slide into a plastic chair. Ira and Josh are waiting. I place the palms of my hands over my ears to muffle the noise. The whole room is spinning. "Just breathe. Just breathe," I keep telling myself. But the heavy aroma of Indian herbs and spices exacerbates my distress. I can't breathe normally.

Ira strokes the back of my neck, but I interrupt his overtures and dash back to the bathroom again…and again.

I forget about the others on the bus until my second son, Adam, taps me on the shoulder. Behind him I see his two taller brothers, Aaron and Jordan. I have no idea how long I've been in the restaurant, but their scrunched-up foreheads tell me all I need to know. I walk over to the counter and ask the clerk for two plastic bags. I place one inside the other and head back to the bus.

As the bus continues on its journey, Jordan, my youngest son, tries to make me smile. He points out a public bus that is jammed with people both inside and on the roof. It reminds me of a cartoon comic strip and I crack a faint smile.

My detour has done little to relieve the mounting discomfort in my body. I squirm back and forth in my seat as Ira holds my hand and utters a few words of comfort. I realize that the most confident man I know feels just as helpless in this Third World country as I do. After living on different continents for months, I draw comfort just being next to him.

More time passes. Perhaps it is an hour or is it only fifteen minutes. I can't tell.

I lean into the aisle and demand, "Josh, please take me to a hospital!"

Josh shrugs his shoulders. He is busy practicing the medieval Hebrew *piyyut* that he will be singing at his wedding, only three days away, and making calls regarding tonight's Thanksgiving dinner that his American friends are preparing. He dismisses my appeal and instead calls a gastroenterologist. The Indian doctor advises that I simply take antinausea pills and wait until morning. My fears escalate.

"Josh, you need to listen. I *need* to go now!"

But Josh just tells me to be patient. It has been months since I was back in the States, but I wish that I were there now. I would have the freedom to drive myself to a hospital and the comfort of knowing where to go.

We finally reach New Delhi after 8:30 p.m. The guard has closed the neighborhood gate for the night and won't allow the bus to take us to our small hotel, which is only a few blocks away. Residential areas throughout the city follow this practice of restricting vehicle access during specified hours. My frustration propels me out of the bus, onto the sidewalk.

"Oh Mom, you're so ridiculous," Josh yells from the doorway. "Get back on and wait for my friend to drive you to the hotel." I glare back at him but don't say a word. I am inconsolable. The emotional side of my brain struggles to cope with the nonstop, torturous pain that has taken over the rational part.

After countless surgeries, I can differentiate between levels of pain. And I can't fathom why everyone is ignoring my cries for help. I keep moving forward, but the pain slows me down and I stumble to the ground. Aaron, my third son, hops off the bus. I stare at his bearded oval face and look into his bold hazel eyes.

"Please help me."

Adam and Jordan step off the bus next. All three look at me with the same tearful eyes I saw when I was in the hospital for abdominal surgery years ago. I can see they understand but feel powerless. None of them knows how to find a reputable doctor or a modern, clean hospital. After touring India's Golden Triangle for just a few days, how would they know where to take me?

Defiantly, I shuffle back to our small hotel, the Ahuja Residency. I limp up two flights of stairs to our tiny guest room, using the banister to maintain my balance and pull up my weight. I enter the room and collapse onto the bed. I look up and see Ira, the boys, and Adam's fiancée, Rachel, hovering over me.

Below me, on the ground floor, Josh's American friends are eating Thanksgiving dinner. I need to be by myself, so I order everyone to go downstairs. Despite their pleas to stay by my side, my sons, Rachel, and Ira finally leave for dinner. Ira eventually returns. I can only guess that he ate.

"Ira, please find me a doctor," I say as the tears flow down my cheeks. "I'm scared."

Ira seems less self-assured than the man I married over thirty-five years ago. He abruptly tells me to wait for Josh. But I can't wait. I storm out of the room and totter down the winding marble staircase. I look over my shoulder and Ira is not there.

Why is everyone so unresponsive? It's like they're all stuck in quicksand.

When I arrive at the bottom of the steps, I'm covered in sweat. Suddenly I see Rachael, Josh's soon-to-be wife, pull up in her car. I drag my feet toward the driveway.

"Please…please take me to a doctor now!"

Josh runs out from the party and sees me pleading.

"Where's Dad?" Josh asks.

"He's up in the room. I can't stand the pain."

"Should I get him?"

"I can't wait. Let's go."

I crawl into the backseat and lie down. I flinch as each stabbing pain strikes. Rachael wants to stop at a closer hospital, but Josh insists on taking me to the one that his doctor recommended. As we drive up to the emergency room, I see a modern building with large windows that reflect in the light of the moon. I feel a sense of relief.

At the entrance, an attendant helps me into a wheelchair and pushes me into the stark, empty ER. Only one other patient is visible. Unlike an American hospital, which requires mounds of completed paperwork before admission, this hospital offers immediate admission and puts me onto a narrow, old-fashioned bed—a crank moves it up and down. When I roll onto my right side, I see streaks of dried blood splattered on the cream-colored wall. A nurse makes several attempts to start an intravenous line to rehydrate my parched body.

The doctor on call, a young Indian woman with a high-pitched voice, orders an ultrasound and blood tests. The first round of IV painkillers has almost no effect and I continue to roll from side to side, fidgeting. Two male doctors several yards away argue. I can't decipher their speech. I hear only sporadic words—"infection…kidney stone…appendix."

The blood-test results come back in a flash and show that my leukocyte count, neutrophil count, and urea levels are elevated, while my lymphocyte count is lower than normal. No one tells me what these numbers mean. Based on what I overhear, I assume that I have an infection.

I wait patiently for the IV fluids to fill my bladder so that an accurate ultrasound can be performed. A petite attendant with crooked teeth pushes me in a wheelchair to an adjacent building for the test. The cool air makes me shiver. I sit parked in the examining room for five or ten minutes until a yawning technician enters the room and runs the test.

Just as I'm moving back to the ER, I feel the need to pee. I ask to be taken to a restroom, and the next thing I know the toilet basin has turned scarlet red.

"Oh shit!" I scream.

I look in the mirror at my straggly brown hair and pale face streaked with tears.

"What the hell is going on?" I ask out loud.

Is this a bad dream? I pinch my thigh and reaffirm that I am awake.

I'm wheeled back to the ER and ask Josh about Ira. Apparently, Ira's in a taxi on his way to the hospital.

The doctor with the irritating voice informs me that the ultrasound reveals a dilated and swollen right kidney and ureter, plus a lodged kidney stone; additional stones in the other kidney and the blood tests confirm an infection.

Once again, the two male doctors talk. This time they're closer, so I can decipher more. The shorter one, a surgeon, insists on running a CT scan to rule out appendicitis, while the taller, heavier one, a urologist, thinks it's not necessary. A few minutes later the attendant is placing me in a wheelchair. I'm on my way back to the other building for a CT scan.

When I return to the ER, Ira is waiting. His face is drawn and dark circles are forming shadows under his eyes. He affectionately kisses and embraces me. I squeeze him with all of my strength and slowly release.

I lie down and close my eyes. I reminisce about the first time I met Josh's soon-to-be bride, Rachael, who also lives in India. We were in Josh's Bangalore apartment talking about my job prospects and my future relocation to India. I was taken in by her unmistakably caring personality and admired her waist-length, glossy black hair, which was braided neatly behind her back. My eyes captured the simple gold chain with two petite charms—a Star of David and an elephant—hanging just below her collarbone.

My thoughts are interrupted when the urologist, a middle-aged Indian with a face marked by maturity, clears his throat and nonchalantly recommends that the lodged stone be surgically removed. I ask him whether it would be safe to wait until after I contact my sister-in-law, Shari, an American internist, but he arrogantly stomps away from the curtained area. *What will happen if I can't reach her?*

The doctor had provided minimal information, and without the Internet or a doctor who communicates, I'm lost. I want to check out the doctor's credentials, the hospital, and treatments for kidney stones. But it's not possible. I stare at the dried blood on the wall. The throbbing in my head is keeping rhythm with my heart as my worries spiral out of control. *I cannot remember anyone having a surgical procedure for a kidney stone. Do doctors perform this procedure in the United States? I glance down at the grimy floor and terror strikes. Will the operating room be cleaner? What type of anesthesia will I be given? Might I die?*

Moments later, the doctor returns. I'm being admitted to the hospital, the surgery is scheduled, and my nightmare is playing out exactly as I feared.

2

My journey was set in motion years ago. In most respects, my family life could not have been better in 2007 and 2008. After leaving suburban Chicago in 2000, we had settled into the laid-back lifestyle of Boulder County, Colorado, without any regrets. We were easily able to commute to our second home in the mountains only a ninety-minute drive away. Our periodic escape to Summit County became an essential part of our family's existence.

Josh was busy working as a venture capitalist in Bangalore, India. An American correspondent had profiled Josh—and his adventurous soul and hard work—in the *New York Times*. Our second son, Adam, was establishing himself as the fitness editor of *Men's Health* magazine, and was well on his way to becoming a prominent journalist and editor.

Ira and I were just a few years away from being empty-nesters. Aaron attended the Leeds School of Business at the University of Colorado, and Jordan was deciding whether or not he should graduate early from high school. Both were immersed in their educational pursuits and had active social lives that limited their time at home. It was impossible not to *kvell*. I was bursting with pride over our sons' accomplishments.

Aaron, Josh, Adam, and Jordan, 2008

My career was on hold as I struggled to cope with an agonizing and tormenting pain in my right hip that made walking a block or two almost impossible. Hip arthroscopic surgery in Vail, Colorado, with an unexpected micro-fracture repair in the fall of 2007 necessitated two months on crutches and almost a year of physical therapy. A dreaded hip replacement would follow in the spring of 2009. My physical limitations disappointed me, and I feared that I might never be able to use my K–6 teaching license again.

So I deviated from my career path as an elementary school teacher and headed into higher education. I used my persistent sales skills to propose new class offerings at the University of Colorado at Boulder and at Front Range Community College. They were eventually approved following a lengthy screening process. During the spring semester of 2008, I found myself standing in front of two very different groups of college students, teaching Jewish history classes—a class in early Jewish history at the community college and one in modern Jewish history at the university. A lack of enrollment and a change in personnel led them to drop my classes the following semester, but I was unwilling to abandon my new career path. I convinced the head of the education department at the community college to hire me as the new Intro to Education instructor. This kept my teaching career alive as I recovered from my second hip operation.

I was secure because Ira was well on his way to establishing himself as a successful Colorado lawyer. For over twenty years he had built a notable career as a high-end commercial litigator in Chicago, followed by his "of counsel" position at Kutak Rock, a prominent law firm with offices in Denver. Next, he was a sole practitioner who split his time between litigation and serving as the outside general counsel for one of his clients, a high-end ski-industry retailer.

But the effects of the recession hit home when Ira's major client, a family-run business headed by former Olympic skiers, decided that the expense of an outside general counsel wasn't in the budget. I'll never forget the evening when Ira came home early from work looking as if he had been hit by a lightning bolt—ashen and shaken.

I quickly defrosted one of our treats—a specially shipped Lou Malnati's pizza from Chicago—and made a spinach salad with Ira's favorite sweet-and-sour dressing. I topped off the meal with a batch of homemade chocolate-chip cookies. As we savored our dinner, I tried to allay Ira's fears.

"You've bounced back before."

Ira shook his head and replied, "I just didn't see this one coming."

"Neither did I."

There was a brief pause and then Ira responded, "My desk is piled high with pending matters, many of which just evaporated a few hours ago."

"You've saved them millions of dollars. I'm certain one of the client's sons will call tomorrow with a better explanation."

"You're right. It can't be as bad as it sounds."

I tried to be optimistic, but deep down I had my concerns because this family's behavior was so abrupt and unanticipated. I was perplexed. For years they wrote glowing e-mails, stroking Ira's ego with incredible accolades and unusual signs of affection that usually would be reserved for family members. His relationship with the family grew deeper as he held the hands of two of the sons through hotly contested divorces. I kept asking myself, *Why did this happen?*

At least from our perspective, a genuine friendship existed. If the relationship had indeed been sincere, it didn't seem possible that any of the family members would act in such a callous and thoughtless manner. Suddenly, after daily communication, it was as if Ira no longer existed. I could only speculate that saving the expense of Ira's monthly retainer and legal charges really was at the core of their decision.

Months later, I was just a few feet away from Ira when I overheard him talking to one of his former law partners. I vividly recall Ira's poignant words: "My faith in people has been shaken. How could I have ever trusted that family?"

Ira's stellar career had included arguments before many federal and state appellate courts, the Illinois and Colorado supreme courts, and the United States Supreme Court, and he had an impressive record of reported cases. I will never forget flying to Washington, DC, in March 1988, leaving Adam and Aaron, who were suffering from chicken pox, with a nurse from Highland Park Hospital. No way was I going to miss this incredible opportunity for Ira, barely in his mid-thirties, to showcase his oratory skills before the Supreme Court. I couldn't have been more proud of him when the decision came down in his favor that June, with only Justice William Rehnquist dissenting.

Ira was composed but forceful as he delivered his arguments, armed with only a yellow legal pad with minimal notes recorded on a single page. With lightning speed and accuracy, he fielded all the questions the Supreme Court justices threw at him. When his allotted time was up and the red light came on, I was in awe of what he had accomplished and regretted that we hadn't insisted that his parents come to watch.

Decades of enjoying the fruits of Ira's legal expertise had diminished the economic fears that plagued the early years of our marriage. Now, unexpectedly, the recession was killing business and most law firms were struggling, as corporations and individuals cut back on paying large fees. Partners and associates were being laid off and fired nationwide, and Ira's legal contacts were downsizing, relocating to inexpensive rental space, and searching long and hard for business. The long-term future appeared unpredictable if Ira were to remain a sole practitioner. As a result, Ira started to explore positions with a set salary.

"How's Dad doing these days?" Josh inquired a few months later.

"Networking and lunch meetings are his new game plan. Aaron recommended LinkedIn. Does it do anything?"

"Yes, it can connect Dad to others. Is he applying for jobs online or contacting headhunters?"

"Both," I replied. "But law firms and companies are looking for women, minorities, and people with disabilities, not a white guy over forty."

"Maybe he should start to think outside the box."

"What?"

"Consider working for an Indian company."

When I got off the phone, I told Ira about my conversation. We both shrugged our shoulders and simultaneously said, "India?"

"You have nothing to lose," I said.

From that moment on, Ira began to communicate with Ritvik, a headhunter in India. We never thought he'd be employed by an Indian company. Absolutely not! But Josh was living in India, so seeing our eldest son more often would be a wonderful perk, and that thought was driving this far-fetched consideration. Ira had active cases with existing clients, so we focused on a future time when Ira's cases would be resolved either by settlement or final court disposition.

As the months passed, I became cynical. Everything I read or saw on TV painted a bleak picture. Bankruptcies, mortgage foreclosures, and unemployment were escalating. I met a shoe saleswoman at Dillard's who had an MBA and previously had owned a profitable business. And I heard troubling stories of successful individuals committing suicide after they found themselves locked out of their career paths. I trembled with fear when I heard the story of a prominent lawyer in Washington, DC, who shot himself after learning that he had lost his job.

Every few weeks, we saw more and more "for sale" signs popping up in residential neighborhoods. When it came close to election time, it seemed as if the "for sale" signs were in direct competition with the candidates' signs. One fall morning as I was driving to the health club, I saw several county sheriffs' cars parked haphazardly in front of the home of one of our neighbors. When I returned a couple of hours later, I saw the contents of the entire house on the driveway and front lawn. A light round of snow flurries followed by sleet added an ominous covering to our neighbor's possessions. Foreclosure and a life in crisis were just a few houses down from ours.

I feared that the current recession would ultimately turn into a devastating depression. I had trouble sleeping and tossed and turned throughout each night. We had house payments, car payments, insurance payments, taxes, utilities, everyday expenditures, and college tuition. *Would being employed by an Indian corporation provide more job security?*

After exchanging e-mails and phone calls with several different outsourcing companies, an offer appeared imminent. The job would enable Ira to further develop his business skills while utilizing his legal expertise in an innovative way. Outsourcing, the bane of many Americans, might become the underpinning of Ira's new career. The contemplated position would put him in charge of several hundred Indian lawyers and support personnel who performed legal work for American and British corporations. The exact parameters of the position remained in flux for many months as different layers of this enormous company involved themselves in the bargaining process.

Would we have to move to India? It was hard even to say where we would live because each segment of the negotiating process brought about a different scenario. My life, the one that I had planned and was in the midst of living, was on the verge of becoming a distant memory.

3

Ira was going to India. He didn't have the official offer yet, but somehow I knew that it would soon become a reality. He would leave…and what would I do? I tried to envision different scenarios.

I could travel as Ira's companion.

Yeah, right! This was possible—only if I was independently wealthy.

Or maybe I would just stay in the United States and he'd travel back and forth.

More daunting was the idea of living and working in India. Ira and I could follow in Josh's footsteps. Josh, in his twenties, had dived headfirst into Indian culture. Ira and I were in our fifties. The whole idea seemed insane. Tossing away an established American life and relocating to a Third World country didn't seem logical for a middle-aged couple. When Josh had accepted a job in India, I wept for days. I feared that our family would become fragmented and that our moments as a cohesive family would become distant memories. I couldn't say anything because it was, after all, his life. But now Ira and I were potentially causing an irrevocable schism. Living halfway around the world from most of our immediate family seemed ludicrous.

By far the safest choice for me was staying put. Ira was free to pursue this job, and I could continue my life as if nothing had changed. But I would have a part-time husband; each of us would need to fend for ourselves when we weren't together. This alternative position was equally unsound. As a married couple, we derived our happiness and security by living life together. If I wanted to live a separate existence, I would ask for a divorce.

None of the options fell under the category of "the secrets of a successful marriage." But I would be selfish if I told Ira that he could not pursue this fascinating career path. Just like Josh had chosen his way years ago without any interference from us, I didn't feel comfortable telling Ira not to take the job.

Too many sleepless nights went by without any resolution, and the lack of rest began to play tricks on me. One minute I felt that an Indian adventure was something to look forward to—a new challenge for the next stage of our lives. And in a blink, I'd change my mind and feel like our cat, Chloe, who likes to hide under the bed. Whenever Chloe doesn't want to be bothered or is afraid that we're going to take her for a much-dreaded car ride, she positions herself under our bed, knowing that she's out of harm's way. Unlike Chloe, however, I had nowhere to hide.

Chloe, our adorable cat

This wasn't an easy time for Ira, either. Some days the Indian company led Ira to believe that a contract was in the offing, while other days he thought that the deal was sinking like a ship that had hit an iceberg. This went on for weeks as the structure of the job changed and the anticipated time that Ira would need to live in India fluctuated. The company treated Ira as if he were Geppetto's Pinocchio, controlled by the whim of a puppeteer. Oftentimes he was told that someone would call at a specific time but the phone never rang. He would wait and wait. Without seeming too impatient, he eventually sent e-mails to a contact person in India who then provided an excuse. Some were ridiculous; some seemed genuine. But all of them became old after months of the same act.

Frustration mounted whenever promises were made and broken. Words such as "tomorrow," "later today," or "we'll call soon" turned into triggers that created skepticism. We learned that these words simply meant "an unspecified time in the future" and weren't an actual promise. Ira and I could only chuckle and make bets about when the next stage would occur.

Ira remained intrigued over the prospect of being the legal head of a legal process outsourcing (LPO) company. Over the years, he had watched as the cost of litigation skyrocketed. By using qualified lawyers employed at a lower hourly rate, clients could decrease their costs. Ira was excited to take over the reins of India Sourced Technology's (IST) LPO while it was still in its infancy. IST was one of India's largest companies and a global leader in technology with revenues in the billions.

After months of discussion, negotiation, and uncertainty, Ira received a written contract in December 2009. I felt like I was acting in a Disney World commercial when I asked, "How does it feel to be the new delivery head of the IST LPO?" Ira hadn't won the Super Bowl, but he was beaming when he said, "I can't wait to mentor hundreds of Indian lawyers and also have an impact on the legal profession."

Now I was faced with one of the most difficult decisions of my life: What was I going to do?

4

*M*arital bliss. Suddenly the idea took on new meanings: awkward and unnatural. Ira would be living in India for approximately half the year. His trips to India would be in thirty-day increments and interspersed with travel in the United States and possibly the United Kingdom. This exciting new job certainly differed from anything that Ira had done before and came at a time when the US economic situation still looked grim.

If the compensation had been greater, I might have considered forsaking my career and periodically traveling from place to place with Ira. Since that was not an option, I needed to decide quickly. On the one hand, if I stayed in the United States, I would have the luxury of maintaining the status quo—but I'd rarely see my husband. And I knew I would miss Ira dearly whenever he was traveling. After almost thirty-five years of marriage, I couldn't fathom being apart for more than a week or two. On the other hand, if I opted to leave my job and follow Ira to India, my life would be on the edge and unpredictable. I had no guarantee that I'd be able to secure an Indian job, and living arrangements remained a giant question mark. I was heading out into uncharted waters without even a buoy to keep me afloat. My time with Ira now would be limited to the whims of his new company.

I stared at the mountains outside my window, looking for solace. How could I consider leaving the awesome Colorado Rockies? We had a home in the Front Range and another one in the mountains. This was our family's version of the American dream. All that Ira and I had planned was now called into question. Bit by bit my life was starting to unravel, and I wondered if it would ever be the same.

My heart drew me to the core of my existence—the memorable family moments. In particular were the Jewish High Holidays in the fall and Passover in the spring. Since relocating to Colorado, our sons and their significant others had swarmed there to taste the delectable foods that were part of our family's traditions. At great cost to a potential career path, I had invested decades of my life in nurturing and raising our four sons. I couldn't speculate on what effect our Indian adventure would have on the underpinnings of our family.

Chanukah 2008

To a certain extent, I dismissed emotion and sentiment and viewed the bigger picture through a rational lens. In which location would I be able to spend the most time with Ira? Ira was the center of my life and had been for most of my existence. At the tender age of eighteen, my monumental decision to marry him had caused a rift with my parents. Their illogical animus for Ira was evident, and my mother was angry that I wouldn't allow her to make *all* of the wedding decisions. I returned home for summer break after my freshman year of college, and they had cancelled my wedding dress, the photographer, and the wedding-day festivities. This situation left me off balance and resulted in Ira's parents scampering to make alternative arrangements.

Our wedding day in 1975

With no parental support, I turned to my future in-laws to loan me the money for the remaining two and a half years of my under-graduate education. Ira and I lived meagerly on food stamps and a tight budget. My maturation into adulthood went hand-in-hand with my ability to cast off my parents' heavy yoke. From that point until now, Ira and I looked to one another for unconditional love and support.

How could I consider being away from Ira for longer than necessary? We were an inseparable couple—teammates who together met each of life's challenges. Based on his company's representations, if I opted to go to India I would be able to spend more time with him. More importantly, I realized that life in a Third World country would be tricky for Ira and that my presence could make the transition easier. The adventurous part of my soul focused on the impact of an international teaching job on my career path. I dreamed about teaching in a foreign country. The buzzwords "making a difference" would ring true and not be hyperbole. No doubt, my two master's degrees and teaching experience at multiple levels were assets.

My mind kept spinning like a dreidel. Would I win or lose in this game of unpredictable outcomes? I had to decide: Go to India or stay in the United States? Leave my life or leave my husband? Start new a career or try to survive through the recession?

5

I started compiling a list of prospective schools and asked Josh to confer with his contacts to create a recommended list. There were no American schools in Bangalore—only international schools following a British, Indian, or International Baccalaureate (IB) curriculum. The private schools catered to foreigners, relocated Indians, and affluent Indians looking for better teachers and foreign teachers. According to Josh's sources, the average Indian teacher earned a monthly salary of 50,000 to 60,000 rupees—$1,200 to $1,400 a month—while foreign teachers brought in more lucrative salaries. No one knew the going rate for an American teacher with two master's degrees and certification.

I contacted each school by e-mail and then waited patiently for their responses. I received numerous e-mails expressing interest. This was in sharp contrast to applying for a teaching position in Colorado: Recessionary times had created a surplus of teachers as school districts around the state down-sized their teaching staffs.

One school stood out in particular because it asked for information that violated U. S. employment laws. The administrators wanted to know my date of birth and how long I would be in India, and they requested an electronic picture of me. My curiosity got the best of me. Were they looking for a strikingly attractive woman or an old maid? Despite this unusual request, I was extremely encouraged. The responses from the prospective schools energized me and lessened my trepidations about living in a foreign country. This could truly be the key to igniting my career.

Was it possible for me to find a teaching job during Ira's first trip to India?

I had no idea and I didn't have anyone to consult, but I estimated that it might take two months to find a job. That meant I would be spending one month living with Ira and another month with Josh in his Bangalore apartment. I could handle the month when Ira needed to be in India but had serious reservations about the second month when he would travel elsewhere.

Could I survive India alone?

What would I eat?

How would I find my way?

Would I be safe?

It didn't take long for more doubts to consume me. I had limited experience traveling outside my home country. Decades of conforming to a traditional marriage limited my independent travel experiences to less than a handful of memories. I had traveled solo more in my youth than as an adult. For nine years I went to summer camps in northern Wisconsin and frequently flew to visit teenage friends who lived in other states. With Ira and the boys, I visited other countries, but other than a month at a summer camp in Zermatt, Switzerland, when I was fifteen years old, I had *never* lived abroad.

Was I lucky or not to have been under Ira's protective wing?

Should I have been more autonomous?

I was genuinely nervous and uptight over the prospect of doing something as simple as boarding an airplane by myself in India even though I had traveled to many foreign countries with the companionship of my family.

My knowledge of India was limited to the stories and pictures that Josh shared with us. My main concern was hygiene and food. Josh had already suffered many gastrointestinal illnesses, including bouts with E. coli and dysentery. Perhaps it was irrational to consider going on such an unusual journey. Yet something intangible kept driving me forward despite my trepidations.

As I vacillated from one option to the next, Ira encouraged me to make *my own decision*. He listened patiently as I verbalized the pros and cons and flatly refused to provide his opinion. Yet in the end when I decided to travel to India, his expressionless face was replaced by a glowing smile.

The more I thought about altering my life, the more I realized how much security I would lose in my new surroundings. My car, so associated with the freedom to go wherever I wanted, was returned to the dealership. This was the first time in decades that I wouldn't have my own wheels. Soon the effects of my decision created even more anxiety. My job security was stripped when I told my supervisor at the community college that I wouldn't be returning. Having taken the time to build both a curriculum and my reputation over the course of four semesters, I was crushed. I said good-bye to my tutoring students, a few of whom I had worked with for years.

The centers of my existence—my children and my homes—were also being thrown into the fray. Our two youngest sons, Aaron and Jordan, were now being asked to maintain two homes while they attended college. I had confidence in their capabilities, but felt guilty that this enormous burden fell upon their shoulders at a time in life when responsibility is usually limited to taking care of yourself and going to school. The comforts associated with being on my home turf would soon be just a glimmering memory.

Making the necessary phone calls to family and friends became an arduous task. We faced a rigid wall of opposition as people attempted to sink our optimism.

"Why would you go *there*?"

"You'll *never* survive."

"You're setting yourselves up for failure."

"Have you lost your mind?"

Only a handful of our friends were supportive and politely agreed that it would be a wonderful experience. For the most part, it was us against the world. To counter this onslaught of opposition, I referred to our new career paths as an *adventure*. The pervasive negativity, however, did cause me to momentarily pause to reflect on our sanity. We had *not* lost our minds.

A Bug Hitting the Windshield

6

Travel days in the Bornstein household are notoriously chaotic. The day we left for India was no exception. The smallest agitation caused the two of us to become unglued as we incessantly snapped at one another.

It was not easy to say, "I'll see you in two months" to our sons and our friends. The only time I remember saying such words was when I went off to summer camp in Eagle River, Wisconsin, when I was a child and a teenager. As a youngster seeking new freedoms and experiences, I welcomed the adventure openheartedly. This time around, as a parent leaving children behind, I was fraught with mixed feelings. My heart was heavy as I gave the last hug and said, "Good-bye."

Standing in line at the Lufthansa airlines counter, I was in awe of what we were about to do. I continued whispering my new mantra.

"New adventure…new adventure…new adventure."

We made some last-minute phone calls. I swallowed hard and cleared my throat before dialing Ira's parents.

"Sandy, are you sure you want to do this? There's still time to change your mind," my father-in-law prodded.

"We've always been partners. I'm not letting Ira go by himself," I forcefully struck back.

My mother-in-law countered with her overriding concern for my well-being. "Please be careful! Don't venture out by yourself."

After a few rounds of small talk, I said good-bye and handed the phone off to Ira. I was becoming increasingly annoyed with anyone who was the least bit unsupportive.

I was relieved when our two-day journey to India was behind us. We disembarked from the plane and found our way to the expansive line waiting to go through Indian customs. Like a periscope checking all four directions, I perused the waiting area. One common feature became immediately apparent—the vast majority of the passengers were men. *Where are the women?* This initial observation often came to mind throughout my time in India.

Like most international visitors to India, we arrived in the middle of the night. We quickly gathered our suitcases and headed outside to locate our driver, who was among the throngs of people holding signs with names and company logos. Just like two ducklings waddling behind their mother, we followed the short man dressed in a faded uniform to his car. The compact car had a minuscule trunk. Ira and I looked at one another as the driver tried to figure out how he was going to load four large suitcases, two briefcases, and a backpack. Before we knew it, three suitcases were fastened to the top and we were on our way to the Adarsh Gardens apartment complex in Jayanagar, a residential area of Bangalore.

Although we had been forewarned about Indian drivers, the real-life experience didn't match up with what we had read about or been told by Josh. It was far worse. I clutched Ira's forearm as the driver weaved between the cars and trucks on the road. He honked his annoying horn whenever he went through red lights and rarely stayed within the painted lines while swerving from one side of the road to the other. Many of the auto rickshaws (three-wheeled, motor-operated mini-vehicles) had no lights, and most of the trucks had no rear lights. Countless times Ira and I gasped when a vehicle flashed before our eyes and our driver veered off his intended course within seconds of rear-ending the obstacle in our path.

Even as we risked our lives in the car, darkness couldn't mask the extreme poverty or the massive piles of garbage we passed.

When we arrived at our apartment complex, it was a few hours shy of dawn on a Sunday morning in late January. The adrenaline in our bodies was soaring as we gladly exited the car. Security guards wearing wool hats, gloves, and heavy jackets greeted us at the front gate. Ira and I were dressed in jeans and long-sleeved shirts. There was a bit of coolness in the air, but it hardly warranted the winter attire, we thought—the temperature was in the high fifties.

Our new home was at G Block, Flat 501. How ironic that Ira and I would find ourselves in the same apartment complex that Josh had lived in when he first came to India to work as a college intern and then again when he moved to Bangalore in 2003. We were now confined to a small area that was about the size of our former master bedroom suite, but it was more than sufficient to meet our daily needs.

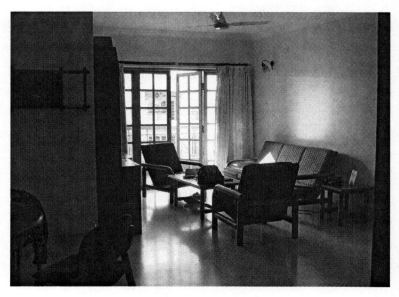

Adarsh Gardens flat

Our new home had some unusual features. Most striking was the simple kitchen. Accessories included a petite refrigerator, an electric pot in which to heat water, a small microwave, a one-burner propane cook plate, and an Aquaguard apparatus that treated the water coming into the flat. Modern conveniences—an oven, a stove, a dishwasher, or a disposal—were missing.

The two shower stalls were equipped with a bucket and a cup so an individual could take a bucket shower. To economize on water usage, you'd fill the oversized plastic bucket with water and then used the cup to bathe yourself. It was commonplace during my stay for acquaintances to openly brag about how few cups of water they use when bathing their entire bodies.

The electricity that flowed to the outlets was not constant. Each wall outlet had a switch that you pressed so the electricity would run to it, and countless times I'd stand befuddled, trying to figure out why an appliance didn't work. To create hot water, we had to hit a switch fifteen to twenty minutes before using it. A few times I had to take an ice-cold shower because I failed to leave sufficient time for the water to heat up.

It was common to lose power for an hour or more each day. One of the Adarsh Gardens employees made it sound as if it happened at the same time each day. While that scenario seemed annoying, it was something I could tolerate. On the second day, however, I learned that the power outages were actually random events that could happen multiple times a day. Fortunately, a generator provided electricity in the bathrooms and for two small sconces in the living area.

The Adarsh Gardens complex sat on a narrow parcel of land that was cordoned off by a fence with barbed wire at the top. To enter, we came through a locked gate that had several security personnel manning it. The tropical landscape received meticulous daily maintenance, and the gardeners kept it exceptionally clean. Children enjoyed a small playground near the entrance, and adults had access to an outdated and extremely limited gym situated near the outdoor pool. It had been decades since I last saw the belt apparatus that was designed to remove hip fat with its jiggling motion.

After exploring the cloistered world of Adarsh Gardens, my curiosity was piqued. *What would I find outside the gates? Were my mother-in-law's fears for my safety justified?*

7

The day after we moved in, a car came at 7:00 a.m. to pick up Ira. I was on my own until he returned after 9:00 p.m. I could now appreciate the apprehension that our cat Chloe felt when we first introduced her to our home in Colorado. For a few days, we kept her in our bedroom so she wouldn't be totally overwhelmed by the expansiveness and complexity of the house. When the space outside our bedroom suite was opened, she conservatively accepted her freedom as she clung to the walls for support and cautiously sniffed as she took each step. Instead of leaping and prancing up and down the stairs without any reservation, she took a few steps forward then retreated before proceeding. She repeated this pattern until her comfort level was established. During my first visit to Bangalore, I was reenacting Chloe's steps of trepidation.

I tested the waters by slowly, apprehensively venturing out of our flat to explore the neighborhood. In sharp contrast to the apartment complex were the never-ending garbage piles and dilapidated buildings that lined the busy and extremely noisy street just outside the gate. The cobbled sidewalks were in disrepair, so paying attention to where I was walking was very important. It was as if I was back in third grade playing hopscotch, jumping from one square to the next. This game was considerably more challenging because one wrong move would land me in garbage in a rat-infested gully. The air was thick and dusty and filled with a scent of excrement and burning sewage.

My recently cleaned body felt itchy from the dirt that was quickly covering my perspiring skin. Most of the locals either were wearing sandals or had no shoes at all. I felt considerably safer in my tightly tied gym shoes. Cars, buses, motorcycles, electric rickshaws, and trucks whizzed by me as they mercilessly maneuvered from one part of the road to the other with horns blaring nonstop.

As I walked, I saw that the neighborhood was a hodgepodge, including some nicer buildings and a few single-family homes interspersed with street people and garbage-filled empty lots. Zoning was irrelevant here. It looked as if no one had bothered to pick up any garbage in decades, and well-dressed men were openly urinating against buildings. As a Westerner used to seeing the positive effects of legislation that curbed land, water, and air pollution, I was appalled to see such a total disregard for the environment.

My sense of feeling out of place was heightened by the fact that I was stared at by practically everyone I passed. *Was I being self-conscious? Perhaps I was overly self-conscious. How could I not be?* Practically everyone on the street was Indian, so I stood out from all the other women. I wasn't wearing traditional, colorful, Indian clothes. Instead, I was sweating profusely in my light gray Ralph Lauren T-shirt and a pair of faded blue jeans.

After my brief but eye-opening tour of the surrounding area, I retreated to one of the wooden benches near the playground inside our complex's main gate. Most of the people who walked by avoided eye contact and only a handful dared to even respond to my soft, friendly Western-style greeting of "Hi, how are ya?" It was mid afternoon and I couldn't imagine why women were swarming like bees to the front gate.

Within a matter of minutes, the mystery was solved. In several waves, children dressed in different uniforms suddenly appeared, walking next to the adults and heading back into the complex. Several of the children looked directly at me with smiling faces, while most of the adults ignored my presence. I wondered if there was some type of cultural explanation for this frosty reception.

One woman, dressed in khaki pants and a woven top, didn't share the others' unfriendliness. She sat next to me on the bench while her first-grader played on the adjacent playground equipment; we started to converse.

"I haven't seen you before. Welcome to Adarsh Gardens."

"Thanks. It's so nice to talk. No one is making eye contact. Is there some cultural issue that I should know about?"

She giggled slightly and said, "Oh no. Don't be concerned. Most of the people are Hindi-speaking maids who are afraid to make eye contact with Westerners. I'm the rare exception. I'm not working right now."

"Wow, that's a relief. I couldn't figure out why everyone was ignoring me. Can I ask another question?"

"Sure. Go ahead."

"I'm seeing so many different school uniforms. Are there that many options?"

"Most of the children attend private schools. Everyone is striving for the best education."

Our conversation ended abruptly when her daughter needed to use the restroom.

Back in the flat, I thought about dinner. The promised cook never materialized, which frustrated us, but there wasn't much we could do. For the first day or two, we relied on the food that we'd brought from home. Granola bars, dried fruit, crackers, oatmeal, peanut butter, and candy became the staples of our daily nourishment.

During dinner we shared our day's experiences. Ira heard my preview of the surrounding area while I learned about his first day at the Electronic City campus about an hour away. He had spent time with Vinay, the new head of Knowledge Services, the division of which the LPO was part. Vinay lived in Texas and was selected for this position after the former Knowledge Service head, Rishi, resigned in December. Ira's employment negotiations had been conducted with Rishi, among others. This was Ira's first opportunity to meet his new boss. Ira was introduced to several India-based employees, including a man named Suraj.

Our second day in India was a national holiday. Ira's gasp woke me up.

"What's wrong?" I asked quickly.

"Uh...uh...I saw something kind of big and dark moving in the next room."

"Where are you going? Please don't go!" I pleaded as Ira thrust himself into the adjoining room.

"I can't believe it!" Ira screamed. "I never thought I'd find a…a…a…"

"A what?" I bellowed back.

"A monkey was sitting on the dining table. He took one look at me and just scampered out the door."

"You've got to be kidding. No way! A monkey? Oh my God."

"I'm going to lock the door and I'll be back in a second."

I trembled as I yelled, "Maybe your parents were right. I can't handle wild monkeys in our apartment."

Ira tried to reassure me that everything would be okay, but I continued quivering as we embraced. I hadn't completely bolted the patio door the night before. I couldn't stop wondering, *How would I react if I was by myself?* I was used to the security blanket of an alarm system that alerted us to anything that penetrated our living space. Now the burden had shifted back to me.

Who would have thought that a monkey would enter through a fifth-floor, partially closed balcony door? Not me! Did the neighborhood monkeys climb from one balcony to the next like security guards checking for an open doorway?

I picked up the apartment phone and dialed Josh.

"Are you coming soon?" I whimpered.

"Yeah, is everything okay?"

"I thought you were kidding. There are real monkeys here. I can't believe it."

"Did you forget that you're in India? Just calm down! I'll be there in forty-five minutes."

I was vulnerable. I tried not to concentrate on my new feelings of isolation. I looked back to the early settlers of America who left everything behind in their old countries. Those people went months or even years before receiving a single letter from a loved one. Emotions were curtailed by the sheer fact that people had to be patient. I was living in the twenty-first century, so it was commonplace to communicate daily with people around the world. I was unglued over my inability to talk to family and friends. The Adarsh Gardens flat was not wired for the Internet and I didn't have an international phone. I couldn't wait to visit Josh's apartment so I could use the Internet and make phone calls.

One of our first acquaintances in India was Josh's friend, Monica, a gregarious Westernized Indian with shoulder-length, jet-black hair and eloquent dark eyes, who happened to be a neighbor in Adarsh Gardens. She came to our apartment to check on us and to help us talk with the Adarsh Gardens staff. Her command of Hindi allowed us to communicate more effectively, and she forcefully explained our needs to the manager and the housekeeping staff. We learned that our promised cook would never be coming and that we should order dinner from the fast-food pamphlets that were left in our flat. Ira and I hadn't eaten fast food in decades and we certainly weren't going to start now. Maybe we'd consider a pizza or two, but not Indian fast food or McDonald's for our daily dinner. Nor was I in a position to cook on a Bunsen burner or without an oven. I controlled my quivering lip until Monica and the unwanted staff left. I was overcome by a flood of doubts.

8

As I planned for the next day, I paced back and forth in our flat. Out of ten possible international schools, I had five scheduled interviews and two or three more pending. In the United States, I had applied to dozens of public elementary schools and had received almost no response. My first interview was scheduled the next morning. *What should I wear to the interview?*

I called Rachael, Josh's girlfriend, for her advice. Although we had yet to meet, we had grown acquainted over the Internet and also by phone. Rachael was born and raised in New Delhi. She was an ongoing source of information and agreed that I should avoid skirts. I settled for a monochromatic linen pantsuit that was both comfortable and practical. I carefully placed my choice on the bed in the spare bedroom.

The next morning, as I approached the gate to the first school I sensed a distinct aura of primness and properness. I signed in and received a visitor's pass to hang loosely around my neck. The guard directed me to an adjacent building that housed the administration office for The Karnataka International School (KIS). All of the secondary students were dressed in formal uniforms—the boys in shirts, ties, and pants, and the girls in tailored blouses and skirts. Some of the students even wore blazers. The primary school's uniform was slightly less formal. The boys had matching shirts and shorts while the girls wore simple blue dresses.

The first part of my visit included a brief tour led by my HR contact, Simona, a young, energetic, and friendly woman. The usually foul-smelling Bangalore air was masked inside the gates by the lovely, sweet fragrance emanating from purple flowers that were just starting to bloom. If you didn't look past the towering perimeter walls, you could easily imagine that the school was in a Western country, far removed from the poverty, cows, stray dogs, and filth that lay outside the front gates.

First I interviewed with the principal, a middle-aged American dressed formally in a suit and tie. His office was large, yet inviting. I was thankful that the ceiling fans kept the room moderately comfortable, since I was still adjusting to the warm Indian days and attempting to cope with the overwhelming sensations of jet lag. The discussion was cordial but centered on topics focusing on my family and parenting strategies. Though many of his inquiries would be prohibited in an American interview due to employment laws, in India I had no choice but to answer.

The director, a stern-looking woman with a tight smile, was dressed in a dark, tailored pantsuit that had a masculine appearance. She graciously shared facts about the school and then questioned me on a few education-related topics. Months after the interview, I remained troubled by some of her probing personal questions. *Why were there no limitations on asking about health history and daily medications?*

After eating lunch in the school's cafeteria, I was escorted to the primary unit building to meet the two middle-aged department heads—an Indian woman, Pari; and a Brit, Elizabeth. Part of this interview focused on the influence that the University of Colorado had had on my teaching philosophy. The smothering air of condescending conservatism along with the overabundance of personal questions made me wonder if this school was a good fit for me.

Jet lag was taking its toll and the bright afternoon sun was draining me as I waited in the shadows of trees for the driver to pick me up. The interview had far exceeded the thirty minutes that Josh had anticipated. I was at the school for over five hours. Panic started to set in.

What did the driver look like?

What kind of car was he driving?

Why didn't I write down the license plate number?

When a white car pulled into the driveway, the driver looked familiar so I climbed into the backseat. It took well over an hour to return to Adarsh Gardens.

For the next day's interview, I headed in the opposite direction—back toward the airport to Chatura International School. This school, a highly respected one that also catered to an upscale clientele, was located in an urban area and situated on a considerably smaller plot of land. The students wore Western clothes and the high school students were free to come and go as they pleased through the guarded gate. Whereas the first school had a British feel to it, this school felt more American. After a few brief introductions to the primary director and the principal, I was asked if I was interested in replacing a teacher who was leaving at the end of February. After responding yes, I arranged to go back in a couple of weeks to discuss compensation and terms and to meet one of the founders of the school.

My interview time was short and sweet—less than thirty minutes.

I was perplexed. *How could they hire me without an employment visa that required a visit back to the United States? Why wasn't I asked about my background?* After the interview, Josh arranged to have the driver take me back to the flat. During the ride, I forced myself to stay awake because I was afraid to fall asleep in a foreign country with an unfamiliar driver.

Shortly after I returned, Monica, our bubbly new neighbor, dropped off several different dinner entrées packaged in a multitiered metal container, which she referred to as a "vessel." Additionally, she provided tasty, wheat flatbread that was packaged in aluminum foil. A short time later, Josh brought other Indian dishes that his maid had prepared. Ira and I savored our vegetarian feast.

"How're things going?" I inquired of Ira.

"I'm meeting tons of people every day. It's a bit overwhelming, as I'm trying to develop a better idea of the bureaucracy."

"Are you the only American?"

"Yes, except for two newly hired LPO salesmen. But next week when we travel to Pune, a few prospective American and British clients will be stopping at the campus. I'll probably have some late nights."

"Your hours remind me of your trial-prep days. Pace yourself. Be careful not to overdo it."

I was delighted that Ira's first few days were going well, and I looked forward to the next day's interview at Star Innovative International School.

The Star school did not cater to the well-to-do. Rather, it offered a progressive education to children of the rising middle class. The director of the school, an older, distinguished-looking Indian gentleman with silvery hair and a soft voice, sat with me for an hour-and-a-half discussing shortcomings in the Indian educational system and his vision for changing the situation.

His ambitious desire to have me instruct his teachers on the modern methods and theories of education was premature—he didn't know if he had sufficient funds for a salary, couldn't offer acceptable living accommodations, and couldn't provide transportation from Josh's apartment. If money hadn't been an issue, this position would have been an incredible opportunity to make a difference for an entire school, not just an isolated classroom. Despite his sincerity, though, I never heard back from this school even after sending a couple of follow-up e-mails.

9

I was in India for just over a week when Ira was asked to take an extended trip to Pune. Not since being in the Middle East had we encountered such a large military and police presence at an airport. Prior to entering the airport, we had to show identification and our tickets to a fully armed soldier.

After receiving our boarding passes, Ira and I split up to go through the separate security lines for men and for women. Men were openly screened with a wand while women waited patiently in line to be checked in a curtained cubicle. While standing in line, I was constantly annoyed by women acting as though they had the right to march to the front of the line without waiting their turn. Some of the women in line glared intensely at the perpetrators, but no one uttered a word. After the third such occurrence, I was tempted to trip the next offending person, but was afraid of the consequences if I was the cause of turmoil.

I was eager to visit Pune, which is approximately 150 kilometers from Mumbai. After our hour-and-a-half flight from Bangalore, we drove about an hour to the IST campus, a fortress with an electrified, barbed-wire fence. Uniformed guards armed with outdated rifles that could have been housed in a museum staffed the security station at the main gate.

It became apparent that my presence was an issue. I didn't have the required badge. After the guards spoke among themselves in a Hindi dialect, we were told to go to an older campus called IST Phase 1 about twenty minutes away. Ira took out his computer and showed e-mails confirming my expected presence and our reservation for a room at Phase 2. After additional phone calls and discussions over a protracted period of time, we were told that we must stay at Phase 1. This required Ira to commute to Phase 2 daily. Ironically, the person who confirmed our written reservation was the same person who made the decision for us to stay at Phase 1. This situation reminded me of our living arrangement in Bangalore. I wasn't allowed to live at IST's Electronic City campus so Ira had to commute from a secondary location.

Walking back to the car, I said, "I never imagined I'd be considered a security risk."

"I honestly don't understand. IST is touted as a 'family-friendly' company," Ira huffed.

"Had I stayed home, you could've lived on the Electronic City campus in Bangalore," I said. "You'd have had zero commute, wireless Internet, and restaurants, instead of fretting over a nonexistent cook. Here, you have to commute as well."

Ira cradled me in his arms and responded, "Sweetheart, I'd rather be with you. We're in this together. Did you ever think you'd work at an international school?"

Despite Ira's reassurances and optimism about my future career, I couldn't stop questioning my decision to come to India.

From the main gate of Phase 1, guards directed us to the hostel/guesthouse. Along the way, I felt at home as we passed a Subway restaurant, a Baskin-Robbins, and a small commissary. When we reached the top of the stairs, I saw an amoeba-shaped pool, a fully equipped gym, and tennis courts that in many respects resembled those in a first-class resort. Our well-appointed room included a spacious bathroom that provided hot water *all* the time.

Standard features of a modest hotel room—a TV, twin beds, desks, two chairs, a small refrigerator, and the tall cabinetry you'd typically find on a cruise ship—made me feel as if I was on vacation. Because our accommodations were on the campus, we never experienced the power outages that were common in Bangalore. *Hallelujah!* I could use electricity without any interruptions and was living in an air-conditioned room.

But I was flustered and annoyed with my inability to communicate effectively with people around me. I slowed down the pace of my speech, used more hand gestures, and listened more intently to what was being said. Even when I made a concerted effort to bridge the gap, my efforts were unsuccessful—neither party had a complete understanding of what the other was saying. *Would I ever reach the comfort level that Josh had achieved?*

My daily walks exposed me to the sheer number of groundskeepers. Everything was done completely by hand without the use of *any* modern tools. Men on their hands and knees cut the grass with sheers and trimmed the foliage with hand tools. Women, dressed in matching forest-green saris with orange trim, swept the grass and walkways with handmade whisk brooms. Another crew of women spent countless hours placing each of the thousands of rocks that formed a perimeter around the pool area into a bucket and then washing them. This mindless mission took several days to complete.

Dinner was problematic. Restaurants were located over thirty minutes away and the hassle of hiring a driver and finding our way wasn't worth the bother. Within walking distance, we found only *one* decent restaurant, the Lemontree Hotel restaurant, across the street. Both the assistant manager and manager of the restaurant took special interest in us since we ate dinner there almost nightly.

Oftentimes our idea of a certain menu item was very different from the Indian chef's idea of the dish. I picked gingerly at lasagna that had large chunks of carrots, beans, and peas mixed with a tomato sauce that was more Indian than Italian. Before I could decide whether to make an issue of my poor choice, the manager, having seen my actions, promptly came to the table and offered a secondary option of an Indian fish meal and a complimentary cappuccino.

On a regular basis, I took advantage of the recreational facilities, using the gym and swimming pool, though they were open for only a few hours before work and a few hours after. *How strange. Didn't they trust their employees to limit their exercising during work hours?* Whenever I went, I was astounded by the ratio of men to women—about ten to one.

Since average daytime temperatures were in the low nineties and the evenings hovered in the fifties, the icy-cold water in the pool stunned me. I can't remember immersing myself in a body of water that chilly since my days as a Camp Nicolet camper swimming in Franklin Lake in Eagle River, Wisconsin. To warm up, I swam in hyperdrive. Goose bumps and chattering teeth were my norm.

Through my goggles, I observed several other brave swimmers. One plump woman wore a maroon swimming suit that went to her knees and covered her arms to her elbows. The men, on the other hand, wore very small suits that resembled Speedos. There was no seating around the pool. When I returned to my room, my skin was still bright red and blotchy.

Everyone experiences wake-up calls that make one sit back, reflect on life, and possibly rethink the direction one is taking. Sometimes these scenarios stimulate a sense of appreciation arising from the sudden loss of something that one previously took for granted. In recent years, my orthopedic problems made me realize how grateful I was when my body was fully functional. I quickly learned how vital it was to be pain-free in my shoulders, feet, knees, and/or hips. The limitations caused by continuous pain took a tremendous toll on my ability to live an active life. Although I was not happy with the shots, surgeries, and physical therapy, all of those procedures ultimately resolved the issues. I learned that I should never take my health for granted.

Now I faced a different type of challenge, one that was the result of being separated from family and friends. To a certain extent, this was reminiscent of our move to Colorado ten years earlier. In that situation, we left behind close family and friends in suburban Chicago and adjusted to our new life in Colorado. This time around, Ira and I were alone in dealing with the language barriers, the social issues, and a totally different set of cultural values. And while Ira was busy with the demands of his new job, I spent most of my hours by myself.

Solitude is manageable and welcome for limited periods of time, but it grows old very quickly. I'd always admired Thoreau for his willingness to explore the meaning of his life at Walden Pond. Like Thoreau, I was listening to the beat of a different drummer by following my own path. I had been in India for only a few days, but I was certain that the experience would have an impact on my life. My longing to learn more about Indian culture initiated an open dialogue with two Indian women.

The first was a slender, petite woman with short black hair. I frequently saw her running on the treadmill in yoga pants and a Nike T-shirt as her young daughter sat holding a Minnie Mouse doll and a small book. The second was an IST consultant whom I met while swimming in the pool. She was one of the brave souls trying to learn how to swim in the unheated pool. Unlike the first woman, who had once lived overseas and was comfortable dressing in contemporary Western clothing, this woman, who lived in her mother-in-law's home, always dressed in traditional Indian clothing. Both women were in their late twenties.

In the middle of the week, I was leaving the exercise facility at the same time as the young woman and her daughter. The girl was eager to share her picture book with me. I sat down on the floor as she read me a few lines.

I turned to her proud mother and said, "Wow, she reads beautifully. I don't want to be rude, but I'm curious about how she can read and speak better than many of the adults I meet."

"I'm not offended. English skills are dependent on social class. Public schools provide a substandard education. Those students have poorer English skills. Everyone with money sends their kids to private school."

"Is that why security guards, taxi drivers, and store clerks struggle with English?"

"Yes."

"Now it makes sense."

"Have you visited any Indian schools?"

"Yes, I visited an assortment of private schools in Bangalore."

"Did anyone tell you that only some schools are run by educators? Religious institutions and corporations also own schools. The Mercedes-Benz International School is just a few blocks from here."

Our small conversation tested the girl's patience. She was tugging on her mother. My remaining questions would have to wait. I politely excused myself and returned to my room.

Life on the campus became monotonous. I initiated whatever conversations were possible. After swimming one afternoon, I talked with the traditional Indian woman.

"I'm impressed that you're taking lessons. Didn't you learn as a kid?"

"No, and I can't think of anyone who knows how to swim. I'm sure you had opportunities," she responded with a curt British accent.

"Opportunities…is that because American women have less limitations than Indian women?"

"Being a woman is a disadvantage in most places. In India, it's more of a burden."

"How so?"

"There's a bias, even before birth. Many families abort female fetuses even though doctors are prohibited from revealing the sex of fetuses."

"If female fetus genocide is prohibited, why are there more males?"

"I'm not sure. But people with money usually find a way around rules."

"It's odd for me since I see more men all the time."

"Male children always have the educational benefits. Without a solid education, women have fewer job prospects and tend to stay home."

"Education is the key to success everywhere."

Our conversation came to an abrupt halt when she realized the time. She needed to be home for her son.

Engaging talks only went so far in diminishing my cabin fever. Until I mustered up the courage to take an auto rickshaw or taxi, my exposure to the outside world would be limited. When the weekend arrived, I was eager to discover the world outside the gate.

10

We sat back and relaxed while our driver, a tall, thin, white-uniformed man in his early thirties, drove us to Sinhagad, a 300-year-old fortress located approximately twenty-five kilometers south of Pune. The driver, Anil, a product of the Indian public school system, took the initiative to improve his English by conversing with his foreign passengers. We became his new teachers as we traversed the countryside and visited Pune's highlights on Saturday and Sunday.

Along the way, Anil stopped at a roadside vendor and bartered for red grapes wrapped in newspaper. We were apprehensive about the elongated grapes, which Anil sprinkled with bottled water; normally, I scalded all of the fruit I purchased from food vendors and stores. While Ira and I munched on this sweet delight, I remembered our youngest son, Jordan, upchucking on the cruise ship after he ate strawberries provided by our private tour guide while visiting the Peterhof Palace in St. Petersburg, Russia. I wondered if I was tempting fate. Fortunately, this time we didn't have any problems, which only made it easier to rationalize the next time when I questioned whether I should eat a forbidden fruit.

After parking, we hiked uphill with our driver, now layered in a black leather jacket, to an eventual height of 1,350 meters. Splotches of manure were everywhere and the manmade steps were steep and irregularly spaced. A pack of donkeys and a few stray cows were our companions, along with Indian families and couples who were intent on hiking and picnicking. Most of the Sinhagad fortress had been destroyed over time, so our memories and photographs are of bits and pieces. Our guide had little knowledge about the significance of this historical site.

After leaving Sinhagad, we took an alternate route through farmland and small villages. The traffic slowed on a stretch of road where young women were using sledgehammers to break apart large rocks. I swallowed hard as I watched these construction workers swinging away repeatedly as the sun beat down on their muscular bodies. Farther down the road, another crew of women sat on the ground hitting rocks together to make gravel for a new road that was being built parallel to the existing one.

We made one stop in a small village where the residents lived in tents and makeshift structures with pieces of metal or cloth for roofs. Satellite dishes prominently adorned each apex. Inside one of these primitive structures, an older man squatted on the ground making tools. In an adjacent area, other men were taking an afternoon respite from the heat. Cell phones were ubiquitous, despite the poor living conditions.

The next day, we ate lunch at the German Bakery, a crudely designed, tented restaurant situated on a busy intersection in Koregaon Park. Once inside, we saw that everyone ordered at a designated counter in the bakery area and then picked a seat in the adjacent room, which was furnished simply with long tables and benches. We weren't provided a receipt or a number for our food. Eventually, we were served our omelets and rock-solid wheat toast when a waiter yelled, "Who ordered two omelets?"

Eggs, a staple of my American diet, became taboo. I was reluctant to purchase eggs in a store since they were neither date-stamped nor refrigerated. With a daily temperature hovering near ninety, I didn't want to gamble with the freshness factor. Hidden within one of our lengthy conversations with Anil was a discussion about his uneducated wife, who was born in a tiny rural village.

"I was just seventeen years old when I married. Does that seem young to you?" he volunteered willingly.

"Nowadays, it does. But did you marry awhile ago?" I politely responded.

"Yes, I've been married fifteen years."

"That's wonderful."

"My wife was only fourteen when we married."

Ira and I both raised our eyebrows and glanced at one another quickly. A brief pause followed, and then I said, "Um…really…that seems kind of young. I'm assuming that your marriage was arranged."

"Yes. Our parents made the choice."

"Did you see a picture of her or get to meet her?"

"No. We accepted our parents' wishes."

"If you weren't happy, could you have said no?"

"Our parents had the final say. I married a girl with the mind of a child. You can't have sex with a girl. We grew up together."

The conversation was becoming too personal. Ira quickly took the lead and changed the subject. I had married young, but this took marrying as a teenager to the extreme. Looking back and reflecting on the maturity level of the average American high school freshman, I shook my head.

Originally, I was going to return to Bangalore with Ira, but my second interview at Chatura International School necessitated that I leave earlier. This flight became the first of a series of pivotal moments in which I developed a new level of independence and confidence. Just months ago, I wouldn't have considered traveling alone in a Third World country. Now, I was less than a day away from boarding a domestic Indian flight.

We were dropped back at the IST campus in the late afternoon. Ira and I settled on eating dinner across the street. The manager waved at us as we found our regular spot and looked over the menu.

"After I leave, will you eat on the other campus with your colleagues?"

"It depends on the length of the meetings."

"You seem upset. Is it my leaving or something else?"

"I'll miss you. It's not any fun to eat alone."

"I know," I said. "That's one of the reasons I came. A month of eating by myself would be torturous. Is there anything else?"

"I'm worried whether my managers will follow my directions."

"How so?"

"They're so eager to impress potential clients that they tend to embellish what we can offer."

"I hope they tone it down."

"I've made it clear that there are ethical issues that can't be ignored. But I'm not sure they understand."

Ira was becoming more settled in his new position. The LPO leadership was working together to create new strategies, which hopefully would be tempered by Ira's legal advice. Ira received an e-mail from Suraj, one of the LPO managers, confirming the LPO's quarterly budget. Money was allotted for numerous trips to India plus more than a dozen US domestic flights. The travel budget was to be divided between Ira and the two American salesmen, with the bulk of the international travel allotted to Ira. I felt intense pressure to find a teaching position so that I could be with Ira as much as possible.

11

On my first full day back in Bangalore, I went to my interview at Chatura. This time I met with one of the founders of the school, Rita, a woman who had possessed a unique vision in the 1980s when most of the Indian private schools were religious institutions. I was immediately welcomed by this affable woman, whose educational views were influenced by the West. Her desire to remain a hands-on leader in the development of Indian education was still apparent, much like a parent who waits in the wings and offers useful advice to adult children whenever they need a helping hand. I also briefly spoke with the principal. "We will be contacting you soon" were his parting words.

In the evening, I accompanied Josh to an art gallery. Ira was still in Pune. It was awkward following my eldest son around the gallery. I didn't know anyone. Josh's popularity was evident by the fact that he went from one group of people to the next and at least someone in each group knew him. I wasn't referred to by my first name. My new label was "Josh's mom." What a twist.

Hadn't my children always been identified as Sandy's sons or Sandy and Ira's sons? I was *kvelling*. Josh, a foreigner, had found his place in a culture quite distinct from that of his upbringing and was accepted without any reservations.

Life sometimes can be all about coincidences or being in the right place at the right time. What a fortuitous moment when Rita walked in. She took a second look as she glanced in my direction. In a city of more than 5. 5 million people, neither of us ever dreamed of crossing paths with one another that evening. It was a worthwhile encounter. I learned that it wouldn't be possible for the school to hire me immediately. Her comments confirmed Josh's contention that immigration laws made it necessary for me to return to the United States for an employment visa. The principal would be contacting me soon regarding the fall-term position. Josh gave me a quick high five when he heard my recap as we climbed into a taxi. A warm glow moved through my body as I imagined teaching in India and I wondered what the defining moments of my teaching journey would be.

Later that week, I was shaken by the February 13, 2010, bombing at the German Bakery in Pune. Six days before this cowardly terrorist attack, Ira and I had sat in that dining room peacefully eating our omelets. We had been surrounded by a diverse group of individuals who were there to enjoy good food and a friendly environment, where strangers from all walks of life shared picnic-style benches and tables.

While confronting the events of this bombing, I struggled with the random uncertainties of life. *Is there a spiritual quality of fate that ultimately controls what I am destined to experience or is my life's journey dictated by both good and bad luck?* What I do know is that I have the freedom to make my own choices. Attached to this concept of free will is the hope that whatever I do on a given day will have a positive outcome and that my inner strength will ultimately give me the fortitude to deal effectively with any obstacles that I encounter.

Three weeks passed quickly and Ira was leaving India in a week. For business reasons, he could never remain in India for longer than a month. For personal survival, I needed to become more comfortable with navigating the nearby streets. I remained fascinated by the auto rickshaws that continually puffed out black and gray smoke.

Driving an auto rickshaw was a tough business, except for those who rig their meters to rip off patrons. Josh said those individuals were usually easy to spot because they wore nicer clothing and jewelry, had newer shoes, and boasted electronic devices, such as fancy mobile phones. He recommended that I avoid hiring a driver who went out of his way to attract a Caucasian's attention. We were frequently harassed by drivers who would ask if we wanted a ride and then follow closely behind us as we walked. This intimidating approach did not encourage ridership. Instead, we preferred to head the other way.

One of my greatest fears was becoming stranded or lost. Hiring a rickshaw and taking a journey wasn't in my comfort zone. Josh thought I was acting like an infant and told me to grow up. Contrary to Josh's stern rebuke, numerous Indian women provided me reassurance when they told me I had good reason to be fearful of Indian streets.

When the alarm clock rang the next day, I didn't want to wake up, even though I had two interviews scheduled. I opened my eyes and my vision was distorted by an aura of sparkling lights. It didn't last long, but I knew a migraine would follow on its heels. Ira immediately could see that something was not right as I lay comatose on the bed.

He leaned over me and whispered, "Are you okay?"

"Uh, I should be all right—just give me a second or two."

"Why don't you cancel your morning interview at Questor Academy?" Ira urged.

"Let's see what happens."

After I finished showering, the familiar pulsating sensation was beginning in the back of my head. I ate a small breakfast before swallowing a pill. I put on my sunglasses and headed out the door.

I tried to rest while the vehicle lurched in and out of the morning traffic. I was in my own little world until the car stopped and the driver gently nudged me from my sleepy state. I gave myself the familiar pep talk: "You can do it!" I exchanged my sunglasses for my regular glasses and walked into the building for the interview.

I was escorted promptly into the director's office. The tall, broad-shouldered woman had a Muslim-sounding name. She candidly mentioned that they were opening up a new school. On the surface, this position sounded intriguing, similar to the one at Star.

The position would be supervisory and would involve training teachers. When I asked where the school would be located, she slurred the letters together so that the name of the city was unrecognizable. When I asked if I could commute from Bangalore, she chuckled. I had revealed my ignorance of Indian geography. The school was far away and off the beaten track. She handed me her card and politely told me that I would hear back from her. That ended up being the last time we communicated.

By the time I was chauffeured to my afternoon interview at Millwood International School, the headache and slight fever had gone away. The school looked out of place amidst the fields that touched its periphery. The grounds resembled a small office complex. Unlike the open-air facilities of the past two schools, this campus had several modern metal-and-glass buildings that glistened in the afternoon sun.

The security was intense. The inhospitable guard immediately used a metal device to scan under the car and then instructed me to go inside the guardhouse. They interrogated me and examined the contents of my purse. Next, I was greeted by a receptionist in the administration building, who asked me to sit in an air-conditioned waiting area with modern black furniture. Then, I waited…and I waited.

The school director, a dark-haired man with a receding hairline and sharp jawline, finally introduced himself. He talked about how his teachers were compensated and the contrasting pay scales for Indian teachers versus foreign teachers. I had participated in many interviews, but none, either in the United States or India, ever started with the topic of money.

I peered intently at the director to catch some subtlety in his body language that would give me a clue to his intentions. I sat erect and calmly asked, "Why are you spelling out the differences?"

"There are two important facts. You're an American but I'm interviewing you here. You're considered an Indian employee," he curtly replied.

"I seem to be missing something. How am I considered an Indian when *I am an American?*"

He stared down at the table and said, "If I met you at a job fair overseas, you'd be an international teacher."

"So, if you hire me here, I wouldn't receive any benefits, such as visa and travel costs or housing."

He made eye contact and said, "Yes, except you would receive an international salary. If you're interested, we'd have you come back to teach a class."

"But an employment visa can only be obtained in the United States. You want me to absorb all those costs?" I questioned.

"Yes."

"What about my salary?"

He took out a small scrap of paper and jotted $36,000 on it. He then handed me the paper.

The director escorted me to another building, where I was introduced to the primary unit's principal. I extended my hand to a tall, Caucasian woman wearing a stylish, tailored dress. She curtly arranged for my tour and handed me her business card as she dashed out of the room.

Josh's friends told me that this school paid the highest salaries in town, yet I had serious reservations about a place that was trying to categorize me as an Indian when I was undoubtedly an American.

I continued to think about this as I remembered my dinner plans.

Shortly after we'd arrived in Bangalore, we received an invitation for Shabbat dinner from the Chabad rabbi. Our schedules had not permitted us to visit him until now. As the sun was waning on the horizon, I returned to the car and provided instructions to the rabbi's house.

After knocking on the door, I was greeted by an Indian woman dressed in a purple sari, who was taking care of a baby that was crawling about. Shortly thereafter, the rabbi's young wife, Shira, appeared with a cell phone in her hand. She was wearing a floor-length, brown, patterned skirt and a matching, long-sleeved over blouse that partially concealed her mid-trimester pregnancy. She motioned for me to sit on the beige leather sofa while she completed her cell phone conversation in Hebrew.

My attention was distracted when Shira's toddler, Maor, tapped my shoe with his large, striped ball. Within no time, I was sitting on the floor rolling a ball to him. I continued to play with Maor and talk with Shira and her husband, Ariel, until Josh and Ira arrived.

The rabbi and his wife entertained us like long-lost friends. Ariel's outgoing personality matched his jovial, round face. My preconceived image of an orthodox rabbi with a full beard and a hat were accurate. He wore both, as well as a dark suit and simple tie. Ariel came from the mystical Israeli city of Safed and his wife was raised in Jerusalem. Both appeared content in their spacious and modern Bangalore residence, but they were looking forward to returning to Israel for the birth of their second child.

Life in Bangalore was a cultural shock for Westerners, and I couldn't imagine the impact it would have on observant Jews who follow every dictate of Jewish law.

"How difficult is it to maintain an Orthodox lifestyle in India?" I bravely asked.

"Many things are in short supply. Kosher wine is one. More challenging are products like kosher meat and kosher milk."

"Have you become vegetarians?"

"For the time being, we are living without meat and relying on fish as our main source of protein."

"How do you get milk for Maor?" I inquired.

"We milk a cow."

I looked out the back window expecting to see a cow. I saw nothing. With Ariel's strong Israeli accent, I wondered if I had heard him correctly.

My bewilderment must have been obvious. Ariel said, "You seem confused about something."

I blushed and meekly answered, "I don't see a cow outside."

Ariel and Shira laughed. "It's not in our backyard. We go to a nearby dairy every week to milk the cow."

My inability to deal with heavy accents was not limited to Indians. Israeli intonations were also troublesome.

Shortly after Josh and Ira arrived, the three men chanted the evening service in an adjoining room that had a selection of books and a small *aron hakodesh* with a Torah inside. Normally I participate in the Friday night service, but Orthodox Jews require a *mechizah* and one was not visible. I whispered the Hebrew words to "Lekhah Dodi" and "Shalom Aleichem" and hummed some melodies as I sat in the adjacent room. My Jewish identity, which was lying dormant in India, was rejuvenated in this small religious sanctuary on the outskirts of Bangalore.

12

Ira and I became vagabonds. We wandered from Adarsh Gardens to Pune and then back and forth between Adarsh Gardens and Josh's apartment. At the four-week mark, I settled into Josh's apartment and Ira flew off to London to meet with clients before he went back to the States. Josh's spacious, three-bedroom place had a garden with lots of shade and was double the size of the Adarsh Gardens flat. Even when all of the windows were closed, it was nowhere near as stuffy or as hot as our first apartment.

The main room was very comfortable, with seating that faced a wall unit with a flat-screen TV. Perpendicular to the living area was the spacious dining area, which included a small alcove that led to a balcony. The bedrooms were off of this main area. Each was furnished with a comfortable queen-sized bed, a ceiling fan, and had its own full bathroom. There was a narrow kitchen with a door leading out to a washing machine and drying lines and a rack.

Josh had moved to this apartment after living in Adarsh Gardens for a few years. To immerse himself in Indian culture, Josh had made a conscious effort to rent an apartment in a small, freestanding apartment building rather than in one of the gated communities that attracted Westerners. Likewise, he purposely picked a place that was within walking distance of UB City—an upscale shopping mall with Westernized restaurants. The hustle and bustle of city life was right outside his doorstep, including the amplified chanting that emanated round-the-clock from the local mosques and madrassas.

In the United States, I always avoided the South. A hot, sticky climate is a wonderful breeding ground for bugs and lizards and miscellaneous other creatures. From the time I could utter my first word, I was averse to any living thing that crawled on the floor, walls, or ceilings. This irrational fear reached its peak when, at five, I was sitting on the floor in the family room of our Highland Park, Illinois, home and looked down to see ants crawling all over me. I even remember the pink, fluffy slippers that were overrun by that army of large ants. I'm not sure if I ever wore them again.

Tiny ants and bugs were everywhere in India, including in my bed at Josh's apartment. The bed was ghastly until the floor was mopped thoroughly, the mattress shaken out, and powdered pesticide was placed around the perimeter of the room. More challenging were the bugs on the kitchen's black countertops. I avoided leaving anything on the counter and prepared my food on the kitchen table in the other room. This was not a problem until one of Josh's roommates decided to invite a few friends over for breakfast. One of them, a young Ivy League graduate, left flour and batter all over the kitchen, and the residues of spilled syrup, pancakes, and juice coated the table.

Latta, Josh's cleaning woman, didn't come until many hours later. In less than an hour, bugs infested almost every surface. The reason bugs were everywhere was that most people didn't lift a finger to clean up their own messes. Someone else had been hired to do it. In this case, I couldn't wait. I cleaned off the table as soon as the horde appeared. Then I smashed each new column as the ants paraded in organized groups across the table.

I slowly became adept at walking to various parts of Richmond Town. I graduated to handling congested streets and continued expanding my turf. The streets in the neighborhood were very narrow compared with the main streets that were just a few blocks away. Horns blared throughout the day and night as vehicles sped by, honking at every intersection. Stop signs were nonexistent.

One day as I was walking back from one of my daily ventures, a young Indian man driving slowly on a motorcycle turned my way, put his right hand to his mouth, and blew kisses at me. I stood as stiffly as a statue as he continued down the empty side street. I couldn't help but feel a warm glow in my checks and a sense of gleefulness. If nothing else, I imagined that I was twenty years younger. That night when I used Josh's Vonage phone to call our home in Colorado, Ira couldn't stop teasing me. I certainly had no immediate plans to divorce Ira and run off with a suave Indian man riding a motorcycle. Josh's response made me reflect on my newfound independence: The man probably considered me a loose American woman, based on a common misconception that *all* American women are sexually permissive. Now I would be suspicious every time a man gave me a suggestive look.

Whenever I became fearful on the streets, two memories instantly popped open. One was the Rogers and Hammerstein song *"You'll Never Walk Alone."* I hummed this melody and softly sang the lyrics as I held my head up high.

I was consoled by this song's lyrics. Who knows what prompted the recollection so many decades after I'd first heard it. Whenever I doubted myself, I also remembered the childhood story, *The Little Engine That Could.* I'd read this classic repeatedly to my four sons and decades later, the message of the book was ingrained.

Recollections of my sons' childhoods put into perspective how they had matured and developed their promising adult lives. The days of sitting and reading classics to them were in the distant past. Each was well established in his own adult life. Now for the first time in years, I had an incredible opportunity to actively participate in Josh's world. Ira and I knew that Josh's budding relationship with his girlfriend, Rachael, was growing more intense even though a two-and-a-half-hour flight separated them. It didn't surprise us when Josh asked our advice on engagement rings. He was planning to propose to Rachael on the beach in Goa, India in two weeks.

A week before that occurred, Rachael flew to Bangalore for the weekend so that we could finally meet. Aside from the years she had spent attending the highly acclaimed National Law School in Bangalore, she had lived her entire life in New Delhi. She currently worked as a corporate attorney for one of New Delhi's most respected law firms. Until Josh returned from Goa after his engagement became official, I clenched my lips and refrained from saying anything about a new chapter in the Bornstein family.

From the moment Rachael entered Josh's apartment, we could see the love that they shared. It was heartwarming to watch them walk hand-in-hand and amusing to hear them talk in jest. When they gazed into each other's eyes, the magnetism was apparent. Rachael's demeanor contradicted the stereotypical image of a passive Indian woman. Her confidence and intelligence were visible whenever she spoke. She took interest in everything that we told her and sat for hours looking at hundreds of family photos stored on my laptop.

After knowing me for only a couple of hours, she insisted that I join them when they traveled to Goa the following week. She knew that I would be alone again when Ira took a second trip to Pune. I refused the invitation because I was aware of Josh's intentions. Her persistence and gentle spirit made it difficult to say no, especially since Goa was one of the places I wanted to visit. By the end of the weekend that we met, we were sad to see her leave. Our paths were now intertwined and we would soon be welcoming our first daughter-in-law into our family.

As planned, Josh proposed to Rachael during his trip to the beach. For years, Josh had told us that he loved taking time off to frolic along the seashore and enjoy the company of his friends in this resort community, which sat on India's western coastline and had a notable Israeli presence. I was happy that such a romantic place had become the backdrop for this memorable occasion.

Josh and Rachael discussed possible wedding dates and locations. The last weekend in November was selected. A wedding at the notable sixteenth-century Paradesi Synagogue in Cochin was considered but quickly discarded due to logistical issues. Rachael's synagogue in New Delhi became the logical second choice. No matter where I was living, I would be traveling to New Delhi for the celebration of Josh and Rachael's wedding next Thanksgiving.

13

A few days after dinner with Ariel and Shira, I received an e-mail invitation to attend a Purim party. I was on my own. Josh was traveling with Rachael and Ira was in the United States. This was another defining moment. If I wanted to attend the party, I needed to arrange for a taxi. In America, I wouldn't think twice about doing so, but in India my fears of getting lost or being ripped off weighed on my mind.

Purim, a Jewish holiday, recalls the story of Queen Esther. When our boys were younger, they would dress up in costumes and we would attend the *Megillah* reading at Congregation Beth Shalom in Northbrook, Illinois. There we'd shake our *groggers* to blot out the name of Haman, an evil man who wanted to exterminate the Jews of ancient Persia. The boys' favorite parts of the holiday were eating the *hamantaschen* that I prepared and hanging out at the Purim carnival on the weekend closest to the holiday. After we moved to Colorado, these family traditions fell by the wayside.

All of the Israeli guests arrived at the Chabad Purim gathering in colorful and creative costumes, and they all spoke Hebrew fluently. I regretted that

I never mastered my Hebrew. Ariel read from the *Megillah*, a scroll with the story of Esther written in Hebrew. It was the first time that I had attended a Purim service that didn't include the handing out of *groggers*. It seemed strange that people would clap. A gesture I usually associated with approval was now being used to show disproval.

Jews often remark how comfortable they feel wherever they go because Jewish traditions are common worldwide. To a certain extent this is true. I have been in synagogues throughout the world and sensed God's presence during the services; and I've felt symbolically connected to the people standing nearby. Yet in this scenario, something was amiss. At first I couldn't put my finger on it. *What was missing?* Ira and my sons, of course. Jewish holidays are always meant to be celebrated in a community setting. But the core ingredient for me—my family—wasn't present. I longed to be back in Colorado rolling *hamantaschen* dough in my own kitchen and then filling it with jelly or melted chocolate.

As I lay in bed later that night, I had mixed feelings about the day. On the one hand, I was incredibly sad that I wasn't in Colorado to share this joyous holiday with my family. On the other hand, I was growing as an individual. Until now, I had been leery of going off the beaten path by myself because I was worried and anxious over unknown consequences. I was proud that I'd found a way to communicate with the dispatcher and the driver with minimal effort. I had passed a major hurdle. I was learning to be more receptive about taking chances.

Josh continued talking with his friends and business associates about my educational background and my desire to find employment. Out of nowhere, I received an e-mail one morning. Apparently, my résumé had been forwarded to a potential employer and the school wanted to meet with me immediately. Josh flagged down a rickshaw outside his apartment. I was on my way with my damp hair flapping in the breeze. When Josh and I reached the school—it resembled a large store—I was on my own.

Once inside, I looked around and realized that I was in a preschool, a place I had no intention of working. I didn't want to offend Josh or his friends, but I told the receptionist that I was no longer interested in the position. I was out the door before she could reply.

How was I going to select a vehicle to take me home? From a distance, how could I determine if the driver was dressed too nicely? Out of the corner of my eye, I saw one going in the opposite direction on this wide boulevard. He immediately turned about and headed my way. "Oh no!" Josh would rule this one out because the driver was going out of his way to stop for me.

"Where are you going?"

"Uh...Richmond Town...Richmond Road...near the TNT building," I said reluctantly.

I breathed deeply and climbed onto the upholstered bench. I hoped all would go well.

I was astounded. The driver could speak English, a true rarity in the population of auto rickshaw drivers.

Once I was situated in the middle of the seat, clutching my purse for dear life, he asked, "Where are you from?"

I hesitated to reply and then softly stated, "United States."

From that moment until I arrived at the TNT building near Josh's apartment, we engaged in a nonstop dialogue. His fluency and his ability to comprehend challenging words and concepts impressed me. I asked him if he had learned English in school. He told me that he had studied the basics but improved by talking with customers.

After I complimented him on his English, I continued the conversation by asking him about his fellow drivers. "Whenever I'm in a rickshaw it seems as if the drivers don't know any English at all. Is that true or are some of them pretending?"

"I'm different. I like talking to my passengers. I want to improve my speaking skills. They are not pretending. Most do not understand English and don't care to learn."

When the vehicle was stalled in traffic, two women in an adjacent auto rickshaw hopped out while their vehicle was idling in the middle lane. My driver chuckled.

"Ha! What do you think that's all about? Did those women not like the driver?" I asked.

"No, it wasn't the driver. It was the meter."

I couldn't believe my own ears. My driver was being candid with me about meter tampering. During our remaining time together, he asked many questions about life in America, especially about driving rules and penalties for infractions. His interest in knowing about places where there were driving rules with enforced consequences grabbed my attention.

Toward the end of my ride, the driver asked what I was doing in Bangalore. He thought it was hilarious that I would be looking for a job in India. Since he considered it so funny, he told me that it couldn't possibly be true. Like an old record stuck on a scratch, he kept repeating, "Why would any American want to work in India?" By the end of the ride, I still had not convinced him. I must admit that I frequently asked myself, *What in the world am I doing here?*

The ride seemed shorter than I expected. His meter was accurate because it was almost identical to the amount on the meter when Josh dropped me off.

14

It's not easy to develop new friendships when you are in your fifties under any circumstances. So imagine what it was like to be in a foreign country with limited opportunities to interact with people. I couldn't rely on Josh to be my social director forever. If I had any hope of living and working in Bangalore, I needed to start networking and meeting other people.

Fortuitously, the Overseas Women's Club of Bangalore became a portal. This group hosted a variety of social and charitable events. Every Thursday morning from ten to twelve, the club hosted an informal coffee at which foreigners could get to know one another.

After my positive experiences in the taxi and auto rickshaw, I mustered up the courage later that week to flag down a rickshaw. By providing Kiran Hospital—a building across the street from the women's club meeting place—as the destination instead of the five-star Leela Palace Kempinski Bangalore Hotel, I was possibly short-circuiting an unethical driver's natural tendency to rip off a foreigner. The strategy worked like a charm. I was charged the appropriate fare, forty-five rupees ($1.10), based on Josh's calculations.

Two American women greeted me. They were seated near the entrance to a terrace situated off of a large, breathtaking garden with a cascading waterfall. I ended up speaking with one of the women, an older expatriate from America, for a very long time. Decades ago, she married an Indian man and opted to remain in India after he died. She understood that the adjustment period was a slow and cumbersome process, and told me not to hesitate to call her.

From there I helped myself to some green tea and a couple of crackers, and I proceeded to mingle. Groups of women were sitting and standing throughout the large room. *Where should I start?* The women in the first group were from all over the globe—Finland, England, Canada, and the United States. The Overseas Women's Club boasted a total membership of over 900, and nearly a hundred were attending today. Almost everyone was in India due to her husband's job. Unlike Ira, almost all of the husbands were India-based employees of American or international companies, so the wives had visas that were tied to their husbands' employment visas. As a result, the women had deluxe accommodations, cars, chauffeurs, and servants. All of the women I spoke with sheltered themselves from the day-to-day life of India.

None of the women I met had ever taken a rickshaw—with their husband or by themselves. All were content to have a company driver take them wherever they chose to go, which seemed to be limited to a small radius from their homes. The perks offered by the corporations appeared to be the main incentive for their relocation. The costly price tag of educating expat children at private schools was a bonus that was hard to pass up. Several of the women asked if I would be interested in joining them for lunch. *How could I refuse?* So I dined in the hotel with nine other women who hailed from different parts of the world.

Seated across from me, a European woman with short brown hair and a radiant smile was telling everyone that she finally received her possessions after waiting for eighteen months. Before coming to Bangalore, she'd packed all of her things into a large container and had brought only one suitcase. Even though she was told *not* to place a car in the enormous container, her husband had opted to put the family car inside. It was hard to believe that she would disregard such an obvious restriction. *How did they think custom officials would react to the car?* It took a year and a half of negotiating over a hefty tax before she could obtain her possessions. When the container was finally released to her, all of her summer clothing was missing. She joked feebly that Indians were wearing her favorite designer outfits in Mumbai.

The trek to the hotel added another notch on my belt of confidence. In the process, I met a new group of people who had one thing in common with me—learning to cope in India as a Westerner.

The interview process became a never-ending journey with multiple twists and turns. Words associated with time took on a different meaning in India. Even a word with an exact meaning, such as "tomorrow," did not necessarily mean tomorrow. Josh continued telling me to be patient but persistent. This only added to my feeling of being in constant limbo.

The Millwood International School—the one that wanted to consider me an Indian employee instead of an international employee—contacted me and asked me to substitute teach. I accepted the assignment to teach several primary music classes. I laughed. I had never taught music.

After arriving at the school, I was briskly handed a one-page, handwritten lesson plan for five different classes. The instructions were sketchy and incomplete. Two of the classes required the use of recording software. *Where was this software and were there any instructions?*

Fortuitously, a lanky young man dressed in khaki pants and a button-down shirt walked into the classroom. He signed onto the school's computer but was unable to find the program or the microphone. The principal peeked into the room and read my body language before I could utter a word. She glanced at the lines that I had circled and highlighted. She shook her head and said, "There's no way I expect you to follow this. Do what you can." I was relieved. I mumbled under my breath, "I hate subbing."

This school had only a handful of Indian students. The vast majority of the students were North American, European, and Israeli. It was a pleasure to teach in a brand-new school with class sizes that averaged ten to fifteen students.

During my breaks and at lunchtime, I visited the staff lounge and mixed with the other teachers. Most of the teachers were also expats who had signed two-year contracts at an overseas job fair. They were all provided private accommodations a few miles down the road in a modern apartment complex. Most of these foreign teachers were in their late twenties and thirties and were wearing business-casual outfits. They preferred working for international schools because they were able to save a substantial amount of money due to tax incentives, and because they were no longer subject to the No Child Left Behind legislation that stymied most American classroom teachers.

The eldest teacher, a balding middle-aged man with glasses, had worked for several decades as an international teacher. He planned to return to the West Coast of the United States and build his dream house with the money he was stockpiling. Tutoring students and teaching in Arab countries for the past several years had been his most fruitful source of revenue. He encouraged me to travel there next. Silently, I knew this was never going to happen. Jews are forbidden in the countries he mentioned.

No one from the administration came to observe my teaching. The principal was more concerned about the fact that I would not accept a check for payment. With a visitor's visa, it was not possible to open a bank account. Without a bank account, I couldn't cash a check.

"It's not possible to pay *you* by check, but could we write a check to your husband or son? Maybe call it a consulting fee?" the principal suggested.

"You can write a check, but you can't label it a consulting fee. It's unethical for either one to accept it."

"Okay, I'll give you cash."

She instructed me to close the door and proceeded to count out five crisp 1,000-rupee bills.

"I truly enjoyed working with the kids. Do you anticipate anymore fall positions?"

"Nope. We're all set with our staff. And since you didn't accept a check, we won't be calling again."

I was content. The international nature of the student body and the class size made the job quite appealing, but I was uncomfortable in what I perceived to be an unethical environment. Comparatively speaking, I was paid exceptionally well for a day of substituting. The 2010 rate for a Boulder Valley School District sub was $94.50. I was paid 5,000 rupees—close to $125.

15

Josh was attending an all-day conference that Saturday and then flying to New Delhi in the evening to see Rachael; he would not be returning until Monday. Gold's Gym was closed on Saturday for its monthly maintenance. *What was I going to do?*

Josh arranged for a driver to come early on Saturday so I could go on a journey to Belur and Halebeedu, a little more than 200 kilometers from Bangalore. Belur and Halebeedu are considered to be two of the three most outstanding Hoysala temples out of over 150 temples in southern Karnataka.

Josh assured me that the three-hour car ride would be worth enduring to see these ancient sites. I rationalized the situation by saying to myself, *What else am I going to do?* Second thoughts crept into my head before my trip when I spent most of the night in the bathroom with terrible cramps and diarrhea. I had been so careful overseeing everything that I consumed. I had dined in one of the best restaurants in Bangalore with Josh and his business partners, and now my stomach was rebelling. As I lay in a coiled ball, rocking back and forth, I reviewed all the foods I had eaten. Perhaps it was the gazpacho, since it was a cold entrée. My luck—I was sick the night before going on my first solo road trip.

The driver arrived punctually at 8:00 a.m. I did not eat breakfast for fear that I would be sick in the car. I packed granola bars, trail mix, bottled water, and a roll of toilet paper for my private expedition.

The driver created a constant rhythm of speeding up and slowing down in navigating the unpredictable roadway. Sloshing gasoline in the tank kept to the beat of the starts and stops. We encountered many trucks, buses, and rickshaws, and an assortment of carts being pulled by either horses or oxen. All of these slower-moving vehicles needed to be passed. Sometimes the driver was cautious; other times, his passing actions were cavalier. Frequently, it seemed like we were on a one-way road, as numerous drivers decided to pass a slow vehicle in unison. The gaps between head-on traffic were too close for comfort. Every passing car seemed to enjoy playing a game of chicken with the oncoming traffic.

I didn't have a map and had no idea where I was at any given time. The three-hour trip ended up taking four and a half hours. When I stepped out of the car, my knees and my back were stiff. My driver, who did not speak English, pointed in the direction of the main entrance. Before reaching the gate, I was instructed to remove my shoes and leave them in the custody of an older gentleman dressed in a tattered and stained white sarong with a matching top. It was easy to recognize my shoes, since all of the other shoes were worn-out sandals.

As I removed my socks, my driver raised his hand and waved it back and forth. In broken English, he kept repeating, "Ammerricn, Ammerricn, sooocks, sooocks." He then pointed to the bottom of his right foot. His gestures took me by surprise, but I appreciated his suggestion. The pavement was scorching. Everyone else was barefoot. I was happy to have my socks.

Before reaching the metal detector at the entrance, I was told to leave my cell phone behind. There was no place to check the phone. I went back to the driver. He was reluctant to take my phone, but eventually agreed to put it in his car. Fear and anxiety quickly overcame me. *Without my phone, how would I find the driver when I wanted to leave? How could I contact anyone if I needed help?* I was exceptionally vulnerable as I walked into the temple.

Josh had suggested that I hire a guide. By sheer accident, I found the place where the tour guides waited. I arranged to have an English-speaking guide escort me for the mere cost of 200 rupees, roughly $4.50. The guide was on autopilot. His remarks were well-scripted and followed a prescribed, memorized format. He used a laser pointer to direct my attention to what he was describing. His limited command of English prevented him from answering my questions completely. I could take only so much before I just politely nodded and smiled whenever he provided a new fact.

The structures at this site dated back to the twelfth century, during the reign of the Hoysalas. The intricate carvings were made from soapstone. This material formed an iron-like firmness when it was exposed to the environment. The craftsmanship was outstanding and truly had withstood the test of time, except for the portions that were either missing or incomplete. Each of the figurines was unique. They were placed on the structure in an interlocked pattern. I was overwhelmed with facts and accumulated a treasure trove of amazing pictures. My uneasiness subsided when I was reunited with my driver.

When we reached Halebeedu, the eleventh-century capital of the Hoysalas, the driver dropped me off and once again disappeared until I was ready to leave. The shrine was located in a gardenlike setting that included a lake and an archaeological museum. After touring the area, I became parched from the blazing heat and returned to the car. Instead of driving back to Bangalore, the driver took a short detour and parked the car in front of a sign with the words, "*Parshvanatha*" and "*Shantinatha Basadis.*" It was a

Halebeedu

small site with only a couple of buildings. After we were back on the road to Bangalore, I nursed the remaining ounces of my water. I frequently dozed off during the five-hour ride as a way of dealing with the monotony of the trip.

Finding an appropriate bathroom was always an issue on an Indian road trip. Oftentimes bathrooms were just holes in the ground that I squatted over, and they usually didn't provide toilet paper or paper towels. My under-estimation of the time factor caused me to miscalculate the amount of bottled water and food that I needed. Having a non-English-speaking driver in a rural part of India made these basic needs problematic.

While I was in the car, I recalled one of our family hikes in Summit County, Colorado. To our dismay, we were inadequately equipped and ran out of water after we became lost on the way back to our car. A not-so-friendly US Forest Service ranger came to our rescue and scolded us. After that, I always made sure to bring sufficient water, especially when we had four boys in tow. I chastised myself for being negligent and not being better prepared.

Once inside Josh's apartment, my first stop was the bathroom. Next, I slowly began drinking bottled water. I took a tantalizingly cold shower that removed the itchy salt, the grime, and the dust. I had a throbbing headache coupled with hot and cold spells. I went to bed early and awoke in the middle of the night with another round of diarrhea.

Josh provided me with World Health Organization rehydration packets that contained a powdered electrolyte mixture easily added to bottled water. These packets became a lifesaver during future bouts of sickness. My mood matched the melancholy selection of songs that I played on my iPod—"Dust in the Wind" by Kansas and "I Am a Rock" by Simon and Garfunkel.

An unexpected call from Ira lifted my spirits. In two days, he would be flying back to Bangalore to meet with prospective clients. Instead of waiting for my return trip to the States, I would see Ira within a few days.

16

The doorbell rang at 4:00 a.m. Ira could barely put down his luggage before I attacked him with massive, unyielding bear hugs and moist, penetrating kisses.

"I'm so happy that you're here," I bellowed.

"Me too!" Ira said as we looked into one another's eyes.

"Did you get any rest on the plane? You look a bit pale and your eyes are glassy."

"I slept a bit, but it's never enough on an international flight. In three hours, I have three consecutive conference calls. And Suraj wants me at the Electronic City office by 10:30."

I looked down at my watch. "Are you kidding? Is that even possible?"

"We'll see," Ira said as we walked into the bedroom.

"What's so important?" I asked.

"Probably nothing."

"I never thought that you'd lose so much of your autonomy."

"You're worrying too much," Ira responded.

I was beginning to resent his employer. Ira was not a machine. He needed time to recoup after two days of intense international travel. Somehow his superiors conveniently took extra time off on travel days, but Ira was expected to be on the go constantly. I was disappointed that during Ira's week and a half back in the States, he didn't have the chance to ski or attend a University of Colorado basketball game. His job had become all-consuming and left almost no time for a social life.

I was delighted that I could share my remaining two weeks abroad with Ira. Now we could both travel to meet Rachael's parents in New Delhi and also return to the States together before the start of Passover. Back in Colorado, Aaron already had taken the initiative to do the "Kosher for *Pesach*" shopping. Shortly after my return, I would need to prepare everything for the holiday from scratch. None of my food preparations could include any corn products or leavening agents. Matzah meal, matzah cake meal, and potato starch replaced basic ingredients such as flour, baking soda, and baking powder.

With little time left in India, I focused my attention on networking with expats and Josh's contacts and following up on my teaching options. I had had such a wonderful time at the women's club meeting at Leela Palace that I decided to become a regular at the Thursday morning tea. Dealing with rickshaws was now more manageable. I frequently chuckled at the craziness of it all. When I would sit at a stoplight, the annoying hum of the rickshaws and motorcycles drowned out my thoughts. Everyone was so closely jammed together you could actually "reach out and touch" whatever or whoever was alongside you. It resembled the start of a marathon in which all of the runners are on each other's heels waiting for the starting gun to go off. Well, in this case, the drivers were revving up their engines, waiting for the light to change. Ready, set, *go!*

At tea one Thursday, I talked with a group of women from the Netherlands. They all appeared to be struggling with life in India and were awaiting the time when they could return to Europe. Just about every foreigner was under contract for a designated time period ranging from eighteen months to three years. Their lives were similar to those of military personnel or international teachers who lived with few possessions and hopped from one place to the next.

In addition to the weekly meetings and charity events, this women's group organized book clubs, special dinners, and field trips. Ironically, the club was providing a weekday field trip to IST's Electronic City campus, which included a tour and a lunch. As Ira's wife, I was prohibited from visiting the same campus during the work week. Once again, I was marginalized by IST's policies.

With less than a week until I was scheduled to go back to the States, my future was still up in the air. My hopes for an Indian teaching job now rested in the hands of two different schools. One was KIS, the first school I visited—the one with British overtones where I underwent a marathon interview process. The other was the one with the progressive and liberal attitude toward curriculum and dress.

With verbal offers on the table, it was wise to explore possible rental situations. Ira's employer didn't allow me to live in Adarsh Gardens when Ira was traveling outside of India, and Josh's apartment was far from both schools. Ira e-mailed his contacts at IST to see if they could provide any assistance. He was advised to check the employee bulletin board for potential apartment leads.

I was furious. Every expat I had met at the Overseas Women's Club was provided housing assistance because all foreign employers understood the difficulties that expats faced in India. The most pressing issue was that landlords expected a deposit that equaled ten to twelve months' rent and an additional broker's fee equaling a month's rent. Nevertheless, we could not afford to make a poor decision. A reputable broker would need to be consulted when I returned.

I packed my clothes for my journey to the United Sates and thought about the progress that I had made in adapting to Indian life. At the same time, I was looking forward to celebrating Passover with Ira, Josh, Aaron, and Jordan. Josh would be traveling back a few days after we did, stopping first in Chicago to visit Ira's parents. Disappointingly, Adam was unable to take any time off since he was going to be on a photo shoot at Vail Resorts just a few days before the holiday. At least we would see him for a couple of days when he skied at Keystone. I couldn't wait to be reunited with my family in the glorious Rocky Mountains.

Casting a shadow on my positive outlook was an unsettling feeling that lingered deep inside me. *Would all of the pieces of the puzzle fall into place so that Ira and I could find contentment living separate lives for weeks at a time or was this farfetched idea headed down a disastrous path?*

Driving on Black Ice

17

If I clicked my heels together like Dorothy in the *Wizard of Oz* and was magically transported halfway around the world, my return would be instantaneous. But Ira and I traveled the conventional way—and spent over twenty hours on two different planes. No matter how long it took, though, I would agree with Dorothy: There truly is no place like home.

Two months is a long time to be away. My house was not as tidy as I would have liked, but it came nowhere close to imitating the rampant pollution that was part of daily life in India. I was thrilled to again use a simple device like the vacuum instead of one of those wispy, handmade Indian brooms; and I was relieved that bugs were not daily visitors. I welcomed the ability to spend time with Aaron and Jordan, to eat whatever I wanted, to bake foods in my oven, to brush my teeth with tap water, to soak in a hot bath, and to sleep in my own bed.

That first Indian experience made me realize how lucky I was to be born an American. My lifestyle and opportunities were dramatically affected by this simple fact. I cherished each and every one of the modern conveniences that were part of my life, and was appreciative that my sons had had an American upbringing and education. To put it simply, I was immensely grateful to be home.

Since our first trip to Keystone Lodge in the 1970s, Ira and I had developed an attachment to Summit County, Colorado. In 1987, after a small hiatus from skiing, we took our three small children to Keystone in the summer to look around. We were instantly sold on the child-care facility when we met the loving director, Jonna Wooldridge. All of our children learned to ski at the Keystone Ski School. Both Aaron and Jordan were riding the chairlift when they were only three years old, and Josh and Adam became ski instructors when they were in their late teens.

Now that we were back in the States, Ira and I longed for a trip into the mountains before the ski season ended. Although his business schedule remained intense and at times unforgiving, it was possible to drive up in between Ira's business calls and then make a few runs midday when most of his colleagues were sleeping in India. Ira needed a diversion from the everyday grind. I was on an emotional high as I skied with him and Aaron and Jordan.

Years ago, my sons had labeled me the "Energizer Bunny." I rarely stopped. On this outing, I didn't think twice about where I was in relation to the rest of the family and accidently skipped the designated last meeting point before skiing to the midpoint lift. When I reached the lift, I was surprised: the rest of the family was not trailing right behind. The seconds turned into minutes. Something was amiss. *Ira mentioned that he had a slight headache. I didn't think much of that. More likely, someone had fallen and time was needed to put a ski or two back on.*

My phone rang. I missed the call. I glanced down. It was Josh, probably calling from Chicago. I breathed a sigh of relief. *Should I say anything to the two ski patrolmen who were standing near me? Uh, what would I say? I had no idea whether anything had happened.*

My stomach tightened. The phone rang again.

"Is Dad with you?" Aaron questioned.

"No!" I blared.

"He's not here. Jordan is hiking up." My heart pulsated. My skin was damp. Time crawled.

The phone rang again. I answered. Aaron's voice echoed, "Dad's in bad shape. Call the ski patrol!"

I skied to the lift operators. *Calm down, calm down.* "My husband's injured!"

"Where?" the shorter one asked.

"It's the steep face on Wild Irishman."

"What's he wearing?"

I couldn't visualize anything—his jacket, his ski pants, or his helmet—everything vanished.

Trembling…sniffling, I said, "I can't remember."

"That's okay."

I slid onto the next available chair.

Bad shape. What did that mean?

Was he bleeding?

Had he hit a tree?

Globs of snot oozed out of my nose. I shook. *Snorkel-snorkel.* My mitten smeared the rest on my face.

The phone rang. "Dad's head…Where are you?" Aaron roared.

"I'm coming!"

Droplets were pooling in my eyes. My vision clouded. My goggles fogged up. My jellylike legs wobbled as I skied down to their position. Heavy wet snowflakes fell. Wind hit me head-on.

A Good Samaritan was waving people away. Skis were placed in a big X uphill from Ira. Aaron and Jordan were standing near three men in red jackets emblazoned with white crosses.

Ira was yelping, "Help me! Help me! It's too tight!"

A neck collar secured his head and a strap held his right arm above his head. His body was tied firmly to a sled.

What was too tight? Was it his head? What had happened?

Jordan had hiked up the mountain calling, "Dad, dad, where are you?" No one responded.

Then Jordan had found him on the side of the run, dazed. Towering over his fallen father, Jordan had watched Ira's hazel eyes roll back and forth. Ira's skis and poles had come off and were now lying haphazardly on the steep mountain slope. He had tumbled or flown several yards. No trees were nearby. His helmet was on his head. Ira didn't know anything. He didn't recognize Jordan. He drifted in and out. During a lucid moment, Jordan heard the words "my right arm."

Traumatized, Aaron and Jordan told the ski patrolmen about the arm. Their main concern was the head injury. Ira couldn't answer simple questions. *Where was his memory?* The boys and I looked at one another. Our tears crystallized. Ira's words made no sense.

The ski patrolmen wasted no time. One pulled the sled. The other two cleared the way. Skiers and boarders alike yielded as the patrollers took the sled and made their way to the medical clinic.

18

We waited. I was handed a plastic bag with Ira's long-underwear top, turtleneck, and sweater, which had been sheared off his body. Another bag held his long-underwear bottoms, ski pants, and coat. His ski boots and helmet were on the floor. All of Ira's possessions were with us, but he wasn't. Aaron updated Josh in Chicago and Adam in Vail.

What happened?

Was it skier error or a medical problem?

Was it a hit-and-run accident?

The doctor came out. The X-ray confirmed a severely shattered shoulder. Ira's irate behavior indicated brain trauma. Ira needed to be evaluated at a hospital. He remained agitated and combative, and the doctor mentioned the possibility of a traumatic brain injury. An induced coma was mandated.

I wasn't prepared.

What happens if he never regains consciousness?

Stop thinking the worst.

Ira exhibited courage and a love of life.

I have to remain strong and positive.

Aaron and Jordan were furious that the ski patrolmen didn't listen to them. They sputtered, "Why did they make daddy hurt more?"

I stood up and the room swirled around me. Aaron and Jordan grabbed me. Someone handed me ginger ale, crackers, and a barf bag. Then we walked alongside the gurney as they wheeled Ira outside. Snow prevented a helicopter ride, so a Flight for Life ambulance was used instead. Tubes ran out of Ira's nose and mouth. We heard rhythmic beeps. The boys leaned over him. They stared into Ira's haunting eyes and kissed Ira's pallid face.

I climbed into the passenger seat, sweating, trembling. Three medical personnel scrunched into the back. Each one introduced herself, himself. Moments later, I couldn't recall any of their names. The youngest questioned the range for the ventilator. There was a disagreement. The older paramedic conveyed her opinion. The two others agreed. I turned to face the back of the ambulance. They were taking turns pumping the hand ventilator. They were keeping Ira alive.

One minute we were enjoying an incredible day. Now we were all heading in different directions. And the next twenty-four to forty-eight hours would be decisive. I couldn't lose Ira. I called a few family members and close friends.

The ambulance arrived at the ER. My vision was blurry. My head was pulsating in an erratic rhythm. I sat myself down in the waiting room. A female chaplain escorted me into an empty room.

She asked, "Have you reached clergy?"

I shrugged my shoulders and replied, "It's almost sundown and close to the Jewish Sabbath."

As she exited, she said, "I'll try."

Within minutes I was talking with the assistant rabbi. I told him Ira's Hebrew name. The *mishaberach* prayer would be said. The rabbi's endearing words connected me to something comforting, although the feeling vanished quickly.

My insides were as tight as an over-wound watch. The slightest beeping sound became deafening. The antiseptic smell was annoying. The brightness made me reach for a pair of sunglasses.

Ira's face was expressionless. His cheeks matched the stark white sheets, and he was motionless and cold. Tubes and wires formed an abstract maze, as medical personnel constantly assessed his monitors.

Could he hear me?

Could he feel my touch?

I sang to him. I caressed him. I wiped his random tears. I prayed. *Would I have the strength to deal with whatever happened next?*

19

Aaron and Jordan arrived. They clung to me like young tiger cubs embracing their mom. My cell phone rang and rang. Bad news traveled at lightning speed. My mom called. I became queasier. Our relationship was erratic, with a long list of ups and downs. A year or two without speaking was common. She had chosen not to interact while I recuperated from hip-replacement surgery. Something sparked her today. My heart was beating faster and faster. *If my mother called, she probably thinks Ira is going to die.*

None of the other calls was as intense. My brother Ed offered to fly out. The remaining callers sent good wishes. Santosh, one of Ira's managers from India, and two American executives, Bala and Vinay, called. We spoke few words. IST offered no support. I became detached.

The ER doctor told me that the CT scan showed no brain abnormalities. Surgery was not needed. I breathed a huge sigh of relief. *I'm glad that Ira was wearing a helmet.* This was the *first* ski season that we opted to wear helmets instead of knitted ski hats.

Technicians scanned the rest of his body. Thank God. The injuries were just his shoulder and the concussion. *Oh, but what did he say about an aneurysm?* I needed to know more. My major fears were lessened. *How long would he remain in the coma? Would there be any long-term effects?* Patience became my companion.

Adam arrived. His arm was around Rachel's back when he entered the room with his college buddies, Neema and Joe. All three were in Vail with Adam for a *Men's Health* photo shoot. Kayla, Jordan's girlfriend, also came to the ER. She treated everyone to Subway sandwiches. Aaron and I spent the night in the trauma center. We nodded on and off on our metal folding chairs. The beeping of the cardiac monitor and the rhythmic drone of the ventilator reminded us to remain alert. Adrenaline kept me going. My arch-enemy—an inability to sleep—was now my friend.

The doctors reduced the amount of sedating drugs they were giving to Ira. He was becoming aware. He was gasping more often. His eyes started to flutter. His toes were twitching. He was pulling on the arm restraints. He squeezed our hands whenever we talked to him. Random tears continued.

Ira wanted to speak. He couldn't. The tubes were uncomfortably lodged in his mouth. I handed him paper and pencil. He scribbled the words, "SET ME FREE." He shook his arms. The arm restraints curtailed his attempts. Tears streamed down his cheeks. His eyes looked wild and full of terror.

Nurses came into the room often, keeping tabs on Ira's progress. They had bet one another on how long it would take for Ira to come out of the coma. We shook our heads in disbelief.

Finally the tubes were removed. Ira could talk and breathe on his own, although his voice was raspy and he dozed off repeatedly. He remained in a daze, with limited comprehension of what was happening around him.

This life-threatening episode was behind us. Serious concerns remained. When the attending physician arrived, he asked if the family had any questions.

"Is it possible that an unknown medical problem caused my husband's accident?" I asked.

"Has he experienced any other blacking-out episodes?" the doctor asked.

"No," I replied.

"It's unlikely that anything medically occurred."

"How do you know for sure that there isn't a medical cause?" Aaron countered.

"We don't. But there's no history so you shouldn't worry," the doctor casually remarked.

"What about his arm? Shouldn't it be in a sling and be iced?" Adam asked.

The doctor looked down at his shoes and said, "Oh, has no one come in yet? I'll contact the orthopedic doctor."

The doctor turned toward the doorway. I interrupted his departure by shooting off another troubling question. "Is a cardiologist going to come in to discuss the aneurysm?"

"I'm not sure what follow-up, if any, needs to be done. I'll get back to you."

The doctor looked down at Ira's chart, wrote a few words, and then walked out of the room. Ira continued fading in and out of consciousness. He tended to repeat himself, asking the same questions over and over. He reminded me of my Aunt Saerre, who was in her nineties. Ira continually asked for his work Blackberry and computer. I instructed the boys *not* to bring Ira's computer or phone to the hospital.

Fortitude was necessary. It could take days, weeks, or possibly months before Ira recovered from his shoulder and brain injuries.

20

Despite my pleas to let me stay the next night, the nursing staff flatly refused. I reluctantly left and drove home with Adam. I was sleep-deprived and falling asleep became a chore. As I entered a dreamy state, the phone rang. It was Ira. He was disoriented and wanted to know where I was. Abruptly, he hung up the phone, leaving me bewildered. A call to the nurse's station yielded vague reassurances that everything was all right.

I tried to sleep but couldn't. I was fixated on everything that had happened and soon became agitated. *Why were the doctors not interested in making sure there was not a medical reason for the accident?* Suddenly, I became obsessed with the word "aneurysm." *Didn't people die of aneurysms? Shouldn't we know more?*

I walked around my house. I was like a lost person driving in an unknown area without a road map. I turned on the computer and researched aneurysms. My efforts were fruitless. I quickly saw that I was searching too broad a term. As the sun started to rise, something clicked. *Why should I struggle to make sense of this by myself?* I e-mailed one of Ira's doctors, hoping that he would respond to my message, which was flagged with a red exclamation point.

The telephone rang. It was Ira again. He had no idea where he was. Josh called next. He had remained with his grandparents in Chicago and would be in Colorado by lunchtime. He had been up most of the night researching aneurysms and wanted to know what the doctors had told me.

On the way to the hospital, my sister-in-law, Shari, called. She echoed the same concerns. Her inquiries to the attending physician netted a minimal response. She wanted my permission to contact her father, a renowned cardiologist on the East Coast. By the time I reached the hospital, I had talked with Shari's father as well as with the doctor I contacted by e-mail. Both agreed that Ira should be transferred to the University of Colorado Hospital.

Paperwork was signed. An ambulance was ordered. Less than an hour before the ambulance arrived, the nurse put a sling on Ira's arm and provided ice for his shoulder. We never saw a cardiologist or an orthopedic doctor.

At University of Colorado Hospital, Ira underwent a new round of testing and was seen by numerous doctors. They explored and then ruled out reasonable explanations for his accident. The neurologist ran more tests and the new tests detected a small contusion inside his brain. The doctors continued to monitor his cognitive ability by asking questions. Delays in processing were apparent. Some of his responses were comical. It was years since Bill Clinton had been president, but that was Ira's initial response when asked for the name of the current president. All of his missteps were, within a matter of a few seconds, self-corrected. His shoulder was placed in a new sling and iced on a regular basis.

During a conversation with Ira's internist, we learned that the heart aneurysm had been detected six months earlier by Ira's Boulder cardiologist. Without any regard for Ira's future well-being, the cardiologist chose not to share this vital information. From this point forward, Ira's heart was periodically assessed for changes and doctors advised him of warning signs that would require an immediate trip to an ER.

We never determined an exact cause for the accident. None of the hospital tests revealed any underlying medical problem that could account for his blackout. If Ira had made a tactical error, it was presumed that he would have instinctively used one of his arms to brace himself for the fall. Instead, his injuries suggested that he had abruptly crashed into the mountain, leading with his head and shoulder. Due to his amnesia, we will never know conclusively what happened.

Our best hypothesis is that skiing at a high altitude just a couple of days after returning from back-to-back trips to India had hindered his abilities. Jet lag, compounded by a challenging workload and the natural stress of being 10,000 feet above sea level were most likely the culprits. In retrospect, when Ira experienced a migraine aura, we should have headed back. Or, better yet, we shouldn't have squeezed in our ski fix before Passover.

21

Passover, one of Ira's favorite holidays, began the day after he was transported to University Hospital. We considered ignoring the seder, but Passover was the *one* holiday that Ira always had looked forward to since he was a young child. As we mulled over our options, we questioned whether it was possible to skip a holiday that symbolized hope, especially this year. How could we disregard something that was so entrenched in Jewish symbolism and the traditional value of remembering the past in relationship to the present and the future?

Coincidentally, the senior rabbi at our synagogue called as the boys and I were sitting in Ira's hospital room on Sunday afternoon talking about our Passover options.

"How's Ira doing?"

"It's been a rough two days, but he's out of the coma," I replied.

"I'm glad to hear that. How long will he be hospitalized?"

"We transferred him to University Hospital. We'll have to wait and see what the new doctors say."

"I wish him a speedy recovery."

"Yes. *Halevai.* Can the synagogue help us in any way for Passover?" I inquired.

"Hmmm. You can always join us at the synagogue family seder."

"That's not an option."

"Please give my best to Ira and have a wonderful Pesach. *Hag Sameach.*"

I disconnected the call and said, "We're on our own for Passover."

"Huh? Didn't the rabbi offer any assistance?" Josh responded.

"Not really. He invited us to the family seder. That's not happening. I'm not leaving your dad for a minute."

"Mom, are you surprised? Other than Rabbi Levy, who moved to New York, no one ever called me when I was hospitalized three times in high school," Aaron said.

"It's disappointing. I wish we were back in Illinois near a Jewish community that cared."

"Mom, we're not. We have one another and that's what matters," Adam said.

"I knew we'd be on our own. I asked Veronica, the day nurse, to locate a room for our seder. I'll give you guys a list of what you'll need to bring."

For over thirty years, my preparations for Passover always involved a substantial amount of cleaning, reorganizing, cooking, and baking. Despite all this intense work, the holiday always gave me tremendous satisfaction, as I modeled traditions that I hoped would be passed on to future generations. As our children matured, they learned to lend a helping hand, especially after we moved to Colorado, where we didn't have any extended family.

On Monday evening, a table was set in the conference room. Instead of china and crystal on a festive tablecloth, an array of paper and plastic products on a bare table sufficed. We placed *haggadahs* at each spot. At center stage was our Israeli seder plate with all of the symbolic items, along with a medium-sized bowl heaping with *charoset*—a mixture of chopped apples, nuts, kosher wine, and cinnamon. Spread around the long, rectangular table were a bowl of shelled, hard-boiled eggs, a bowl of saltwater, gefilte fish, horseradish, a black-and-white box of Yehuda matzah, a specially designed matzah cover with three compartments, an *afikomen* bag, Ira's *Kiddush* cup from his bar mitzvah, and a large bottle of Mogen David concord wine. Our main entrée was sliced corn beef and some turkey that Josh brought from a Chicago deli. Dessert was imported from one of our favorite Jewish bakeries, Leonard's Bakery, in Northbrook, Illinois. I was so proud of my sons because they prepared and delivered everything to the hospital while I remained by Ira's side.

The plastic cups were filled with kosher wine. Ira recited in Hebrew the *Kiddush*, the blessing over the first of four cups of wine that are drunk during the seder. As Ira walked over to the adjacent sink to fulfill the customary ritual of washing his hands, I glanced around at our small gathering—our four sons plus Aaron's girlfriend, Natalie, and Jordan's girlfriend, Kayla. The pleasure of being together as a family became the source of great joy and happiness. To put it simply, it was more important for us to stay by Ira's side than to stand in the kitchen preparing for the holiday or attending a synagogue seder. The rituals of reorganizing and cleaning my kitchen, using glass dishes, and preparing a wide assortment of Pesach foods lost their importance when I held his hand there in the hospital.

We passed a bowl of saltwater around the table for dipping our sprigs of parsley. As we recited the Hebrew blessing, I was grateful for every food that was harvested from the ground. After living in India and recently witnessing Ira's comatose state, simple things in life had a new meaning. When Ira took the middle of three matzahs, broke it into two, and then wrapped one of the pieces in the *afikomen* cloth, I watched the brittle matzah crumbs splinter onto the table. This reminded me of the masses of poor Indians who were forced to make do with just crumbs and scraps of food.

Josh read the opening words of the Passover story, "All who are hungry— let them come and eat. All who are needy—let them come and celebrate the Passover with us. Now we are here; next year may we be in the Land of Israel. Now we are slaves; next year may we be free."

A chill ran down my back and goose bumps formed on my arms. Our family underwent its own metamorphosis as each of us grappled with the meaning of life and death. Having watched Ira lying in an induced coma hovering between life and death, we knew what it meant to be a slave to our worst fears. Now we were free to look past this dark moment with the joys of freedom and a future with our family remaining intact.

It was a miracle. Ira could hardly gather his thoughts in a meaningful way one day and the following day he was sitting at the head of the table leading a Passover seder in English and in Hebrew. The meager spread of foods did not dampen our spirits. We read and sang songs without giving a second thought to the hospital surroundings. One of Ira's favorite songs, "Dayenu" (which translates as "It Would Have Sufficed" or "We Would Have Been Satisfied"), took on a new layer of meaning. We were grateful that our lives were not shattered by Ira's accident and that we were still together as a family.

Ira remained alert during most of the evening, except for two or three times when he nodded off. As Aaron went around adding some wine for the fourth cup of wine, everyone was smiling. *On Friday afternoon, who would have imagined that this would be possible?*

Ira smiled as he read the part titled "Conclusion of the Seder." The closing line—next year in Jerusalem—and the singing of the corresponding song in Hebrew seemed to evoke an unanticipated sense of euphoria.

When we finished the song, I leaned over and whispered in his ear, "What were you thinking while we were singing, *'L'shana haba'ah b'y'rushalayim'?*"

"I'm not exactly sure. I'm just content to be alive, to be here with you, and to have a future."

We all felt the same way. Just a handful of days before, Ira's entire existence and future were in limbo. If he had died, his past would have been reduced to our memories. By remaining alive, Ira's past was once again merged with the present. He would remain part of our family's future.

Near the conclusion of the seder, as everyone was singing "Chad Gadya" in Hebrew, my eyes drifted over to the English translation. I skimmed over the cumulative tale that illustrates how stronger creatures consume the weaker ones, ending with the Holy One overcoming death. To some, this song is symbolic of all the larger nations that have unsuccessfully tried to destroy the Jewish people. This Passover, I saw the song in a more personal light. Ira and I had endured varying degrees of adversity during our life together, some having more significant consequences than others. The agony of watching Ira's motionless body in an induced coma was the latest episode, and our family was indeed fortunate that Ira had eluded the Angel of Death. Forces way beyond my grasp controlled his destiny and Ira had prevailed.

The following afternoon, Ira was discharged from the hospital. We arrived home in Superior just in time to start the second seder. Four days after my world started to unravel; my family was in our home, safe and sound. As a united group, the time had come to cherish and revel in each and every precious moment together.

22

Ira suffered for weeks at home as his body responded to his injuries. Much like the recovery process after a devastating earthquake, it was slow and deliberate. Ira reluctantly succumbed to my nagging that he take medication and dutifully follow the doctor's orders not to move his arm. His shattered right shoulder needed time to heal; his arm, bent in a constant right angle, rested in a sling attached to a contoured, immobilizing black cushion. Every movement caused pain and discomfort, which the prescribed narcotics only partially relieved.

Just about everything became a challenge and he fatigued easily. In bed he couldn't lie on his sides, and his right shoulder throbbed when he was on his back. Propping pillows under his arm eased the pain slightly, but the discomfort and pain from the injury took many agonizing and sleepless months to resolve.

Josh extended his stay for a couple of weeks so he could lend a helping hand. If I needed to run errands or get some exercise, Josh made sure that Ira wasn't left alone. When I drove Ira for medical appointments, Josh took care of whatever needed to be done around the house.

The HR department at IST contacted Ira regarding his going on short-term disability. He resisted taking *any* time off and instead chose to continue working. Within a day of returning home from the hospital, he was making phone calls and responding to e-mails. I was happy that he was remaining mentally alert and finding ways to distract himself from the intense discomfort. But I wanted to baby him. He needed rest, because, after all, his body needed time to heal from the trauma it had endured.

None of the people Ira spoke with on a daily basis realized the full extent of his limitations. Only a handful of IST colleagues even asked how he was managing. Most didn't show the slightest interest. Instead, Vinay and Suraj sent e-mails and made phone calls to press Ira to assess what he had accomplished during his time in India and the United Kingdom. We heard some nasty insinuations that my presence in India had compromised Ira's work. This line of thinking was outrageous. When I was in India, I had spent most of my time by myself. None of Ira's previous colleagues or clients had ever questioned his work ethic—everyone recognized his type A personality. I was puzzled.

Suraj went so far as to ask why Ira had needed to return home for Passover and why he was not willing to return to India in June even though he had family wedding parties scheduled for Josh and Rachael in Chicago. These exchanges would have been troubling under normal circumstances, but coming on the heels of a near-fatal accident, I became disturbed by what Ira shared with me. *What type of company took issue with someone's taking time to celebrate religious holidays and a major family event like a wedding?*

Equally disappointing was Suraj and Vinay's new idea to revise Ira's American-based employee status to that of an Indian-based employee. Neither Vinay nor Suraj had been a party to Ira's hiring. Now months later, they were attempting to redefine his job. Not only did they want Ira to give up his American salary and extensive insurance package, but they also were telling him that his main obligation was to assist the two US-based salesmen. Ira would never have accepted the IST position if he had been told that it would be primarily a sales position. *Wasn't his title "Delivery Head" for the LPO?*

In between his conference calls and computer work, Ira continued with a multitude of follow-up doctor visits and also traveled to a physical therapist as often as three times a week. I chauffeured him and maintained his medical appointment calendar. Being his right-hand man consumed most of my waking hours.

In the car on the way back from the physical therapist's office one sunny day, I glanced at Ira precisely at the moment that he jolted himself awake from a catnap.

"Are you all right?" I asked.

"Why?"

"You woke up so abruptly."

"It just happens. I nod off and then wake up. That's the least of my problems."

"Are you sure you're okay?" I reiterated.

"Being in a coma and not remembering several days is more of an issue."

"It's behind us."

"Yeah, but when I look at the pictures Aaron took in the ER, I realize how my life could have ended."

I reached over and touched Ira's arm. "Stop looking back. You're here and I'm here with you."

"But I need to remember that so I value my life more."

"I agree. You need to cling to things that will enhance your life."

A business trip to the United Kingdom was near the top of the list of things that Ira set out to accomplish the following month. Long before the accident, Ira was scheduled to attend this legal conference in May and was now planning other ways to maximize his visit. He was making arrangements to speak to a large, worldwide gathering of lawyers from a multinational conglomerate and also was setting up meetings with prospective and existing UK clients.

"Are you ready for international travel?" I asked as I was checking airfares to London.

"Why not? My doctors say I'll be fine if you're with me. It'd be silly to walk away from potential business."

"I just wanted to make sure. It hasn't been that long since the accident."

"I want to go, especially with you by my side. After everything that's happened, I want to explore London and possibly Paris on the weekend. We need to enjoy life," Ira said.

"What about Suraj? Is he going to say I'm *distracting* you?"

Ira's voice grew in intensity when he replied, "I don't give a damn about him. The doctors are all in agreement. I can't go overseas without an escort."

"That's all I needed to hear. I'll book my flight once you have yours in place."

I looked at this business trip as a way to cast off my lingering fears surrounding Ira's health. Weeks and weeks of sleepless nights had transformed me into a watchman who stood guard over Ira as he grimaced in pain nightly.

The fear of almost losing him made me hypersensitive and overprotective. I hoped that watching him function in a less fragile state would help me loosen up. The side trips on the weekends were an added perk. We could enjoy life to the fullest.

The accident indeed had made an impact on our lives. A day didn't go by without our reflecting on how fortunate we were that Ira survived. Along with these positive feelings came the never-ending questions about our future. It was less than six months ago that Ira had started working for IST, and he thrived on the challenge of working in a different legal environment. It didn't seem prudent for Ira to start looking for another position, especially since his shoulder required a long recovery process. Nevertheless, the thought of being separated, even for just a few weeks, now seemed unnatural and unreasonable after our ordeal. After all, employment choices continued to be limited by a sluggish economy. My body tightened whenever I thought about my pending Indian teaching opportunities or Ira's next trip to India.

Less than two weeks before we were scheduled to leave for London, Ira received a call from Suraj. Other people would be traveling to London, but Ira's trip was cancelled, even though the projected cost was purportedly in the approved budget. Suddenly, no money was available for Ira's travel costs, but sufficient funds could be found for Suraj and one of the American salesmen to travel. Ira was disappointed. Suraj suggested that Ira address a banquet room full of lawyers over the telephone. I laughed out loud when I heard that comment. How could Ira address a large group of people using just a telephone? It would indeed be embarrassing if he told everyone that IST did *not* have the money to send the LPO Delivery Head but could send two people who were not lawyers.

Ira took this decision, which was beyond his control, in stride. He was quickly learning that the freedom and respect to which he had grown accustomed as a private American lawyer were at times nonexistent in a large

Indian corporation like IST. People who weren't lawyers were making important decisions that oftentimes didn't make sense, undermined his legal authority, and potentially diminished his stellar reputation.

I was disappointed that Ira's travel plans to Europe were cancelled arbitrarily without any regard for the fact that *my* ticket was already paid for. Suraj and Vinay quibbled about the charges incurred for the cancellation of Ira's ticket and offered no compensation for the $250 change fee that became my problem. *Was I surprised? Not really.*

As the weeks passed, doctor appointments were less frequent, except for the periodic follow-up appointments with the orthopedic surgeon. Despite the daily physical therapy at home and the visits to see Hetal, the physical therapist, Ira's arm wasn't progressing as expected. An MRI was taken near the end of May. Dr. McCarty, the orthopedic surgeon, didn't hide his concerns when he strolled into the room with the MRI results in his hand. Ira needed to have the torn rotator cuff in his right shoulder repaired if he had any hope of ever regaining full use of his arm. Ira was scheduled for surgery the morning of June 23.

23

When Ira's accident turned my life upside down, I was still corresponding with two schools—Chatura (the smaller, progressive day school)—and the Karnataka International School (KIS, the conservative boarding school). Chatura sent me e-mails that encouraged me to believe a written offer was coming. I sent follow-up e-mails and never received a response. A pattern was becoming apparent. Indian school administrators preferred to remain mute rather than responding with negative e-mails.

If I wanted to teach in Bangalore, one option remained—KIS. *After all that had happened, did I want to teach in India? I was conflicted and still overwhelmed.* My dilemma focused on two key issues—Ira and my career path—and too many unknown and unpredictable variables lingered in the background. If Ira would be traveling for his job, I would be able to see him more often in Bangalore than in Colorado. I assumed that he would need more assistance after the operation in India than in the United States.

Wherever I ended up living, it wouldn't be ideal. I would be with Ira only part of the time. Equally problematic was the fact that I had resigned from my teaching position in December. I was close to securing a contract with KIS but did *not* have any other potential job opportunities. Without looking at any other factors—the unknown and unpredictable, the *what ifs* of life— I was confident that I should continue my contract negotiations with KIS.

Josh and Rachael encouraged me with their phone calls, but my sons living in the States were less than thrilled with my desire to move forward. Adam, Aaron, and Jordan agreed on one point. They did not want their mom to move oversea. They desperately tried to find fault with my reasoning. None of them wanted me to spend a second alone in a Third World country.

Despite their protests, I spent several weeks corresponding with KIS regarding how many days I would need to take off for the Jewish holidays of Rosh Hashanah and Yom Kippur and for Josh's wedding in New Delhi. I was elated when an e-mail reply stated that we had reached agreement and that contract documents were being sent. Unlike an American school, which would require a background check, fingerprints submitted to the local police and the FBI, official college transcripts, and my teaching license, KIS hired me without any verification.

In the middle of my negotiations, I was mistakenly sent the offer letter that would normally be sent to an Indian secondary teacher. The total salary was listed as 790,726 rupees, or $17,329, which was subject to Indian taxation. This was slightly higher than the $1,200 to $1,400 monthly salary that Josh's contacts had said to expect, but it was nowhere near my agreed upon $35,000 annual *tax-free* salary.

If Ira and I would be gone for most of the year, we'd need Jordan to take over the day-to-day running of our main house in Superior and our second home in the mountains. Adam was in Pennsylvania and Aaron had accepted a position with Ernst and Young in Los Angeles, so they couldn't help. This would be a tremendous responsibility for someone who was only nineteen years old. We had numerous conversations with Jordan to make sure that he was up for the challenge. Without any hesitation, Jordan agreed to lend a hand even though he did not want me to leave.

I needed some help and advice with my India plans, so I reached out to others. One memorable conversation was with Caroline, one of the two readers of my graduate-school comprehension exam. She had had a well rounded career, first as a secondary English teacher, then as a primary teacher, and later as a college instructor teaching literacy. Since graduation, I had repeatedly called upon her for advice. After I described Ira's situation and my job offer, she helped me sort through my feelings. Without any hesitation, she asked, "Why do you want to teach in India?"

"I'm not sure," I meekly replied.

"You sound so uncertain. It's unlike you."

I shot back a staccato reply. "Ira's accident…living without him…there are too many unknown factors. It's downright scary."

"Why, then, are you considering this job?" Caroline prodded.

"I can't stop thinking about what it would be like to teach at that school. It's something that someone half my age would do. Maybe I'm having a midlife crisis. Am I looking to reclaim my youth? I don't know."

"Your voice sounds energized even though you have major reservations."

"Yeah, I don't understand it. I can think of so many reasons to walk away, but something deep inside echoes: just do it!"

Caroline probed further. "But will you be able to cope? A month or more without your husband is a long time."

"If I stay in the United States, I might be seeing him less."

"Trust me, living without your husband won't be easy, but regretting a missed opportunity is hard to swallow."

"I know. No matter what I choose, I'll have to find peace with my decision."

After a restless night, I awoke to a beautiful, sunny, mid-May day. A few hours later, I stared intently at the towering Colorado flatirons (mountains) to the west as I sat in my car outside the FedEx office. The signed papers were next to me. Even though Ira had remained neutral throughout my decision-making process, I was having second thoughts.

With Ira's impending shoulder surgery and additional months of intense rehab, was it fair to ask Jordan to handle the extra responsibilities that would now fall on his shoulders? *Could Ira manage without my presence?*

It wasn't just Ira's shoulder that bothered me. I pondered other aspects of his health. Ira's cognitive abilities had returned a short time after the accident, but he seemed more tired. *Would he be even more fatigued after the rotator cuff operation?* A simple thing like food preparation could be a nightmare with just one arm. *What would he eat?*

And I couldn't forget Ira's aneurysm, a ticking bomb with an unknown detonation time. *Yet, wasn't this true of most underlying health problems?* We were aware of the problem and it was being monitored. *How many people walk around each day with a potential medical disaster on the cusp of occurring, without any warning of its existence? What if Ira needed me while I was in India? But wait, wasn't it better that I be in India if he needed me there?*

The cardiothoracic surgeon calmly advised us that surgical intervention might be necessary within a few months, within several years, or maybe never. Statistics demonstrated that only one-third of the people diagnosed with Ira's condition ever required surgery. *Was this risk worth fretting over?*

The whole reason I started this Indian job search was to be close to Ira. But since the ski accident, Ira's responsibilities appeared to be in flux. *Were Suraj and Vinay's new ideas a minor detour? Were Ira's growing aggravations a sign of things to come?*

I was thrilled that I could spend more time with Josh and Rachael overseas. But the largest splash of water that tipped the balance in favor of looking at the glass as more full than empty was the lure of teaching in a Third World country, where my expertise could make a difference. Plain and simple, I wanted to have a *purpose*. I feared that if I stayed in the United States,

I would never find a position that would give me the job fulfillment I was seeking. *But would this decision have a positive or negative effect on my marriage?*

I eventually opened the car door, walked into the FedEx building, and handed the envelope to the clerk. Now the clock was ticking down to my departure date in the middle of July.

24

The school made tentative plans for me to take an Air Emirates flight, stopping in Dubai. As an American woman with a Jewish surname and an Israeli stamp in my passport, I didn't feel safe. Officials were holding Israelis responsible for the recent assassination of a high-ranking Hamas leader in Dubai. I was apprehensive about raising such concerns with the school, but my security was at stake. My children and Ira were against this prospective flight plan, especially if I had to travel by myself. So I contacted the school. All my worries were for nothing. The school was amenable and booked a flight routing me through Newark and then to Mumbai, connecting with a domestic flight to Bangalore.

I received a lovely e-mail from the two primary-unit directors, Pari and Elizabeth, welcoming me. I was going to be teaching fifth-grade English and social studies. A teacher named Mahi would be teaching math and science. (Typically, a fifth-grade teacher in an American classroom would be responsible for all four subjects.) I requested curriculum specifics but was provided only a general overview. It was impossible to prepare in advance.

Ira began communicating with Vinay and Suraj regarding his trip back to India. Several of Ira's managers in Pune and Bangalore were simultaneously asking when they would be seeing him. Ira remained in a holding pattern, as his travel requests to return to India were not immediately answered.

My daily morning routine continued. On Sundays, Tuesdays, and sometimes Thursdays, I went swimming at the Lakeshore Athletic Club-Flatiron in Broomfield. For many years, the heated, five-lane, indoor pool was my primary fitness training site. Secondary sessions took place in the adjacent fitness areas, where I did cardio work and light weight training.

One day at the pool, I started working the lower half of my body by flutter-kicking my way across the pool with my training flippers. My head was erect as I peered out the streaked floor-to-ceiling windows to watch families gathering at the outdoor water park. As my legs kept a constant rhythm, my thoughts jumped back and forth between different parts of my life.

I tossed the kickboard and put a blue buoy between my knees. My arms now took center stage as I jumped decades back in time and found myself in the fall of 1974, reliving episodes of my freshman year at the University of Colorado at Boulder. Ira was graduating the following May and was applying to law schools on the West Coast, in the Midwest, and on the East Coast. We didn't want a long-distance relationship, so a youthful marriage in August was our choice.

I remembered a pivotal moment in early June of that year when my father bluntly asked an unreasonable question. "Who do you love more, Ira or us?" At the tender age of eighteen, I mustered the courage to reply, "This is a question that should never be asked of a child. But if I need to make a choice, I will go with my future. Ira and I are in love with one another and want to be married. You will remain in my past if you are unwilling to accept the present and the future." Within what appeared to be seconds, my original August wedding date was cancelled and my mother told all of the wedding vendors and all of our acquaintances that Ira had broken off the engagement. I couldn't afford to wear the magnificent, lacy, wedding dress I had selected from Bonwit Teller or to be married at the posh Standard Club in Chicago.

Ira's parents took over responsibility for the wedding as well as the financial burden of my living expenses and college education. From that point on, my relationship with my parents and immediate family became dysfunctional. Ira was treated as a pariah and our future children were never treated like the other grandchildren were. Despite all of my parents' irrational and hurtful behavior, Ira and I remained together and I developed an inner strength that I didn't have before.

Toward the end of my swimming routine, I flipped over onto my back. I drew my knees to my chest and sculled toward the other side of the pool. Looking up at the ceiling, a warm glow encircled my body. I recalled tender moments after each of our children was born. How lucky I was to discover my *b'shert* so early in my life and to be blessed with four loving sons. Now we were changing the course of our lives. We were married but we were going to live apart. My body was starting to cool as I continued to skull.

As I treaded water at the far side of the pool, the continuous circular motion of my legs brought to mind the evenness of my life. I was fortunate that neither business nor pleasure ever had separated Ira and me for extended periods of time. Some friends relished their freedom from their spouses and frequently took separate vacations. Other couples voluntarily chose to have careers that placed them in separate cities and were able to accept the lack of time spent together. My traditional values favored a more conventional existence. It was awkward accepting an alternate way of life that focused on spouses having complete independence from one another. Despite my traditionalism, however, Ira's new job caused me to be flexible.

I put my goggles back on and was swimming the front crawl. I varied my breathing from side to side as I kept my eyes on the blue-tiled line below me. But old habits are hard to break, and after decades of turning my head only to the right side I had to remain focused on my new breathing pattern. Otherwise, I would subconsciously revert back to breathing just on one side or accidentally swallow a mouthful of water.

Mentally, I went back in time to the first decade or two of my marriage. It was my choice to stay home and raise four sons. I embraced the idea that I could be the one to instill proper values while at the same time watching firsthand each stage of development. I balanced my child-rearing years by volunteering and by pursuing two graduate degrees. After decades of devoting myself to my family, I strived to do something different. I didn't want to remain in a rut like an outdated breathing pattern. I was determined to follow through on becoming an international teacher.

25

A cquiring a travel visa is usually a straightforward process. But securing an employment visa is more complex. The applicant has to submit a long list of documents to Travisa Outsourcing, following very specific guidelines.

I spent weeks e-mailing back and forth with KIS to make sure all of my i's were dotted and t's crossed. Everything in the application packet had to be perfect or it would be flatly rejected. To avoid a costly trip to San Francisco or the uncertainty of shipping the application, I decided to hire an agent.

When I walked into this Denver office, I overheard one of the employees arguing with a customer on the phone. I just dismissed the conversation as irrelevant and focused my attention on the middle-aged man with oversized glasses who was reviewing my envelope. He was nervous and unsettled over the prospect of obtaining an employment visa for me. I paid the fee—$173 for the employment visa and $139 for the agent fee—and he provided a receipt, noted with the expected return date.

Two days later, Ira underwent reconstructive surgery. Doctors shaved down the bone spurs from his numerous fractures, repaired his torn rotator cuff, and inserted a large screw to reattach the acromion (a part of the shoulder blade). Once again, the arm became totally immobilized. Ira lost whatever independence he had regained and the healing process commenced again. Jordan and I did whatever we could to make life easier because doctors estimated that the sling would remain in place until sometime in the fall— and that a new round of extreme pain would last for weeks. Painful physical therapy would involve untold additional hours. But this setback didn't deter

Ira. Shortly after returning home from the hospital, he was sitting at his desk going through his business e-mails.

The due date for the return of my employment visa passed. With less than ten days until my departure date, I called the visa agency.

"Hi, I'm Sandra. I'm checking the status of my Indian employment visa."

A brusque masculine voice responded, "Didn't I talk to you yesterday?"

"Yeah, but I'm getting kind of nervous. I'm working in India. I'm *not* going on a vacation."

"I'm sick of your harassing calls. We'll let you know when it's back."

I was taken aback by the response and started, "But can't—"

Click. I was disconnected.

Two days later, I learned that my employment visa had been denied. It was less than a week before my departure date. Not only was my employment visa not granted, I also lost the nonrefundable $312.

What was I going to do? I had psyched myself up for the challenge of living and teaching in India and now I had a formidable obstacle in my path. I could enter India on my tourist visa, but I could not work without an employment visa. The race was on and a host of high and low hurdles besieged my attempts to reach the finish line.

I called my sons to tell them the news. From India, Josh blamed the agency for its incompetence. He couldn't stop staying, "I told you to go to San Francisco."

I responded to his cavalier words by saying, "Yeah, Josh, you're right. Not much I can do about it."

My other sons were ecstatic. Their mother had no way to go off to India.

Adam, who rarely thinks of life in Jewish terms, gleefully remarked, "Mom, it's *b'shert*—meant to be. I'll go one step further: It's a sign—a spiritual reprieve."

"Come on, Adam, don't be ridiculous. You never think in such terms."

"Mom, I'm serious. It's a sign. None of us wants you to go. Now God is sending you a powerful message. Just walk away. Better yet, run as fast as you can. We'll all be happy."

"I know nobody wants me to go. Don't you see it's an incredible opportunity? I need to be in India for Dad."

"Come on. He needs you, Mom—now more than ever. How can you even consider leaving? Who knows if he'll ever be sent back to India?" Adam replied.

"Adam, don't make me feel guilty. It's better to be in India whenever Dad's there."

"Being separated is ludicrous. You belong together. Your happiness is more important than any job or career."

"What if my future happiness is tied to my career path?" I barked back.

"That's nonsense."

"After a string of part-time jobs, I finally have an exceptional opportunity. What if I never end up teaching again?"

"Yeah. It's India, Mom. You don't belong there."

"But Josh and Rachael are there."

"So what?"

It was clear where Adam stood on that day and the days that followed.

I also spoke with Marilyn, a contemporary of mine. We met in 2005 when we were both teaching at the Boulder Jewish Day School. She had close to thirty years' of experience in the Indianapolis public school system and was assigned as my mentor. She was ecstatic about my news.

"Hurray! You have a way out of your contract. You can stay home and look for a nanny job."

"A what? Do you really expect me to consider a nanny job?"

"That's better than *any* job in India. There are several posted on Craigslist with great pay. Take a look."

If the best I could do with two graduate degrees was a nanny job, then India looked even better than it had before.

It was not fair that some unknown person tucked away in a San Francisco office had prevented my employment visa. *Was it a bureaucrat in the consulate office or an incompetent person from Travisa Outsourcing, or was Josh right? Did the blame fall on the third-party agency?*

26

I had a simple question with a complicated answer: *What was I going to do?* The Indian Consulate did not respond to e-mails or even answer its phones.

With an urgent red exclamation point and a message that was titled "URGENT, VISA DENIED," I wrote KIS and explained what had happened. I requested immediate assistance.

I took the initiative to book a flight to San Francisco on Sunday with a return on Wednesday. A fresh sprig of optimism arose when I learned that Josh needed to make an unexpected trip back to the United States to meet with clients. To minimize my out-of-pocket costs, I would stay at his partners' home in Palo Alto. Neill and Linda were Josh's venture-capital colleagues.

My anxiety level escalated when I had no response from India that day. *Did they expect me to handle this situation all by myself?* I sent a second e-mail. Once again, only silence. I sent a third e-mail. *It was impossible that no one was working at the school.*

I called Continental Airlines and rebooked my overseas flight to India. I arbitrarily extended the flight an additional week. I was now scheduled to leave on July 28. I would arrive in India just days before the first day of teachers' orientation.

Not only was I frustrated with the Indian Consulate, but I was now becoming disturbed with KIS. I picked up the phone and called Simona, my HR contact at KIS. She was very nonchalant regarding the lack of communication. It wasn't rare for the school's computer server to be out of commission for days and currently it wasn't working, she said.

Simona agreed to forward my e-mails to the principal after they were received. I imagined that someone would call me. Instead, I received a curt e-mail reply from the principal asking me to keep in touch regarding any further document requests. No assistance was offered. Previously, I was reassured in various e-mails that the school would assist me in procuring my employment visa. I had not envisioned being abandoned.

I arrived at Neill and Linda's Palo Alto home on Sunday afternoon. The next morning, I was off to San Francisco with a bottle of water and a banana in hand. I left my packet of documents at the Travisa office and was advised to return at the end of the day to pick up my visa. At the appointed time, I approached the desk. The clerk behind the counter politely said, "I'm sorry." She handed me back my passport.

"I can't believe this. Is there an explanation?" I whined.

The agent shook her head and nonchalantly said, "No, miss. The Indian Consulate never gives an explanation. Usually, more employment visas are rejected than accepted."

"What can I do?" I inquired.

"Call your employer."

I was beginning to wonder if Adam was right. *Should I accept this rejection and just turn my back on my Indian adventure?* I had my doubts. Josh and Rachael were determined. Even though they were on opposite sides of the globe, each researched the employment visa process and reached out to people in the Indian government for possible explanations. Several of their contacts suggested that my employment letter should be rewritten. A new employment letter was drafted and I extended my stay in California to Friday.

While Josh and Rachael were exploring contacts, I called several Colorado politicians' offices. A pleasant woman named Rosalyn in Congressman Jared Polis's Washington, DC, office was excited over the prospect of a Colorado woman going to teach in India. She diligently tried to put me in contact with the Indian Consulate in San Francisco.

Two options remained. Either I obtained an appointment with the consulate or reapplied for a third time through Travisa. The Indian Consulate office was my first choice. I didn't want to lay out any more money.

Even after making the decision to go to the consulate office on Thursday, I had second thoughts. *Was Adam right?* He took serious issue with his brother's insistence that I teach in India. *Were the salary and the experience worth this emotional upheaval?*

On Thursday morning, I drove to San Francisco with Josh and an Indian national. I had not heard back from Rosalyn, but someone else had arranged an appointment at the consulate. With my US passport and new employment letter clenched in my right fist, I walked toward the consulate, where I was greeted by an Eastern European man with slicked-back hair and visible tattoos. We answered his questions, handed over my passport and letter, and then waited.

After a few minutes, an Indian man dressed in a suit came toward us with my passport and the letter. He handed me the passport and immediately spoke in Hindi as if I knew what he was saying. My companion carried on a brisk conversation. He told us to come back in four hours.

Mid-afternoon, I sat across from a seasoned Indian diplomat who had resided in the United States for a year. From the start, I learned that he wasn't obligated to provide a reason for the denial and could have refused my request for a meeting. He claimed that my denial was probably based on the fact that I didn't have a specialized profession. I maintained a faint smile. *Why was I wasting more of my time on this ridiculous pursuit?*

I directed his attention to the letter that I had dropped off in the morning and asked for reconsideration. He asked, "What will you do if your visa is denied?"

I responded, "I will be unemployed." A small knot tugged inside my stomach when I said the simple word "unemployed."

A glimmer of hope became a noticeable flicker when he bluntly said, "You'll hear back by mid-morning."

My cell phone rang shortly before 10:00 a.m. I was instructed to reach San Francisco as soon as possible to pick up my visa. Without a moment's delay, I borrowed a car and was on the highway back to San Francisco for the third time in less than a week. My coveted employment visa was glued into my US passport adjacent to the page with my Israeli stamp.

I sat in the car looking down at the visa. *Was it worth the effort?*

I dialed home and Ira answered.

"I'll be back in Colorado by dinnertime. Any chance you'll be joining me in India?"

"They've ignored my latest e-mails," Ira replied.

Exasperated, I said, "This is crazy. I'm going to India without you."

"There's not much I can do without Suraj and Vinay's approval."

I pounded on the steering wheel as I yelled, "This sucks."

I boarded a plane back to Colorado. The countdown had started—only five days with Ira before I would board an international fight to India. *When would I see him again?*

Adjusting to My New Terrain

27

I drove to the airport while Ira sat silently next to me. Jordan snoozed in the back. It was unnatural for us to go so long without talking. Tears were welling up like lava in a volcano about to erupt. I remained composed until Ira had to coax me out of my seat.

"I'm going to miss both of you," I said as I dabbed my eyes.

"We'll be fine. I'm more worried about you," Ira replied.

I slipped a Kleenex out of my pocket and blew my nose. "Josh will take care of me."

As Jordan removed my luggage from the car, Ira spoke. "Hopefully, I'll see you next quarter."

Tears were gushing when I replied, "But that's not until October."

"Maybe sooner?"

Jordan was staring down at me when I grabbed his lanky body. "Jords, I'll see you at Josh's wedding. Love ya."

Hugs, kisses, and long embraces followed. Ira repeatedly offered to tote my bags into the airport. I insisted on doing it myself. My survival mandated no assistance.

When I turned my back and walked into the airport, I became nauseous and light-headed. It was similar to what I'd experienced in the Keystone Clinic as Ira's comatose body lay in the adjacent room. Plunging, once again, into unchartered waters required me to gain control. I couldn't look over my shoulder for fear that I would gallop back to the car. If Ira and Jordan had called out to me, I'm not sure how I would have responded. I was conflicted.

My inner turmoil had been building for years. Ira's career path certainly had caused an upheaval in our lives, but the crux of my indecisiveness was rooted much deeper. Staying home and raising my children had been an amazing experience while it lasted. People who'd loved raising their kids had warned me that the years would pass in a flash. Indeed, they had. I had attempted to prepare myself for the day when I would become an empty-nester.

Other than a love of learning, nothing else could explain my dedication in plowing through two master's degrees between 1993 and 2005. Nevertheless, I never anticipated that external factors would prevent me from fully utilizing my updated education. I never had attained my dream of having a rewarding career, but instead had sputtered from one job to the next.

Like other women raised in the '60s, I had choices. My choice was unpopular to some—choosing motherhood over a career path. Somewhere along the way, I began to challenge my decision and wondered how my life would have been different had I combined motherhood with a career. Knowing the demands of raising four sons with an assortment of complicated childhood medical issues and living with a high-powered attorney who frequently traveled and spent long hours preparing for trial, I realized that I had made the correct choice for *my family*. The result of my decision was that I could provide a nurturing family environment and prepare my children for adulthood. But a part of me still felt empty and longed for something slightly beyond my grasp.

With my children no longer needing my day-to-day care, I saw a small window of opportunity. I could kick up my heels and do as I pleased. Was I undergoing a midlife crisis, as I had alluded to when I spoke with Caroline? I didn't know. I wasn't interested in divorcing the love of my life (a common response to middle-age questioning)—I simply wanted to see if I could find a sense of individual purpose that was separate from those of my husband and sons. Undertaking this task was risky, but a small voice inside me egged me on despite my reservations and the negative feedback I received from others.

At the airport, I opted to sit in a quiet and somewhat secluded area that was several yards from my assigned gate. I wanted to come to terms with what I was doing. Eventually, I moved closer to the gate. An older gentleman wearing a sport jacket and khaki slacks seated to my right engaged me in conversation when he casually remarked, "I probably shouldn't be saying this, but with my luck, I'll be seated next to her." He was referring to a young woman wearing a navy scarf on her head and a loosely fitted, ankle-length, light blue dress.

We both observed her inability to control her four small sons, whose colorful *kippot*, or yarmulkes, identified their Orthodox Jewish faith. These boys were in their own world, wandering this way and that. Being parents, we sympathized with her predicament. This man—an IBM executive with a passion for music, it turned out—was a welcome acquaintance. Our brief conversation helped me to overcome some of the anxiety that was building inside of me. He encouraged me to look upon my upcoming Indian employment as a time of exploration—even though he clearly didn't envy my upcoming challenges. It was amazing how a stranger could provide such emotional support at a time when I desperately needed reassurance.

Our departure was delayed for security reasons—President Barack Obama's arrival in New Jersey. The layover in Newark was shortened a bit, so I ate and made phone calls. Finally, it was time to board the plane for Mumbai. There was no turning back. I was on my way to India.

28

On the first Wednesday in August, with a gray backpack slung over my shoulder and a black fanny pack (a keepsake from Josh's bar mitzvah) secured around my waist, I gleefully strolled three blocks through the deserted Johnson Market as the sun was trying to peek through the dull and hazy sky.

Positive energy was buzzing through my body as I walked alongside Josh. Like an elementary-school crossing guard, Josh firmly helped me navigate my way across the multi-lane, garbage-infested street to the Fatima Bakery.

We weren't alone. A slender, shoeless woman dressed in a threadbare, pale-blue sari was lying next to a girl wearing a faded print dress that hung just below her knees. A couple of yards away, a short man was squatting next to an open fire cooking something in a metal container. When I looked in their direction, the young girl's dark brown eyes met mine and I saw her mother motion to her. She skipped toward me and then circled around me as if she was playing the preschool game Ring around the Rosie. She drew her hands close to her mouth to mimic eating. As Josh instructed, I continued looking straight ahead and desperately tried to ignore this pitifully emaciated child.

My heart became saddened. Poverty was rampant. Too many Indian children were destined to lead lives without much hope. Many spent their days in squalor and never attended school. Horace Mann's prophetic nineteenth-century American ideas were alive and well in twenty-first-century India. "A child without education is poorer and more wretched than a man without bread." My warm and generous heart was becoming callous to the plight of these Indian children.

Josh and I waited for bus No. 2, the vehicle that would take me to my first day of teacher orientation. Twenty-five years earlier, I had escorted Josh to the designated bus stop where he was to wait for the kindergarten bus that would take him to Hickory Point School in Northbrook, Illinois. I couldn't prevent myself from reflecting on this poignant moment when our roles were reversed. Josh was there to be my guiding light in a foreign country while, decades ago, I was his mother holding his small hand as he entered the unknown world of the public school system. In our respective ways, we each met the unfamiliar with a mixture of trepidation and excitement, but were reassured by love and compassion.

When the old school bus rounded the corner and headed in our direction, my new adventure began. I climbed its steep steps and waved good-bye to Josh. My chest pulsated with excitement.

The sights and sounds mesmerized me. I had a bird's-eye view of areas that were blocked by walls from the view of people going by in cars or on foot. Until then I never knew that cows and goats paid their respects on the graves in Christian cemeteries. I gained a new perspective on the lack of safety on Bangalore streets. Being in the biggest vehicle gave the driver a sense of empowerment as he bullied his way using the sheer size and weight of the bus.

Untold times, the lurching bus came within inches of running into other vehicles, bicyclists, and pedestrians. One abrupt stop propelled me into the aisle and onto the filthy floor. My ooohs and aaahs were ignored as my stomach tightened with fear. The bus's horn was an additional weapon, an irritating sound that the driver deployed without hesitation as he steamrolled his way through traffic. To ease my rising tension, I turned to the words from the familiar kid's song, "The Wheels on the Bus Go Round and Round." I became preoccupied with the lyric, "The horn on the bus goes beep, beep, beep."

Once at the school, I followed the other teachers from the bus parking lot to the administration building. There I waited patiently to meet Dr. Wilson, the principal, and Dr. Diya, the director. Both were happy to see me again and applauded my tenacity in resolving my visa issues. A secondary teacher with a Chinese passport was still stranded in Iceland waiting for her visa to be granted.

The principal talked at considerable length about having to return with his entire family to the United Kingdom in the spring to wrestle with the Indian consulate office. *Hmmm...I wasn't the only one who encountered problems with the Indian government's granting of employment visas.*

"Greetings! Welcome to Bangalore. It's with great pleasure we welcome you to the KIS family." Over and over and over again, I heard this familiar refrain during the first two weeks, as each orientation speaker started his—or her–spiel. I also listened countless times as Dr. Wilson told everyone that "this is going to be the best year of the rest of your life." I was not ready to forsake my own family for the KIS family, but I was eager to become part of this school community. And I knew the climate was ripe for such interaction.

When I learned that KIS was part of a consortium of schools founded by Dr. Diya's father, S. A. Gupta, in 1959, I was elated. What an incredible opportunity to be a part of this man's vision to reform education in Asian countries. KIS was considered the flagship, an award-winning school with an enrollment of approximately 1,000 students. About two-thirds of the students were secondary students (grades six through twelve) while the remaining students were in the primary department (preschool to fifth grade).

My head was spinning. I had been in India for only four days, still recovering from jet lag, and had barely reacquainted myself with living with Josh. Now I was being thrust into a brand-new situation. I was corralled into several long PowerPoint presentations. I met dozens of people each hour and simultaneously received advice on a plethora of rules and regulations.

I was the odd man out. Everyone easily remembered my name. I was the *only* American female teacher on campus. I, on the other hand, struggled to recall names because the sounds of the Indian names were difficult for me to decipher. I constantly looked at people's name tags in order to make sense of what they were saying. Vowels and consonants mysteriously took on different patterns, and sounds melded into adjacent letters, while other names were spelled with too many letters to remember. I was overwhelmed and, at times, embarrassed.

After a long day of meetings, I took the bus back to Richmond Town. On the walk back to Josh's apartment, I didn't have to worry about crossing any major streets. However, my initial steps off the bus were met with potential peril as auto rickshaws, motorcycles, and bicycles attempted to take shortcuts around the vehicles in the right-hand lane. With the help of the bus assistant, my first step onto the pavement was partially protected. From there, I watched my step for lingering minefields—large gaping holes in the pavement and frequent animal droppings.

Once I was on the side street, I gave a sigh of relief. A barefoot boy, no older than six, grabbed my salty arm with his grimy and sticky hands. With his other hand, he motioned to his mouth. Even though my heart told me to help the child in some way, I couldn't. If I showed any sympathy or compassion, I would soon be the Pied Piper and have all the street urchins in tow.

After walking more than a block, he let go and walked away. "Phew!" I said to myself as I turned the corner. I walked by the dilapidated building that served as the local post office and headed toward Josh's apartment building. Inside, I finally was safe.

After two exhausting days of commuting, I was in a no-win situation. I could not stay much longer in Josh's place, but neither could I consider living in an apartment close to the school. Without knowing Ira's future schedule, it wasn't financially smart to invest a hefty security deposit and a one-month broker's fee. I took a cool shower and fell fast asleep, only to awaken in the middle of the night to the pervasive street sounds. I gazed up at the ceiling and watched the fan rotating. The mesmerizing motion of the blades eventually lulled me back to sleep.

In the early morning hours, my lower back was throbbing. Lower-back pains hadn't plagued me in over a decade. I found ice in the freezer and chilled the area. I couldn't physically and mentally handle the long, taxing bus ride each day.

After arriving at school the next day, I mustered up my courage and headed straight to the administration building. I respectfully asked Dr. Wilson for a moment of his time. He kindly agreed. Dr. Wilson understood my predicament—the long, perilous bus rides twice a day, and my living alone in the heart of Bangalore for many weeks each month. As we parted, he promised that an effort would be made to locate a place for me.

I waited in the administration building lobby for my ride to the Foreigner Regional Registration Office (FRRO). The law required that all foreigners register with this agency within fourteen days of arriving in India. Three secondary teachers—Carol, Marissa, and Dylan—joined me on the ride to the government office.

Carol, the Chinese-language teacher, and Marissa, the Spanish teacher, signed contracts stipulating that they would live alone, but when they arrived on campus they were asked to share a two-bedroom apartment. Neither trusted the other. They resorted to locking their bedroom doors and creating territorial spaces in the common areas. There was a tense moment when Carol suddenly recalled that she had unplugged the refrigerator.

Marissa exclaimed, "Huh? What were you thinking?"

"Don't worry," Carol replied quietly.

Marissa moved closer and said, "I just bought perishable food yesterday. I don't want it to spoil."

Carol looked out the window and nonchalantly responded, "We won't be gone long. Don't worry."

I was sitting between them as Marissa glared at Carol, who continued to passively look out the window through her dark sunglasses.

Dylan, the German teacher, broke the silence when he began bad-mouthing the administration. His experience as an international teacher in a variety of different locations made him our resident expert. After less than a week at the school, he was outraged by the lack of hospitality extended to foreigners. He candidly said, "Can you believe I wasn't offered a glass of water when I arrived?" He was deeply frustrated with everyone's inability to answer questions directly and completely.

The three language teachers agreed that Mohan, the estate manager with an engaging smile, was just a "yes man." Mohan, a man of about thirty with small, dark eyes and bangs that made him look like Prince Valiant, rotated his head back and forth and said "yes" when he often should have replied "no." I vaguely remembered meeting him the day before.

All complained vigorously about the intense nature of their "boarding duties." In exchange for their housing and the right to dine in the school cafeteria for breakfast and dinner, each was obligated to devote every other weekend to supervising the boarding students. This was in addition to their twice-weekly commitment to supervise the students' study time. This policy stood in sharp contrast to those of many other schools, where such duties were assigned to others. Since I wasn't offered an apartment, these obligations didn't apply to me. I was wondering how my life might change if I moved to the campus.

Our driver took a red-and-gold bandanna off of the dashboard and folded it so it formed a long, narrow rectangle. He placed the middle over his forehead and tied the ends behind the back of his head. Dylan raised his eyebrows as he turned to face the three of us in the backseat.

"What's he doing?" Marissa asked softly, motioning toward the driver.

"It looks like he's preparing for battle," Carol added.

Dylan was now facing forward and yelled, "Watch out!"

The car came within an inch of the car next to us as it swerved in and out of the busy streets. Our knees made a cracking noise when they smacked into one another. Marissa faced me as her pupils dilated. Carol's eyes remained hidden behind her dark glasses, but I noticed that she was clenching her fists tightly and her knuckles were white.

Our experience at the government office tested our patience. Hordes of foreigners crowded outside the police station that was a holdover from British rule. Only a prescribed number of people were allowed to enter the dilapidated colonial structure at one time. More people squashed together inside, each waiting for someone to take a digital picture and enter his or her documentation into a ledger book. This was just another example of the dichotomy of Indian life—a nineteenth-century bookkeeping process combined with the use of modern technology.

After returning to campus, I heard, "Miss Sandra." I turned. A bald man wearing a white shirt and a tie told me to go to Mr. Mohan's office. I walked from the airy reception area to the corridor with the offices. I knocked on his door. Sitting at a desk at the far end of the oversized office was Mohan.

"Hello, Miss Sandra. I've good news. You can stay in a guest room upstairs."

"Can I see the room?"

"No problem."

Within seconds, I was following a man in a blue uniform. We passed the first floor (the ground floor was zero), which housed Dr. Diya and Dr. Wilson's offices and two glass-walled conference rooms. The next floor had four to five doors on each side of a cavernous hallway illuminated by fluorescent bulbs. The man I was following opened the second door on the right.

An unfriendly, musty odor greeted me. The simple room had a monastic feel. Two contrasting colors tinged the walls—dull white and pale salmon—and large stress cracks traversed the walls and ceiling. An electrical outlet dangled precariously above the bed frame on the wall to my left, and another outlet was similarly unattached on the other side.

I looked toward the high, vaulted ceiling and a storage area above the entryway. Someone had fastened two fluorescent strip lights to the sloping ceiling, and a single fan was anchored in the middle. A door on the opposite side, camouflaged by beige vertical blinds, led out to a small balcony. The modest bathroom was appointed with black floor tile and a black speckled countertop.

The furniture was simple and bare bones. I would have my choice of sleeping on one of the two extremely thin mattresses on dissimilar twin bed frames. A small, round, wooden table with two matching chairs and a petite square table that could double as a nightstand were the only other pieces of furniture. Three modestly sized, fire-engine-red refrigerators lined the adjacent wall.

I raced down the two flights to Mohan's office and told him I would be happy to move in on Sunday afternoon. I politely requested that a wardrobe and a desk be added and that the extra refrigerators be removed. I thanked him for his time and then went to the principal's office to express my appreciation.

29

O n Saturday morning, I attended a special meeting that focused on the fifth-graders' transition to the middle-school curriculum. The fifth-grade teachers and their primary directors, and the secondary director and her staff of sixth-grade teachers, sat on red plastic chairs facing one another in a circle.

The secondary-school director took the lead by calling on each teacher to describe the shortcomings of the students entering the sixth grade. After each synopsis, the fifth-grade teachers gave their feedback. The underlying philosophies of the primary department teachers didn't match up with the expectations of the sixth-grade team.

The middle-school teachers claimed that the students in English could not formulate their ideas into organized paragraphs. Speaking and reading comprehension skills were also called into question, as the sixth-grade teachers discussed examples of the deficits that they had tracked in their students the previous school year. A heated discussion took place over the necessity of having assignments and tests that required answers to be written in complete sentences or paragraph form. The comments for social studies were equally distressing. Significant gaps in learning needed to be filled and the students struggled with test-taking skills. The other core areas—math and science—showed similar deficits.

After the meeting adjourned, some members of the primary staff lingered. Instead of focusing on what the sixth-grade teachers said, these teachers avoided reflection. They comforted one another by claiming that they wanted to retain a warm, friendly environment devoid of too many tests.

The curriculum and textbooks remained a mystery. I couldn't evaluate the situation without having more facts. If the sixth-grade teachers were correct in their evaluations, changes were required. From what was described, one of my previous classes—the lower-socioeconomic fifth-grade students at my first practicum placement at Baker Elementary School in Westminster, Colorado—could out-perform some of these students.

While I sat waiting in the reception area for the afternoon bus into the city, my curiosity was piqued. Recent articles in the United States suggested that international test scores of American students were lagging behind some Asian and European countries. President Obama stated to the press that Americans were in an "education arms race" with India and China. If the sixth-grade teachers' words were accurate, the fifth-grade program did *not* stack up to the education that my children had received in Northbrook, Illinois, or at schools located in Colorado's Boulder Valley School District. KIS might be considered one of the best Indian schools, but I would reserve my judgment until I saw an overview of the curriculum and worked with the kids and the staff.

My background knowledge of international testing was limited to my son Adam's participation in the Third International Math and Science Study (TIMSS). In 1996, Adam was randomly selected as an eighth-grader at Wood Oaks Junior High in Northbrook, Illinois, to take a special math and science exam and then, months later, received a special invitation to attend President Clinton's speech at the local high school. Adam was part of the First in the World Consortium, a title that accurately reflected the intended goal.

Twenty affluent suburban Chicago school districts banded together to enter the TIMSS. The president's visit acknowledged that they had tied for first place in the world in science, and had come in second in math. People proposed various theories to account for this remarkable achievement. The socioeconomics of the communities and well-trained teachers who collaborated with one another were some of the suggested reasons. Undoubtedly, many other explanations were offerred that caused educators to rethink American educational practices.

After the hoopla dissipated, I continued to seek out the underlying factors affecting student achievement. Just tracking my own sons' academic progress, I could see on a small scale how many variables came into play each school year. Now I was anxious to compare my fifth-grade classroom experiences as a teacher and as a parent with my fifth-grade class in India. *Was the assertion by the* Independent Show School Magazine *that KIS was one of the five best international boarding schools in the world warranted? Could this school truly be on par with one of the other four, the Phillips Exeter Academy in New Hampshire?*

I hypothesized that it would take weeks or possibly months before I could draw any conclusions as to how KIS's curriculum and student performance compared with those in Colorado and Illinois, and I realized that many questions might end up unanswered.

I spent three hours waiting for the bus. Being totally dependent on a bus schedule wreaked havoc on my sense of personal freedom. Part of me was rebelling that I no longer had my own car and was no longer capable of going wherever I wanted, whenever I chose. I relied on others and was at the whim of schedules that I didn't control. I realized that adapting was my top priority because only one more week of orientation remained before school began.

Josh didn't leave town for the weekend because Rachael was visiting. They saw my vulnerable state and did what they could to improve my quality of life. What better way than to visit Spars, an international megastore that resembled Walmart. Basic necessities, such as plastic plates, silverware, bowls, plastic storage containers, a hot pot, and dish detergent were the first items I placed in my shopping basket. Food—soy milk, yogurt, cheese, bread, cereal, tea, fresh fruit, and chocolate—soon followed. By the time the three of us hailed an auto rickshaw in a late afternoon downpour, we were each carrying several plastic bags.

After we returned from dinner that evening, the familiar tones signaling an incoming call on Skype brought an instant smile to my face. Sally and Steve, our good friends from college, were frequent Skype buddies. I remained in contact with Sally during her anguishing months of chemotherapy. Now she was reciprocating by holding my hand while I coped with my new life in India and Ira's recovery from his traumatic accident. Their kind and reassuring words confirmed that they were friends I could rely on.

Then on Sunday afternoon, I took a cab from Josh's apartment with my new possessions in tow. It reminded me of being in my late teens when I was on the verge of moving into my college dorm. Butterflies were fluttering around in my chest and abdomen. I was a married woman moving into a minuscule room of about 300 square feet that was 10,000 miles away from my husband.

One of the guards carried my new possessions up to my room. Two pale lizards, each about the size of my hand, chased one another up and down the walls playing their reptile version of tag. The ghastly odor was still present as I tugged lightly on the cord that opened the vertical blinds. I opened the double doors that led out onto the balcony and took a giant gulp of air laden with pollution and a trace of smoke. I turned on the noisy overhead fan.

Organizing was my first step. Mohan had listened to my request and brought in a squat wardrobe with a long, slender key. Without delay, I placed my clothing and personal possessions into this miniature closet, neatly positioned my food and kitchen items on the round table, and put the perishable items into the dirty refrigerator. Until a desk was added, my extra bed would be the resting spot for a mound of books.

Tuffy Tiger, the quart-sized stuffed animal I brought to India, became my mascot. I placed him on the table next to my bed. He wore a pale green vest with the words "I'm a little Tuffy" emblazoned on his chest. I looked to this orange-and-black-striped toy as a sign of hope and encouragement. However corny it may sound, I told myself to be like Tuffy Tiger to cope with my solitude and isolation. My imagination was captured by the stuffed animal's simple name.

My next stop was the bathroom. "I can't believe this!" I screamed.

No one had cleaned this room. Slimy soot, ripe for finger-painting, layered the bathroom floor and the countertop. I saw that the cream-colored tile floor in the bedroom was equally soiled. I turned on the sink and immediately sensed water pouring onto my bare feet. The pipe running from the sink was not connected properly. All I could do was chuckle and say, "Oops!"

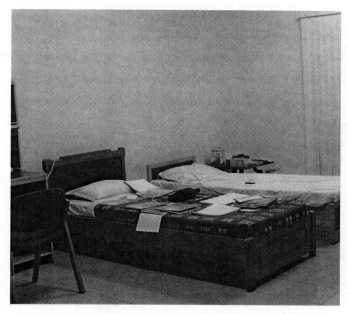

My room after the desk was added

Next I tried flushing the toilet. "Wonderful!" was my next exclamation. The toilet did not flush. I was 0 for 2. I was appalled by the dark yellow stains creating an abstract picture on the toilet seat. Had the toilet seat ever been cleaned or did men use it for target practice?

I then turned my attention to the shower. Brown water with a thick residue sputtered out of the shower head onto the floor and quickly spread to the rest of the bathroom. With no shower curtain or partition between the shower area and the rest of the bathroom, the entire room became a wading pool of brown goop. I was 0 for 3. But I ran the water for several minutes until it became a steady, clear stream.

I dashed downstairs to the reception area. The room was dark and no one was manning the desk. I went into the public restroom to wash the dirt off of my hands. Miniature rolls of toilet paper sat on the countertop instead of paper towels. I picked off small pieces of toilet paper that clung to my dry hands. I filled up my empty water bottles using the water cooler adjacent to the reception desk and marched back to my room.

I waited for Ira's evening call.

"How's life in Colorado?" I asked.

"Not the same without you. Physical therapy is getting easier, but it'll be months before I can use my arm. How's your room?"

I looked out the window when I said, "I'm safer on campus. I can't beat the convenience."

"You don't sound very convincing."

"I'm lonely and this place is a bit creepy. All the teachers live in apartments on the other side of the campus."

"Until you have the Internet up and running, call Josh if you're scared," Ira insisted.

After we said our good-byes, I glanced toward Tuffy Tiger and half-jokingly said, "It's you and me, babe."

Tuffy Tiger

The whirling ceiling fan did little to cool off my room, and I was reluctant to leave the patio doors open because there were no screens. I pulled back the green-plaid, woolen blankets and lay on the pale pink sheets that were streaked with an assortment of faint stains. Tiny droplets of water were forming a body mask that ran from my head to my toes.

I felt like Goldilocks as I moved my books to test the two thin mattresses. Both were equally unpleasant. I stared up at the ceiling. Although
I was not in the habit of praying, I uttered a short appeal to the God of
Abraham, Isaac, Jacob, Sarah, Rebecca, Rachael, and Leah to give me the
strength to meet the challenges that I faced. I took another look at Tuffy
and fell asleep.

30

I n the hours before midnight, howling dogs serenaded me from the
adjacent street. Then the hours after midnight were calm and tranquil.
But by 6:00 a.m., the cars, trucks, buses, motorcycles, and auto rickshaws
became my morning rooster call. It wouldn't be possible to sleep past 6:00
a.m.—I didn't need an alarm clock.

I ate breakfast in my room. On the way to my classroom, I met Mohan. I
kindly reminded him that the additional refrigerators, although quite colorful, should be removed. I smiled and asked, "Can a teacher be a teacher without a desk?" He flashed his infamous smile. I added one more request—a
drying rack. I casually mentioned the issues with my bathroom fixtures and
my need for a cleaning lady.

His eyes widened as he exclaimed, "The toilet and the sink are broken?"

"Can they be repaired today?" I replied.

He smiled and wobbled his head like a doll with a spring neck. I wasn't
thoroughly convinced that this was a positive gesture. I just hoped that the
plumbing worked when I returned.

It was the second week of teacher orientation and five days before parents would come for orientation on Saturday morning. My classroom was
empty except for a computer, a desk, and a chair. Books, materials, and general supplies were nowhere in sight. The library holdings would have been

severely depleted if every teacher set up an appropriate reading corner in his or her classroom. This was in stark contrast to the loads of books that adorn the average American classroom and the stockpiled books tucked away in the school library storerooms. The number of books for each stage of reading was pitiful—only a handful for each grade level—and many of the library holdings were tattered and worn out. The fifth grade had multiple copies of only four books—*Matilda*, *The Family Under the Bridge*, *The Bridge to Terabithia*, and *The Silver Sword*. Considering the stature of the school and the fact that each of my students paid approximately $10,000 for tuition, I expected a more comprehensive selection of books and materials.

To ready the room for class the following Monday would require considerable effort. I was thankful that I had moved onto campus because my life no longer revolved around a bus schedule. I could go to the classroom early and stay late, as an American teacher would do. Ah, it was nice to have some freedom restored.

Many mandatory meetings took place in the auditorium, which was adjacent to the parking lot that doubled as a bus hub. Impressive was the best word to describe this professional-looking indoor amphitheater; it seated well over a thousand people with comfortable theater seats fastened to a sloping concrete floor. Located in the back was a glass-partitioned audio-visual room. The focal point on the raised stage was an oversized screen that could be lowered into place. The sophistication and the elaborate nature of this structure seemed out of place in a school that had a meager supply of library books, classroom materials, and furniture. But wasn't that the dichotomy I saw everywhere? Was it any different than seeing a beautifully landscaped apartment building next to a tent community with no plumbing or electricity?

Dr. Diya, who peered through her glasses, opened each of her presentations with a Calvin and Hobbes comic strip. Countless slides were projected as the administrators rambled on and on. As I looked around, many of my peers were dozing off in this overly warm and stuffy environment, which reeked of pesticide. I had the good fortune of getting to know Asha, another member of the fifth-grade team. She taught math and science for 5B and was also a new team member.

I became uncomfortable during one of the orientation sessions for the boarding staff. The principal discussed the importance of enforcing the rules for boarders, the appropriate way to deal with students, and the consequences for not following the rules. Even though the closest I ever came to a boarding-school environment was my experience at overnight camp, I realized the importance of strict guidelines. I had raised four sons and knew firsthand the importance of discipline. Nevertheless, I wasn't prepared to hear the strict dress code for the girls. Girls were instructed to style their hair a certain way, could not adorn their fingers with nail polish, and could wear no makeup. While I was still contemplating the ramifications of such an inflexible and structured home-away-from-home, the principal moved on to the topic of inappropriate behavior.

When I heard the principal say that one of the *most horrible* things had happened last term, my ears perked up like our cat's. My initial reaction was that someone had gotten pregnant or physically injured. No, that was not the cardinal sin. It was pornography. I looked around the room and everyone was mesmerized. Supposedly, one of the high school boys had brought a hard drive filled with pornographic movies that he shared with his fellow students. The young man wasn't aware that his actions would be considered improper. When his liberal-minded, Western-educated parents were brought in, their response shocked the principal—it was the same as their son's. Without any hesitation, they openly admitted to watching pornography, which appalled the principal and many of the teachers. I can still hear the principal saying that he couldn't believe what he had heard.

There was no shortage of judgmental comments. But I was out of place. I do not endorse pornography, but at the same time I am a realist. Teenage boys have always gravitated to looking at women in sexually explicit poses and whenever possible seek out X-rated movies and magazines. Some pornography may be degrading, but it's hardly the *worst* thing that could happen.

Before the boarding students arrived and school officially opened, the staff was free to sit at any of the long rows of cafeteria tables. I consciously agreed with Mahatma Gandhi, who said "a nation's culture resides in the hearts and in the soul of its people." What better way to become absorbed into Indian culture than to share meals with its people?

The dining hall gave me a jump start in acquainting myself with some of my students, who resided on campus because their parents were either teachers or administrators. These kids ate with their parents but tended to wander around the campus while their parents attended or led orientation sessions.

Arjun, an overly tall Indian boy with large ears, inquisitively approached me at almost every meal. He and his parents, who were both teachers, never failed to say a friendly "hello." Occasionally I would see Arjun playing peacefully on the colorful playground equipment that was situated in the primary unit courtyard. I worried for his safety because packs of wild monkeys frequented the equipment. These primates used the slide and climbed on the jungle gym until one of the uniformed guards chased them away with a big wooden stick.

No matter whom I sat with, my dining companions invariably chastised me for not eating more. Almost everyone piled huge portions onto their plastic plates and no one was shy when it came to taking additional food from the bowls on the table or the buffet server along the adjacent wall. Perhaps these people were generally interested in my well-being. The harsh and critical tone of their words, though, made me wonder. If my religious dietary limitations or healthier food preferences made me eat differently, I didn't want to talk about it. Over time, I frequented the dining hall less and less often. I ended up eating most breakfasts and dinners by myself in my room. I was obligated to eat lunch with my class.

Monday afternoon was the first time I talked one-on-one with Mahi, my team-teaching partner for 5C. Theoretically, we were equals. I was responsible for teaching English and social studies while she taught math and science. Mahi was a heavyset woman in her late twenties with a shiny, round face and a double chin. She wore an undersized pair of wire-rim glasses on

her squat nose. Her glossy, jet black hair was pulled tightly into a high ponytail at the midpoint of her head.

She was half my age but acted as if she were my mother. Instead of talking about how we were going to work together as a team, she ordered me to
do different tasks in a brusque and condescending manner. The harshness in
Mahi's voice suggested that she didn't like to be questioned. She had started
at KIS the year before. For several months she had shadowed different teachers and then midyear she was paired with Kavya, another fifth-grade teacher.
I assumed she felt superior due to her slight seniority.

Every day, I struggled with basic vocabulary. Long ago, the Indians
adapted British English. Thus, words like torch (flashlight), boot (trunk of
a car), stationery (basic supplies), maths (math), duster (white board eraser)
as well as many other words were initially confusing. Likewise, I had to
frequently consult a dictionary for spelling because everyone followed the
British format for spelling—for example, using "colour" for "color."

Four days remained and the textbooks were still missing, and I didn't
have a complete copy of the curriculum outline. I had *no* idea what I was
going to teach the following week. None of the teachers was concerned.
Their main objective was decorating the bulletin boards. Our class had only
one bulletin board, which Mahi had commandeered, and no supplies. The
requests made in the spring for furniture, additional bulletin boards, and
supplies remained unfulfilled even though an additional class was added to
the fifth grade.

Tuesday, the fifth-grade instructors met to discuss the nuts and bolts
of teaching as a team. I learned that it was common practice to follow
the teachers' handbooks exclusively. Now I understood why no one was
concerned about planning for the first week of school. I had visions of the
seven fifth-grade teachers standing by the edge of a pool with our scripts
in hand. Then at the count of three, we would all jump into the water in
unison.

My frustrations grew more intense as we discussed the first week of
class. None of the teachers understood the importance of establishing

a *community of learners*. They were under the impression that a couple of fun activities on the first day of class would be sufficient and that magically the students would feel comfortable with one another and their teachers. American teachers placed a greater emphasis on team building.

The standoffish attitude that I experienced from my co-teacher Mahi was shared by the three other teachers who made up the English/social studies team. Frowns and rolling eyes illustrated their displeasure with the ideas I was sharing. It was as if I were speaking a foreign language or was an alien from Mars. I hoped that meeting my students on the first day of class would mollify my feelings of alienation.

Was I being as pigheaded and ethnocentric as my colleagues were? Yes, to a certain extent. Both my American training and my experience supported my beliefs, while the Indian teachers were doing what they had done in the past. Their methods were totally reliant on the teachers' guides, while I utilized theories and methods that supplemented the teachers' guides.

Elizabeth, the British primary director, became my logical sounding board. She lived on campus; Pari, the Indian primary director, lived off campus. If I had any questions or concerns, I met Elizabeth before breakfast or after school. Elizabeth reassured me that within reason I could be as flexible as I wanted as long as I followed the fifth-grade curriculum. I wasn't sure this would be possible if the three English and social studies teachers were going in a different direction. I tiptoed through this potential minefield by strategizing with Elizabeth and, later on, with Pari.

How could I not be enthused by Elizabeth's unparalleled optimism? She had spent seven years at a school in Thailand and the past year in India. It wasn't just her tolerance of cultural differences that impressed me, but also her compassion. She genuinely wanted to remove potential obstacles from my path. Having lived on campus without her husband the year before, she commiserated with my position. I considered myself fortunate to have her as my boss, ally, and friend.

One day, out of nowhere, she inquired, "Have you requested a drying rack yet?"

I matter-of-factly responded, "Yes, but I'm still waiting."

"Be persistent! It took me three months."

I shook my head and said, "Three months? You've got to be kidding."

She smiled and said, "No joke!"

I sighed and then responded, "Well, I guess I'll be sending all my dirty clothes to the school laundry."

"Not everything! Underwear and socks can't be sent."

I was caught off guard by her response and with incredible disbelief said, "What?"

"Just wash your things when you shower each day."

"Come on. Are you telling me that the kids on campus have to wash their underwear and socks?"

"No, they can send theirs."

"What's wrong with socks?"

It was an unanswerable question. She just smiled and shook her head.

31

The school allocated time for room preparation and finally installed our missing bulletin boards. After just an hour or two, the classroom looked as if a tornado had swirled down and caused everything to end up in disarray. Instead of placing scraps and garbage into the miniature receptacle, Mahi dumped everything on the floor. Almost all of the teachers in the primary unit did the same. It was easy to litter because of the expectation that the cleaning crew would clean up the mess.

I wanted at least one of my boards to be interactive, so I used the concept "You've Got Mail." I cut out different colored mailboxes with flags and placed names on the students' respective boxes. Later, I wrote a welcoming letter to each student and placed it in his or her box.

You've Got Mail Bulletin Board

After I had stapled all of the mailboxes into place, it suddenly dawned on me: Indians did not use this type of mailbox. *Would the students have sufficient background knowledge to understand? In the future, how would I know when cultural differences might interfere with my teaching?* It would be two more days until the dorm students arrived.

In the late afternoon, I hiked to the other side of the campus to the Olympic-sized pool situated between one of the large playfields and the girls' dorm. Along the way, I talked briefly with Jonathan, a Caucasian boy who had moved from the United Kingdom shortly after his father began working at the school. A wiry lad with a fair complexion dotted with freckles, Jonathan had a second home on the playfields—athletics was his calling. We had met a few days earlier when Jonathan absentmindedly ran into me while he was chasing after his soccer ball and said, "Miss…Miss. I'm so sorry. Don't tell my parents."

The pool provided instant relief from another sweaty day. The heavily chlorinated water stripped away the salty residue from my body and my core temperature was stabilized. In my fins, cap, and goggles, I swam contentedly. I was energized. I was at home in the water, and I was reluctant to break away from my private retreat when the designated faculty hour was over.

As I was leaving, I saw the caretaker dipping his hand into a plastic bucket and then throwing powdered chemicals into the pool. No mask or gloves or a scoop...just his bare hands. His safety concerns were nonexistent. I just hoped that someone was monitoring the chemical balance in the pool.

When the final day of prep began, I doubted that everything would fall into place. Only two-thirds of the dilapidated and broken desks and worn-out chairs were delivered by the end of the day. Without any protective gliders, the chairs and desks made a horrendous screeching sound whenever they were moved across the floor. The furniture request was *not* approved, so we were left with an assortment of rejects.

Compared with an American classroom, the space looked cramped and lacked pizzazz. We weren't permitted to put anything on the stark white walls or ceilings. Only the bulletin boards could be used. It seemed equally strange that the bookshelves were devoid of books and games.

After the primary teachers drifted to the waiting buses, I was listening to a selection of Beatles songs on my iPod when I sensed movement behind me. I assumed it was the cleaning people entering the classroom. As I looked over my shoulder, an electrical current ran down my body like a jolt of lightning. It was not a person. I was face-to-face with a monkey.

"Oh my God!" I said. I froze in my tracks. The monkey, with its marble-like eyes, was about the size of a five-year-old. It scampered toward me and skillfully leaped onto the shoulder-high cabinet two feet away. It played with the colored whiteboard markers that stood in an oversized ceramic mug.

I remembered Elizabeth's instructions: Clap your hands and don't show your teeth. Clenching my upper and lower lips together, I clapped aggressively until the monkey rushed out of one of the open windows with two colored markers in hand. My heart pounded.

Part of living in India was learning to cope with wild animals everywhere and anywhere. I remained fascinated by the community of monkeys that shared my habitat. Like a small child awed by a tightrope walker at the circus, I watched families of monkeys scoot along the power line that laced its way from the dining hall to the junior boys' dorm. It was precious to see how the babies clung to the undersides of their moms as they traveled from one building to the next. Despite my curiosity, however, I remained fearful of their unpredictable behavior.

On my way back to my room, I stepped into Elizabeth's office, still shaking.

In a joking manner, I quipped, "Hey, Elizabeth, guess who came to visit me?"

She glanced up from her computer screen and remained silent.

I continued. "A monkey. It scared the hell out of me. Look at my hand. I'm still trembling." I raised a hand and displayed my quivering fingers.

Her eyebrows furrowed. "Are you all right?" she questioned.

"I'm not sure. It was so close. I could hear its breathing."

She motioned to the chair in front of her desk and said, "Please take a seat."

I sat down on the chair. "The monkeys terrify me. I'm not happy with the pesticides, either."

"The monkeys weren't an issue last year. We'll see what happens. The bugs are something else. If they don't spray constantly, we'll be under siege."

"Are the pesticides safe?" I inquired.

"I'm not sure. More important, did anyone tell you about the cobra?"

32

O n Saturday morning, I awoke early. I purposely chose a Ralph Lauren skirt with an abstract pattern that included bold splashes of many coordinating colors and a fitted, Ann Taylor, button-down, purple blouse. This outfit stood in stark contrast to most of my wardrobe, which revolved around monochromatic themes of muted colors and basics—black, navy, khaki, and light pastels.

My everyday taste in clothing had caused a stir with some of my fellow teachers, who didn't hesitate to tell me that I looked plain and lacked color. I agreed. I'd never gravitated toward wearing bright, contrasting colors with patterned designs. These combinations were too flamboyant and gaudy for my tastes. Yet here I was on the verge of meeting my students' parents and I was consciously attempting to *fit in* by wearing the only boldly colored outfit I owned in India.

I combed my thin hair into a ponytail and begrudgingly put on a light layer of makeup. Eeeewww! I preferred not wearing any makeup because my skin was normally bathed in waves of sweat and covered with grime through-out the day. An afternoon and evening of black smudge marks accenting my dark brown eyes was not an appealing thought, but neither was a morning look of dull eyelashes and lifeless lips against a backdrop of pale skin. After taking a last look in the mirror, I briskly dashed to the classroom. As if a fairy godmother had waved her magic wand, the mess and debris were removed and the missing desks and chairs were now in place. *Elizabeth was right. Everything would fall into place.* I carefully wrote a few welcome messages on the whiteboard, went to breakfast, and then joined my colleagues in the auditorium. *I couldn't wait to meet the parents.*

5C Classroom

I paused for a moment and looked at the people entering the doorways on both sides of the auditorium. About a third came with children in tow. Many women wore traditional Indian outfits while others were dressed in Western wear. The men were wearing slacks or jeans with colorful shirts. Two of Josh's business acquaintances made small talk with me as they passed. By the time the presentation began, the auditorium was about two-thirds full.

The lengthy presentation spotlighted both the accomplishments of the previous year's graduating class of seniors and the school's reputation. From there, the parents left the main auditorium, walked across the campus, and entered the primary-unit building, which was next to the administration building. The fifth-grade parents trickled down the long, zigzagging hallway to the music room, where they occupied most of the chairs. After this meeting, the parents and students went to their respective classrooms.

Unlike an American open house in which teachers briefly introduce themselves and the curriculum, we simply welcomed everyone into the room and said, "Good morning, I'm Miss Mahi" and "Good morning, I'm Miss Sandra." Mahi and I mingled among the parents like politicians greeting their constituents. We smiled, shook hands, answered questions, and thanked everyone for coming.

A small number of students, most of whom resided on campus, were present. Pankaj and his father came up to greet me. Pankaj, a short, frail-looking boy with a long, slender face and sad eyes, had moved into the boys' dorm the night before. His proud father, thirtyish and dressed in a colorful polo shirt and slacks, bragged openly about his desire to have Pankaj enrolled in the "best" school in India. Standing next to Pankaj was Kabir, a slightly taller boy who had an enormous smile that almost rocked the glasses off his small nose. Kabir told me that both he and his twin brother had also come from Mumbai to attend the "best" school. Pankaj and Kabir had been paired up as roommates and had just met the day before.

A young Caucasian woman walked toward me, pushing a stroller and talking to a thin girl with green eyes, long eyelashes, and flower-petal earrings. The young girl, Emily, was conversing in French with her mother but immediately reverted to English as soon as the mother and daughter made eye contact with me. In a quiet voice, the mother informed me that her family had arrived in India the past spring and that Emily was still struggling with English—her native language was French. I calmly reassured her.

The last child I talked to was Neha, a taller Indian girl, with long black hair parted on the side. Her high cheekbones partially hid her small eyes.

"Miss Sandra, can I take my books home?" Neha politely asked.

"Yes. Remember to bring them back on Monday."

Neha rifled through the stack of texts and said, "Miss, where's my science book and my social studies textbook?"

"Some are missing or delayed. Please look on the whiteboard for the list."

"Miss, miss, what about our class novel?" she continued.

"Oops, that should be on the list. *Matilda* will be passed out next week."

The last set of parents exited the room. The school year officially had begun. From this moment forward, I was Miss Sandra to my students and their parents.

Meeting the parents and a handful of students primed me for my first class. I was anxious to finally meet all of my students after my two-week orientation. In some ways it was similar to the anticipation I experienced at American schools, but in other ways it was totally different. Teachers generally feel a rush of exhilaration before the first day. I definitely felt that. This school year, I was stepping out of my comfort zone and leaping for a challenge that few women my age would dare to consider. With that scenario came an additional dose of appreciation and excitement.

33

On Monday morning, I opened my door, put my miniature garbage can into the hallway, and then locked the door behind me. I swiped my badge at the reception desk and walked outside. I never thought to ask where the children were supposed to gather after getting off the bus. A pulsating sensation began behind my forehead and my palms became sweaty as I imagined all the possibilities. I scurried to the field closest to the bus parking lot, the one behind the auditorium; it was empty. *Where could everyone be? I couldn't be late on the first day.* By this time the first bus load of students had arrived. I saw small groups of children on the side of the auditorium. I simply fell in step and followed one bunch to a centrally located field, behind the senior boys' dorm.

Rows were forming on the muddy grass for each grade. A foreboding mass of dark gray clouds hung overhead as I scanned the field. A sea of cerulean-blue uniforms with matching hats was visible. A buzz of excitement grew as the kids renewed their friendships and talked among themselves, and the teachers waved to one another in greeting. After all the buses had arrived, Elizabeth commanded everyone's attention. She introduced Dr. Wilson and then in unison everyone responded in a singsong manner, "Good morning, Dr. Robert."

He gave a short speech welcoming everyone to "the KIS family." His parting words included another one of his favorite lines. "May this be the best year of your life."

Elizabeth excused each class one by one. Mahi and I led the 5C class back to our classroom. The students located their assigned seats, arranged in groups of five, and I welcomed them to 5C. In unison, the class said, "Good morning, Miss Sandra. Good morning, Miss Mahi." We took attendance. Eighteen out of twenty were present. We later learned that the two missing girls would join the class later. One was the daughter of the music director, who was awaiting the approval of her employment visa, while the other student wouldn't be arriving until the second term.

Our first activity was to create colorful nametags highlighting the student's favorite place and something that he or she loved to do. The second part of the activity paired up the students so that each could talk with another student and then introduce that student to the rest of the class. Within seconds of reading off an arbitrary list of pairings, a chorus of indistinguishable voices rang out.

"Miss, Miss, she doesn't speak English," a boy whined.

"Miss Sandra, I don't want to be with *her*. Can I switch partners?" another male voice blared.

"Miss, Miss. Why are there *too* many boys in this class?" a soft-spoken girl asked.

I wasn't expecting these reactions to the classroom demographics, even though I was fully aware of the disproportionate number of boys—twelve boys to six girls.

I responded cheerfully. "Everyone needs to talk with a partner. We'll share in fifteen minutes."

Most of the students complied, although I did hear a few moans and groans. When it came time to present partners, a few hands shot up as I heard a new round of "Miss…Miss…Miss."

Kabir, with a warm glow in his eyes and an enormous, toothy smile, popped up from his chair, approached me, and shoved his hand almost directly into my face as he shrieked, "Miss! Miss!"

"Kabir, please sit down. I'm looking for hands, not voices," I calmly responded.

The constant chorus of "Miss…Miss…Miss" was already becoming annoying.

Listening to the students, I realized that the range of speaking skills varied significantly. Some were glib and talked freely while others were less confident. A handful struggled with basic language skills. Emily and two other girls were reluctant to talk because they were just learning English. My attention was immediately drawn to Kamala, a shy Thai girl with a wide nose, flat cheeks, and jet-black, shoulder-length hair kept in place by a narrow plastic headband. She preferred looking at the floor to making eye contact. Kamala was a boarding student who had come from Thailand with her older sister, a secondary student.

When it was lunchtime, I dismissed one group of desks at a time. Without any instructions, the boys and girls quietly arranged themselves according to gender. The boys took the lead at the front of the line while the girls followed in a separate line. The boys and girls rarely mixed together in line. This seemed out of sorts. In America, the boys and girls would probably not routinely segregate themselves.

In the cafeteria, our class sat at the last table and at a few seats of an adjacent table. I opted to sit at the head of the last table. Pankaj raced to take the seat to my left and Emily and Kamala took seats to my right. Mahi sat at the next table with one of the other fifth-grade teachers. The students automatically took the lids off the metal bowls situated in the middle of the table and scooped food onto their plates. A handful of students brought their own food packaged in small plastic containers. Emily and Kamala gingerly picked over their small portions. I assumed first-day jitters were curtailing their eating. With twenty minutes remaining in the period, the students went outside to play.

After lunch, a handful of students were milling around the "You've Got Mail" bulletin board. Some were sneaking a peek at their letters and slid them back into the pocket as soon as they saw me. I pretended I didn't see.

I struggled to remember their unusual names and butchered the pronunciation of several. The three English-language learners came from three different countries—France, Thailand, and South Korea—and their names were the easiest to recall. The vast majority of the children were "day scholars"—students who went home to their parents in the evening.

After school, I spent a few hours in the classroom preparing lesson plans and looking over the students' surveys. I didn't want to rely on just the parents' survey. I wanted to hear my students' voices. I wasn't surprised when I read Emily's. Her biggest concern was "not understanding English," while Kabir worried about the coming year. That response was a bit surprising coming from a ten-year-old. Another student—Neha—had written, "This year I am really looking forward to the trip to Kabini 'cause it would probably be one of the best parts about Gr. 5." Hmmm…I wondered what she was talking about. *What was Kabini?* Even though Jonathan and Kamala were present, neither one of them handed in a sheet. *Was Jonathan forgetful or not willing to share? Did Kamala not understand the instructions?*

It was dark by the time I left my classroom. Back in my guest room, I turned on my computer and heard Skype ringing. I accepted Ira's call.

"Sweetheart, I miss and love you so much," I blurted as Ira's blurred face appeared on the computer screen.

"How was your first day?"

"It was amazing," I said, beaming. Before I could respond further, a typed message in red appeared, stating that the call had been dropped. I tried numerous times to reconnect. Ira eventually called me on my mobile phone.

I immediately answered. "Don't you just love modern technology?"

"Yeah, this sucks. Skype should work."

"The IT guy told me that the school's server needs to be upgraded. What were you asking?" I inquired.

"The kids?"

"It's interesting. Most look Indian, but many were born in other places. Some have traveled all over the world."

"Did everything go okay?"

"It went better than I expected. They were lining up to leave before I knew it. My first day was awesome!"

34

After the first day, we followed the daily schedule with a few minor exceptions. Surprisingly, the fifth-grade students spent *less than half* of their school time in the core classes of English, math, science, and social studies. Three times a week, each student studied French, Hindi, or English as a Foreign Language (EFL). A long list of additional special classes included physical education/swimming, music, art, library, computer science, club activity, drama, yoga, and life skills. In an American school, the specials amounted to a very small percentage of the weekly schedule and oftentimes rotated from term to term. Our fifth-graders spent less than seven hours each week studying English, or approximately half as much time as an American fifth-grader spends.

The fifth-grade teachers didn't view writing as a necessity. Other than a few major papers spread out over the course of the year, the students weren't expected to write on a regular basis. This was the antithesis of an American-based education, where writing stood at the core. I deviated from the team by introducing a writing exercise once a week. A quote from Thomas Edison emphasizing perseverance became the focal point of my first writing lesson.

Emily raised her hand and I called on her. "Miss, I don't understand."

My eyes shifted to the two other second-language learners. Both were staring down at their desks with blank looks. Without pausing, I asked the three girls for their attention. I picked up a book and motioned that they should read instead of write. All three followed my cue and read a book independently. I forgot that the foreign students didn't attend their second-language class during this particular English period.

"That's not fair," an unfamiliar voice rang out.

"Who said that?" I instinctively asked.

I looked around and pinpointed a boy with uncombed hair. He was slumped in his chair.

"I'm sorry. I can't recall your name."

"Miss, I'm Amit."

"Amit, if you were going to a French school, would you be able to understand?"

Some boys chuckled in the back of the room and one voice rang out. "Miss, Miss. Amit used to live in France. He understands French."

I smiled at Amit and continued, "I remember that you were born in the United Kingdom. Did you live in France?"

He looked up at me and gleefully responded, "Yes, Miss."

"Would you be able to follow the teacher's directions if you went to school with Kamala in Thailand?"

He looked around the room and then remained silent. I didn't intend to single out Amit or direct attention to the second-language learners. I was merely trying to make appropriate accommodations for struggling students.

In the coming weeks, the fifth-grade teachers read *Matilda* out loud to the students. I provided them with handouts so they could organize their ideas for the final assessment, which would compare the book to the movie. In prior years, the students listened and answered oral questions. They were never given a notebook to record any information about the novels they read. I was invigorated by the opportunity to demonstrate American organizational methods and sincerely hoped that my students would improve their comprehension and writing skills as a result.

By the end of the first week, I was feeling more comfortable in my new surroundings and the students were likewise getting acquainted with one another and my classroom procedures. Upon entering the classroom, the students would race over to the bulletin board to see if they received any new mail. They often used the ten to fifteen minutes before the first period began to answer the mail they received from me or another student. It was fun to read their letters at the end of the day.

Arjun shared his dreams of traveling. "I would like to go to Nepal because I always wanted to hike in the Himalayas. Yes, there is another place, Canada. I want to see how it snows in the winter."

I could commiserate with Jonathan when he jotted down, "When I came to India five years ago, I missed the food I used to eat. I found the food overly spicy. Now I'm used to it."

Kabir wrote, "Since I am a boarder, I enjoy staying on campus. The best part of living on campus is that I am a boarder. You never feel alone on this campus."

Emily asked for my assistance. Her note read, "Mi sister don't want to eat can you elp me."

While Mahi was teaching math or science, I occasionally observed the kids and tried to pick up clues about their personalities and work habits. From observations, I realized that Emily and Kamala needed significant support and that a handful of others were not at the same learning level as the majority of the students.

At the end of the first week, Emily's mother wrote a general note in her daughter's homework diary complaining about the difficulty of the assignments. I shared the note with Mahi.

Mahi glanced at the note and snapped back, "She *can* do her homework with a little help."

"Is her homework the same as the rest of the class's?" I curtly responded.

She glared at me and raised her voice. "Why shouldn't it be?"

"She's only been in India a few months and *English is her second language.*"

"She can do it!" She brusquely turned her back and walked away.

We had totally different ideas on how to meet the needs of a second-language learner. Mahi was ignorant of the fact that it took approximately five to seven years before a student mastered academic English. I was miffed. With a rigid attitude that relied on the adage "one size fits all," how could she handle *any* peripheral students who were at a different level than the majority? These students needed to be treated with compassion.

While Mahi was teaching science class, I decided to seek out Pari, the primary director, for her Indian perspective. I avoided making a personal attack on Mahi. Instead, my focus was on the well-being of the second-language learners. Pari listened and seemed to understand my predicament, but didn't offer any opinion.

Students who are just learning English have to reach a comfort level that enables them to participate in a setting where dozens of eyes are staring at them. Without listening to anything that I'd said earlier, Mahi put the spotlight on Emily and Kamala later that day.

"Kamala, come on. I know you can do it. What is the answer to number 5?"

Kamala looked at the floor and didn't respond.

"You know the answer. Just say it."

Kamala's face began to quiver and her eyes were moist. Some of the boys at the next table giggled. Without a reprimand, the boys continued laughing and making rude comments.

I left the room. I couldn't interfere in the middle of Mahi's class.

Pari happened to pass me in the hall, so I asked her if she had another minute. Perhaps, a second example would illustrate the problem better. She smiled and said little. *I was extremely frustrated.*

In the afternoon, the situation repeated itself. This time, Emily was pummeled with repeated questions about chemical reactions.

"What is happening in this picture?"

Emily paused for a moment before responding, "I don't know."

"What about this one?" This time she said nothing.

Again the question was asked. By this time, all of the students were staring at Emily, who was cringing in her seat. I could hear some faint whispers in the back of the room.

"She's so stupid," Amit said.

Emily bravely held back her tears until she burst out of the room heading for the snack break.

In the hallway, I calmly asked Emily, "Are you okay?"

Between sniffles she said, "I don't understand."

I gently replied, "I understand. I will help you."

Emily wiped the snot from her face and gave me a warm smile. From that moment forward, I couldn't help but feel an emotional bond with the non-English-speaking students.

Since the first days of orientation, I'd been perplexed by Mahi's behavior but tried to meet her halfway. Now things were morphing into something completely different. Mahi's teaching methods were emotionally abusive. It wasn't possible to force someone to learn something if he or she had not mastered language skills. Short of a miracle, I envisioned a continuous uphill battle that would require true patience on my part.

I volunteered to teach a beginning-level English class during the three Hindi and French periods. I wanted to concentrate on Emily and Kamala's language skills. Elizabeth approved my proposal and added an additional student. I created lessons for the two girls and a friend of Kamala's. These lessons focused on improving their reading, writing, speaking, and listening skills by using a cross section of texts. Establishing a working relationship with these students became one of the highlights of my teaching experience.

Meanwhile, my life was starting to improve. After I pestered Mohan numerous times, the two foul-smelling refrigerators were removed from my guest room and a worn-out student desk with overhead shelving was added. A week or so later, a rickety drying rack was placed outside my door.

After school on Friday, I heard a knock at my guest room door. I was curious. No one ever just showed up to my room. I slowly opened the door. It was one of the school maids dressed in a blue and red sari.

"Hi, can I help you?"

She stared down at the floor and in a soft voice muttered, "Clee noow."

"Huh? Can...you...say...it...again?"

"Clen roooma."

"Oh, you're here to clean my room."

She used hand motions to describe a mop and a bucket.

I didn't have cleaning supplies because I assumed the maid would bring them. It was fruitless to even attempt to explain this. Elizabeth's intervention remedied this new conflict. The woman came three days a week and once a week she would ferry my clothes to the school laundry on the other side of the campus. She was paid 500 rupees or a little more than $10 each month.

Later that evening, I tried to reach Ira by Skype. It rang and rang. Finally, he picked up.

I started to sing, "Happy birthday to you, happy birthday—"

"It's so great to see you—pixels and all. My birthday wasn't the same without you."

"How was Houston?" I asked.

"Frustrating. Suraj and Vinay continue to be clueless about the American legal system."

"I'd be unglued if Elizabeth didn't have an education background. It's bad enough dealing with Mahi."

"Yeah, I'd much prefer colleagues who are inexperienced than decision makers who don't understand."

"I'm sorry it's such an aggravating situation. Did they start up with you again?" I inquired.

"Yeah. Now Suraj is blaming me for putting the May UK conference on the schedule."

"What? Weren't the plans made before you were hired?" I asked.

"Yep, but it's always convenient to blame someone else."

"What's the reason? Is it because you're an American?"

"Who knows? Vinay and Suraj are argumentative with the two American salesmen, too," Ira replied.

"Don't get discouraged."

"I won't. After the accident, I try to take everything in stride."

"Are you managing okay otherwise?"

"Yeah. I just miss you terribly."

"Me too, sweetheart."

During Saturday's lunch, Elizabeth and Marissa asked if I wanted to splurge and have dinner in Whitefield, an area on the outskirts of Bangalore that catered to expats and international corporations. I agreed. That night I was sitting at a large, round table with a mix of nationalities—British, Canadian, South American, Caribbean, Kenyan, and American. Four of the women were teachers and two were wives of teachers. All of our backgrounds were unique and our ages ranged from late twenties to midfifties. I was the grandma of the group.

Wine flowed freely and frequently as the women became more and more relaxed. Five bottles of wine for six women made it an out-of-the-ordinary night for me. I rarely drink, let alone have more than one drink. In 2009, my son, Adam, posted a picture of me drinking a mug of beer on his Facebook wall. The caption read:

Right here is some history. This is my mom drinking alcohol. It may not seem like much, but this is like watching Big Foot, King Kong, and Moses sit down for a cup of coffee. It's something you just don't see. The fact that I had my camera is a minor miracle. Even better, I think my mom passed out three minutes later. Two words: light weight... and suddenly it all makes sense why my dad chose my mom—cheap date (and the fact that he loves her more than anything ...oh details, details).

The inebriated women spoke freely about their constrained lives on campus. Other than Jade, a secondary teacher who lived in Bangalore with her boyfriend, everyone else was subjected to the watchful eye of the school. I couldn't imagine how Elizabeth had remained cloistered in her apartment for almost the entire previous year. She candidly admitted that she was a recluse who rarely ventured out of the compound. Not only did I have Josh's place to escape to on a weekly basis, but I also planned to visit Josh and Rachael in New Delhi, travel to the Taj Mahal before Josh's wedding, and perhaps travel to Goa, the Andaman Islands, and the Himalayas.

One topic of conversation followed another. As new teachers, Marissa and I were warned of lurking dangers. The message was loud and clear: KIS didn't approve of any dissension and monitored whatever it could. Jade knew a reliable source who was aware of the installation of surveillance cameras and audio feeds on campus. Comment after comment suggested that nothing remained a secret. I was happy that my colleagues shared these morsels of information.

Politics and religion, two topics often avoided by Americans, became a focal point. I sat tight-lipped. They repeatedly referred to the areas of Gaza and the West Bank as the country of Palestine. *Huh? Where did they gain that tidbit of knowledge? Had they ever read a mainstream newspaper or looked at an official map of the Middle East?* Their attitudes regarding the Israel Defense Forces (IDF) and the Israeli government sounded as if their information was lifted directly from a Hamas or Hezbollah website. The woman who previously had lived in Gaza prided herself on owning an official Hamas T-shirt.

I was comfortable until the conversation went down the dark alley of radical political opinion. Was it their alcohol-induced high that caused their lack of discretion or sheer ignorance of how their words could make me feel alienated? Whatever the cause, I didn't care. It was simply a treat to have adult companionship. I had already endured too many lonely nights to get bent out of shape over silly comments.

After dinner, our celebration continued back at Sylva's small, off-campus, two-room retreat, which was located in a small village, just a couple of miles from the school. It was a makeshift building with a corrugated metal roof supported by walls of concrete blocks, different colored cloth, and dull metal. My new acquaintances were serious drinkers. They continued their merriment with several more rounds of beer. I had reached my limit at the restaurant with two glasses of wine and was not interested in embarrassing myself. Elizabeth and I returned to campus before the stroke of midnight. The others remained.

The door to the administration building was closed and the bar that locked the door from the outside was partially in place. *How odd. Am I locked into the building every night?*

I spoke with Ira before going to sleep. It didn't look as if I'd see him anytime soon. He filled me in on his conversations with our sons. I was an iceberg drifting farther and farther away from my source. Josh's Vonage phone was the main link to my children. When I didn't go to Josh's apartment, e-mail, Skype, and G-chat were secondary options. But they were dependent on the school's Internet server.

Ira and I were living in different worlds that took us on a trip back in time. I was reliving my college days while Ira was stuck in bachelor mode, forced to prepare all of his meals and keep up the house. *Would these changes in lifestyle enrich our lives or make us grow farther apart? Would I be able to forge friendships that would help me through this challenging episode in my life?*

35

Before the students arrived on their buses, I usually started my day talking with Asha, a middle-aged Indian teacher with two adult sons. A private driver took her to school. Almost all of the other off-campus teachers rode the students' bus. Our friendship had grown since our first encounter during orientation. We had one thing in common: We were the new kids on the block for the fifth-grade team.

Asha's contract had begun at the very end of the previous school year, when she shadowed the team. It was a regular practice to test-drive new teachers by having them assist current teachers for a few months before they were given the responsibility of teaching on their own. While I could understand this practice for novice teachers like Mahi, many of the teachers who went through this process were veteran teachers with many years of experience. Asha was one of these.

By the middle of the second week, Asha's radiant smile and upbeat attitude were gone. Her eyes lacked their usual luster and her frown revealed a sense of sadness.

"Asha, are you feeling okay?"

Instead of responding in a chipper way, she blandly replied, "Not really. I'm not sleeping."

I hesitantly asked, "I don't want to be a busybody…but can you tell me what's wrong?"

Her eyes turned to me. Then she looked away. "I'm losing my confidence. I'm treated like a novice."

"It sounds like the team is smothering you," I responded.

"I'm always watched but never told where things are."

"I can relate to that. I still don't have some assignments, assessments, or answer keys."

"Maybe I'll stop by your room later. I want to see what Mahi posted for math homework," Asha said.

"Come anytime. We can always talk. Maybe you should have a meeting with Elizabeth or Pari," I suggested.

"Thanks."

"I've been meaning to ask someone. What's Kaaabeen?"

"Are you trying to say Kabini?"

"Yeah, that's it."

"No one told you?"

I shook my head.

"In October, the fifth grade is going to the jungle."

"The jungle?"

"Don't worry. We'll have a great time."

We hugged and then I returned to my class.

Talking with Asha helped me feel connected and happy. I wished that the other team members were more receptive.

Later, during English class, I introduced the concept of free writing. Elizabeth had advised me that KIS conditioned students to respond to exact directions and rarely gave them the opportunity to write without a prompt, as American students did.

I began the mini-lesson by writing the word "authority" on the board. We casually discussed what it meant and then I asked the students to locate a word that was hidden inside.

Neha raised her hand and correctly said, "Miss, I see the word 'author.'"

"Who can tell me the connection between author and authority?"

No one said a word and hands didn't move.

"Anyone? Yes, Jonathan."

"Miss, the author of a nonfiction book is an authority on that subject."

"That's true. But what about fiction?" I paused and gave the students time to respond. "Kabir, are you an authority whenever you write?"

"Yeah, I think so."

"Everyone in this room is an authority on certain things. Take out your creative writing book and title the page 'My Authority List.' Then make your personal list. Everyone's list will be slightly different."

I turned on the portable CD player I borrowed from the library. It was broken just like the CD drive on the classroom computer. I was disappointed once again.

I walked around the room. Jonathan was reading a book and couldn't locate his creative writing notebook. I found it stuck between two other notebooks. Some students were writing nonstop. Many students just stared into the air. I provided individual conferencing to help the students capture their hidden expertise.

I cannot take credit for the underlying idea for this mini-lesson. Two writing experts, JoAnn Portalupi and Ralph Fletcher, alerted me to the fact that the word "author" was imbedded in the word "authority." I hoped that this subtle clue inspired my students to write about what they knew best— their own past experiences.

36

I experienced bruising on my right leg that was becoming progressively worse even though I couldn't recall a trauma. It started as a small patch just under my kneecap, and within three days the amoeba-shaped black-and-blue mark, which was approximately three to four inches wide, stretched from my knee almost to my ankle. When my shin and knee joint started throbbing in the middle of the night, I sought medical attention.

Not being on my home turf made my situation more complicated. I showed my leg to Elizabeth. She suggested that I go to the medical center, which was located past the faculty apartments and next to the laundry. When I walked, I was favoring my left leg and limping.

When I entered the two-story building, I was greeted by a pleasant woman who told me to wait for the nurse. A stocky woman with dark hair appeared and asked me to follow her into a small examining room. The nurse asked several questions and then took a spray bottle out of the cabinet.

"What's that?" I questioned.

"Oh, this," she responded as she took the cover off the bottle. "It's a wonderful spray that's used for pain and cleaning a wound."

"Huh. I'm bruised. Why would you put *that* on my leg?"

She shook her head and didn't respond. Maybe she was taken aback by my questioning of her authority. She had served in the military.

She eventually asked, "Does it hurt inside?"

"It hurts in the shin and in the knee joint. When will the school doctor be here?"

"Next week."

"If I want to see a doctor off campus, how do I arrange that?"

She immediately handed me a form and instructed me to obtain the required signatures and then wait at the reception desk while she arranged an appointment.

"Today?"

"If you want to see the doctor, go today," she snapped.

It seemed nonsensical. One minute she wanted to treat me like a small child who needed Bactine and the next minute she was overly eager to disrupt my teaching by sending me immediately to see a doctor.

A KIS driver took me to Kiran Hospital. I registered at the front desk. It was wall-to-wall people. On the way to the orthopedic department, I stopped to use a restroom. The stench emanating from the ladies' room and the murky liquid that was loitering around in the stall made me gag. I was wearing sandals but should have been wearing galoshes. "Yuck!" was my reaction as I looked for Kleenex in my purse. No toilet paper. No paper towels. I had forgotten to replenish my supply of Kleenex. Pieces of notebook paper sufficed.

When I checked into the orthopedic department, it was a chore locating an empty seat in the crowded, dirty, waiting room. No one asked me to complete a medical questionnaire. After my name was called, I visited a young male doctor in a small room with an outdated examining table and limited furniture. The doctor focused only on my immediate problem and didn't ask anything about my prior medical history. *Three* times he asked in a nasal voice if I had fallen out of my bed. It was preposterous that I wouldn't remember such a tumultuous event. Without trying to be disrespectful, I couldn't stop chuckling over his silly allegations and his insinuation that I was intoxicated.

He ordered an X-ray that required prepayment. I stood in a chaotic line that appeared to have neither a beginning nor an end because masses of people were just standing as close together as possible. It was an absolute free-for-all. From there, I waited in another enormous waiting area in the X-ray department. Once again, I was overwhelmed by the sheer number of people waiting in the rows and rows of chairs. I was given a digital copy of the X-rays and then returned to the orthopedic department to wait.

I dreaded another encounter with the doctor. This time another doctor, a middle-aged man with oval glasses and a receding hairline, greeted me at the door. He was professional and asked more pertinent questions. His thorough examination detected tender areas on the outside of my knee that mandated further investigation. Since I couldn't recall hurting my leg, he was concerned that I might have a rare disorder. An MRI was ordered.

In the meantime, he prescribed a leg cream to decrease the bruising, a knee brace, an ice pack, and an anti-inflammatory medicine that doubled as a painkiller. I returned to the haphazard line at the cashier's desk so that I could prepay for the MRI, which cost 6,200 rupees—approximately $135. This was a substantial savings compared with the $1,000 that is usually charged for such a test in the United States. The MRI was scheduled for a few hours later.

I carefully hobbled across the hectic road and entered the Leela Palace. I couldn't resist treating myself to a Western-style meal. After being refueled, I returned to the hospital for round two. I didn't have to wait long for the MRI, but was nervous about leaving all of my possessions, including my diamond ring, in a flimsy cubbyhole with a simple locking system inside a small dressing area. Next, I stopped at the pharmacy counter for a number and then waited in a massive room for my number to be called. Everything was available except the gel pack. No one behind the counter knew where I could buy one.

I didn't have health insurance, a common situation in India. As part of my KIS compensation package, I was allowed to submit $500 worth of medical bills for reimbursement. After completing the required paperwork, I was eventually reimbursed by the school.

After I returned to school, the students and teachers were long gone for the day. I was exhausted, frustrated, and disappointed that I missed *all* of my classes. My knee was throbbing.

I went back to my classroom to collect some of my papers and books.

"Rats," I said under my breath. I still had not been supplied a key to my classroom and I was locked out again. Limping around looking for a security guard was tiresome. I made another request to Mohan for a key.

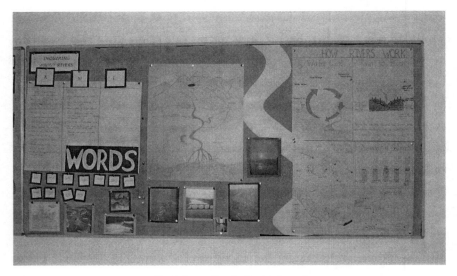

Social studies bulletin board

Inside the classroom, I became instantly annoyed. I had spent hours and hours drawing colorful social studies posters that mirrored the graphics from the textbook, *The River Book,* that had yet to arrive. Mahi, in my absence, had used my water-cycle poster for one of her science lessons. Instead of pinning it back on the bulletin board, it was lying face down on the dirty floor with two chairs on top of it. I ranted and raved about her cavalier attitude toward my work product. I became incensed when I saw the science assignment that was still posted on the white board. The class did an assignment that was almost exactly the same as the one that the English team had planned for the following week. I murmured, "Whatever."

When teachers don't care to communicate with one another, it reduces the effectiveness of the classroom. If the science and social studies classes were studying the same topic, we should have had a team effort in place.

37

I decided to remain on campus for the weekend so that I could rest my leg. The sidewalks near Josh's apartment were difficult to navigate and the restaurant I liked was a mile and a half away. On Saturday afternoon, I visited the girls' dorm to check in with Kamala. Her eyes widened and a full smile crossed her face. She had missed two days of school due to sickness. I opened up my computer and let her watch the social studies videos that she missed. The graphics and pictures were useful, especially since the textbook was still on back order. I talked slowly and clearly. I was able to engage her in a simple conversation, something that I had yet to see in the 5C classroom.

From there, I walked back toward my guest room but made a brief stop at the boys' dorm. Pankaj and Kabir were sitting on their beds reading magazines. Pankaj hopped off his bed and opened up his cabinet to proudly display all of his books and games. His parents had visited earlier to celebrate his birthday. The school restricted the amount of time that boarders could spend with their parents and had limits on what the child could be given. Next, Kabir gave a personal tour of all of his athletic equipment and clothing. I sat down on a desk chair and listened to them talk and talk. I relived the homesickness and loneliness that permeated my life, and I was unsure how ten-year-old boarders coped with living on a campus so far away from home—especially Kamala, who had limited English proficiency. I was happy that I could act as a surrogate parent whenever I visited the dorms.

Back in my room, I looked at Tuffy Tiger perched on the shelf above my desk and proceeded to scroll through the family pictures on my laptop. I listened to Simon and Garfunkel's song "I Am a Rock" over and over.

I resented becoming a hermit. My recent knee injury had limited the time I could spend on my feet. I had my leg elevated most of the time and for now I had stopped swimming. On Saturday and Sunday, I declined offers to join Marissa, Carol, and Dylan on walking tours. Instead, I planned a brief trip to a Whitefield food store. The taxi dropped me off at the Forum Mall in Whitefield. I waited on a bench for Elizabeth to come from church.

"We have great timing," I said to Elizabeth as she approached me.

"I'm glad you made it."

I stood up and walked with her toward the mall bookstore. I repeatedly asked her to slow down so that I could keep up. Next, we walked toward the grocery store. I then followed her down the street to Fabindia to look for clothing. We took an auto rickshaw back to the campus. Elizabeth refused to bargain with the driver for the twenty-minute ride. We were excessively overcharged when the driver refused to use his meter and insisted on a flat fee of 250 rupees. I could have taken a forty-minute taxi ride to Josh's apartment for almost the same amount. I'm glad that the fare was split between the two of us.

As the wind blew our hair in all directions, we spent the time talking.

I faced Elizabeth and asked, "I'm concerned that I'm making too many changes. Can you give me some direction?"

She responded, "It's natural to make changes because you're used to the way you do things in your own culture."

"But is it fair if we're only here for a short time?"

"If the changes are meaningful, don't worry," Elizabeth said.

"I just have so much opposition from the team."

"Use your training to your advantage."

"I wish it were that simple," I replied.

After paying my portion of the fare, I went to my room, elevated my leg, and listened to music. I closed my eyes and visualized a Slinky that pulled outward and constricted inward as it bobbed down a staircase. I was making progress like the Slinky, slowly and methodically. If I allowed anything to tug or distort the symmetrical coil, I would never accomplish what I hoped to achieve.

I toyed with the idea of taking the easy way out. If I simply followed the team, I would have minimal prep time and would grade grammar worksheets and simple one-line answers instead of meticulously grading actual writing.

Taking such a shortcut would disrupt my forward motion and eliminate any hope of making significant improvements. I couldn't forget that I was hired for my expertise and that the school was paying a premium for my American education. I was determined to follow through.

38

T he next week, I returned to the hospital for a late-afternoon visit. The MRI had detected a sprained ligament in my knee, the result of a traumatic injury that I should have recalled. Perhaps I hurt myself one of the times that I tripped on the uneven sidewalks on campus. I needed to be cautious for the next three to four weeks. I was thankful that I didn't have a rare disorder.

The school called an extra meeting for the fifth-grade team during the third week to address issues that Asha and I had raised. The team sat in Elizabeth's office and listened to the test scores of the second-language learners. The students in my special English class were at a first-grade level while some of the other students were at a third-grade comprehension level. I could see that the team didn't want to address these children's special needs. *I was astounded.*

Elizabeth talked about the need to work as cohesive group. The other fifth-grade teachers pleaded ignorance and failed to acknowledge the short-comings of our stifled interactions. No one was willing to admit that any-thing was impeding our team's performance. I glanced at Asha and she looked equally frustrated. *I was discouraged.*

I continued using frequent writing prompts to give my students more opportunities to write. I couldn't resist the one focusing on Helen Keller's words: "Life is either a daring adventure or nothing at all." I derived tremen-dous pleasure by exposing my students to a cross section of personalities and different times in history. By encouraging these extra writing endeavors, I could make a difference in the lives of my students, and these supplementary assignments made me realize why I loved being a teacher.

Later, when I was evaluating the lack of a connection between what was taught and the outcome of the students' work, I realized that part of the problem revolved around listening skills. Too often students didn't follow instructions, and I frequently had to ask students to redo their work. I could understand Jonathan, who sometimes failed to wear his hearing aids, and possibly two other students who struggled with listening skills, but the numbers were higher. *Was it my accent? The words I used? A lack of personal discipline? Or was it something else?*

I had an ah-ha moment when I remembered Elizabeth's comment that Emily, Kamala, and the girl from South Korea were not the only second-language learners in 5C. Other than the few students who were born in the United States or the United Kingdom, the remainder of the students had more than likely learned another language before they spoke their first words of English or they had learned two languages simultaneously. If that was the case, most of the students were technically second- or third-language learners. Keeping this in mind, I understood the compelling reason for the students' struggles with English. If the students' primary language had not fully developed when they started learning English, learning issues would arise. Second and third languages always piggyback on the first language.

My curiosity was stoked. I had the students complete a language survey. The survey revealed that seven students I had erroneously assumed spoke English as their base language had actually started with another language. Additionally, almost everyone in the class had learned a second language during their preschool years, and some were in the process of learning a third or fourth language.

Simultaneously, I tried different ways to modify irresponsible behavior. I inaugurated an open discussion regarding the homework issue. In large red letters I wrote, "Can you name an excusable reason for late homework?"

Some students simply shook their heads and responded in unison, "No!" Others raised hands and waited to be called on.

Neha had a reasonable response. "If you're sick or on vacation, you can turn homework in late."

"Yes, that's true."

I called on Kabir.

"Miss, I have to do my maths and science homework, otherwise I will miss recess," he said.

"Is that why you're in the classroom during recess?"

"Yes, Miss," a chorus of voices responded.

"Any other reasons?" I pried. My eyes caught Arjun's.

"I sometimes am too tired to do my English homework because maths and science are more important," he said.

"Why do you think that English takes a backseat to maths and science?" I asked.

"Miss, what do you mean by backseat?" Amit said.

"Second position or second place."

"You won't yell at us if we don't do our homework," Jonathan said.

The dynamics of a dysfunctional partnership were rising to the surface. This was no different from a husband and wife who use dissimilar approaches in parenting. The children were aware of the disparity between Mahi and me. They invariably played us off against one another. I had to make an effort to short-circuit this unacceptable relationship.

39

On Friday morning, we initiated the routine of having class assemblies during the first period. Until I had attended this first assembly, I was clueless as to what happened during this time slot. During orientation,

Elizabeth had posted a sign-up sheet in the staff room listing all of the available dates and the corresponding topics. Mahi scheduled our class for Friday, September 17. The topic: Yom Kippur.

I was overjoyed with the idea of bringing the Jewish holidays to life for a school population that had minimal contact with Jewish people. I was disappointed, though, that I would miss the performance itself. I had already made reservations to fly to New Delhi in two weeks to celebrate Yom Kippur with Josh and Rachael. I could have remained in Bangalore and attended services at the Chabad House, but I preferred to be with family and not spend the holiday by myself.

During the following week, I put my heart and soul into creating an engaging and informative thirty-minute program. I pulled colorful slides and YouTube videos off the Internet and provided speaking and dance parts for the entire class. As a topic, Yom Kippur was too narrow. I expanded the idea to include basic information about the Jewish people, with a spotlight on the fall holidays. We spent many academic periods rehearsing. It was thrilling to see how the students banded together and took pride in the production.

Friday afternoons were sometimes more challenging than other days because students and teachers anticipated the weekend's arrival. It was unfortunate that the assemblies were scheduled in the morning rather than in the afternoon. During the afternoon break, Arjun and Jonathan were pushing one another around and two others refused to listen to the teacher in charge. Instead of handling the situation on the field, the playground supervisor came marching into the classroom after the break and chastised the students in front of Mahi and me. These students' restless behavior continued into the final period of the day—drama class. This time it was the drama teacher's turn not to enforce any discipline, choosing to send Arjun, Jonathan, and Amit back to the 5C classroom.

Mahi's face was flushed as she glared at the three perpetrators and instructed them to put their heads on their desks. Slowly the rest of the class trickled in and started to gather their belongings for dismissal. Mahi's face was beet red and she walked stiffly, like a soldier. I went around to the different tables to double-check that the students had recorded all of the homework in their diaries and that Jonathan was putting the appropriate items in his bag. The students sat waiting to be dismissed.

Mahi stared at the class from the front of the room and bellowed, "Your behavior is terrible."

Standing in the middle of the room, I scanned the students and saw that most had dilated pupils and wide-open mouths while Arjun, Jonathan, and Amit looked down at their desks.

She continued yelling, "Do you know what you've done?"

I had no idea what she was talking about and was caught totally off guard. There was total silence as all of the students looked her way. She continued ranting in a harsh and sarcastic tone. "Boys, you're damaging the reputation of our class. It's *always* the boys. No special classes next week. You will sit at your desks and *read*. 5C isn't going to be an embarrassment."

I could hear my watch ticking as the students lined up to leave. Mahi led the class to the buses.

It was the start of Labor Day weekend in the States but an ordinary weekend in India. Josh was going to be in town, so I took the school bus to Richmond Town. Then I picked up the phone and dialed home.

"Sweetheart! I miss you so much."

Ira didn't hesitate telling me about the trials and tribulations of being one-armed and the uphill battle he was encountering with physical therapy. I listened.

I interrupted him at one point and asked, "Will you be coming to India soon?"

"Same old same old. I keep on making requests, but most remain unanswered, or Vinay and Suraj claim there's no money for me to travel," Ira answered, disheartened.

"You need to be here for Josh's wedding. Please book a flight. You can always cancel your ticket if Suraj chooses to be honorable and keep his word."

I heard a faint sigh and then he said, "I'll look into it."

Our conversation ended abruptly when Ira had to answer his work cell phone. I went into the living room to spend time with Josh. He was going over our social calendar for the weekend. Josh didn't require food in the refrigerator. He rarely ate at home.

The next day, I took advantage of the Vonage phone like a small child left alone in a candy store. I spent hours catching up. I had missed calling Aaron the previous time I was at Josh's apartment and was happy to finally connect.

"Hey Aaron, how's your new life in LA?"

"I love it. I'm using JDate and meeting so many attractive Jewish ladies."

"Maybe you'll be lucky like Adam. How's living with your cousins?" I asked.

"They're taking good care of me. I still can't believe that you left without Dad. How're things going?"

"It's not easy, but I love teaching. Where else could I teach a Hindu population about Jews?"

I heard a slight giggle and then Aaron said, "Yeah, 'Apples and Honey for Rosh Hashanah' and the 'Aleph Bet' song. I can't believe you taught those songs in India."

"You should see the girls dance to the Chasidic music."

"Mom, you're incredible. I can't believe what you're doing."

"The funny thing is that I didn't ask to do this. I just feel bad that I'll miss the performance."

"Whether you're there or not, you need to feel good about it."

Aaron had flown home for the holiday weekend. If I had been in Colorado, I would have been gearing up with Ira and him for the football rivalry between the University of Colorado and Colorado State University, and I'd have been making plans for a sumptuous Labor Day barbeque with all the fixings. This time-honored tradition would proceed without me.

As a substitute, Josh wined and dined me at two of his favorite restaurants at UB City: Toscanos and Café Noir. He introduced me to more of his friends. Several of them were planning to fly to New Delhi for the wedding at the end of November. I dawdled behind Josh as we walked from place to place.

Throughout the weekend I considered how I should deal with Mahi's outburst. Sending an e-mail was never the desired way to face a growing problem, but I had no choice without Mahi's phone number. After taking great care in picking my words, I drafted a candid note that voiced my concerns about punishing all of the students for the actions of just a few, singling out the boys as being trouble, and using reading as a negative consequence.

As soon as Mahi entered the room on Monday morning, I knew something was amiss. She avoided eye contact and our bare-minimum interaction had dropped to zero. *If it was the e-mail, why didn't she reply or ask to talk? If it wasn't the e-mail, I had no idea why she was so standoffish.*

The silent treatment continued. Elizabeth ended up acting as intermediary because the situation was intolerable. Mahi and I found a mutual free period to air our differences in our closed classroom. I tried to engage her in a constructive conversation. Instead, she went on and on about how my e-mail words were hurtful and demeaning. She continued harping on how I had destroyed her confidence. Then she raised unrelated issues about how I had handled Emily's poor test scores.

"Huh?" was my initial reaction when she lashed out at the note that I had sent to Emily's parents about the 40 percent on her latest first-grade-level spelling test. Emily had not studied; it was necessary to inform her parents. Mahi lambasted me for degrading the child. How ironic, since Mahi was the one who expected Emily to keep up with the rest of the class.

Suddenly, without notice, a stout Indian teacher with dramatic makeup entered the classroom and swaggered to the back of the room pretending to look for something on the bare shelves. She left just as suddenly. Soon another interloper, a heavyset Indian with a stern face, waddled past me and asked Mahi a nonsensical question. I simply gritted my teeth and smiled insincerely. I didn't know how to respond to this odd and unprofessional behavior by fellow teachers.

When it was time for break, Mahi went to the staff lounge and I lingered behind. Asha came in to check the math and science homework assignments.

"So, is Mahi staying on task or is she zooming ahead?" I asked.

"She's at least a week ahead of where we're supposed to be," Asha whined.

"Just follow your instincts," I kindly advised.

Asha hesitated for a moment and then responded, "I don't have a choice, do I?"

"No, neither one of us does."

"I wish that Elizabeth and Pari had followed Kavya and Mahi's wishes. We would've made a great team," Asha said.

"What do you mean?"

"Oh, you didn't know that the two asked to be paired together? The directors were afraid to put two newbies together."

As Asha was walking out of the classroom, I said, "Maybe next school year. For now, I'm just glad we can talk. We can both laugh at the drama."

Before my next class, I walked to the administration building to pick up my latest round of photocopies. Instead of single-sided printing that could be pasted into their notebooks, the pages were double-sided with one side going in the opposite direction of the other. I shook my head. I was finally handed back the spiral-bound KIS planner that had fallen apart during the second week of orientation. Someone had put it back together without paying any attention to the page order. Exasperated, I marched across the hallway to Mohan's office.

"Hi, I'm sorry to bother you. Look at my planner," I complained.

I reached over his desk and placed the thick, blue notebook in his hand. He thumbed through the pages. His eyebrows furrowed and his face became flushed.

"I'm so sorry. I'll have this done again."

"Yeah, my planner mirrors my life here—out of order and upside down."

"Shhh, Miss Sandra. You need to be careful what you say."

I walked out, shrugging my shoulders.

40

*E*rev *Rosh Hashanah*—the eve of Rosh Hashanah—sneaked up on me like an unexpected bandit. My intense focus on school obligations left me unprepared. Leaving the campus midweek was likewise unsettling. I needed to fly to New Delhi on a Wednesday afternoon so that I could arrive before the two-day observance started.

Rosh Hashanah begins the High Holidays, which culminate ten days later with the solemnest day in the Jewish calendar, Yom Kippur. Living in an environment totally devoid of any signs of Jewish identity made my Jewish soul long for the foods and symbols associated with Rosh Hashanah. I craved the simple pleasure of dipping sliced apples into a smooth but gooey pool of golden honey and eating chicken soup with matzah balls.

When Josh and I arrived at the small, inconspicuous New Delhi synagogue on the first day of the holiday, a contingent of Indian soldiers greeted us. They were stationed at the small outpost adjacent to the synagogue. Two Israeli men, who were wearing earpieces, interrogated us as one of the Indian soldiers stood by their side. In light of what had happened in Mumbai a few years before, it was comforting to see that the Indian government was making an effort to protect New Delhi's dwindling Jewish population of fewer than ten families.

Inside the modest Sephardic synagogue, marred with water stains and chipped paint, was a small gathering of Jews—roughly forty or so. A wooden *aron hakodesh* was at the front of the sanctuary while the *bimah* was centrally located. Several Israeli men stood on the bimah taking turns leading the service and reading from the Torah while Ezekiel, the leader of the synagogue, orchestrated each person's portion.

Josh and I each picked up a *mahzor* with fragile yellow pages and frayed binding. Even though the liturgy written on the pages of the Hebrew/English prayer book was in many respects similar to what would be found in an

American prayer book, the overall format of the service was different. Familiar melodies were replaced by tunes that did little to ignite my Jewish passion.

As I stared at the *ner tamid*, I relived my experiences chanting *Haftarah* and Torah portions during the High Holiday family service at Congregation Beth Shalom in Northbrook. These honors connected me to the community and God's presence while simultaneously enriching my Jewish identity.

I could never forget how Steve Stoehr, our former cantor in Illinois, reached out to me after my father died unexpectedly. Steve became my intermediary when my mother refused to provide me with the funeral details. He accompanied Ira, Josh, Adam, and me to the funeral and performed the ritual of *k'riah*, the cutting of the black memorial ribbon, since the officiating rabbi refused to do so. Steve also arranged for a *minyan* to be present each night of *shivah* at our home. My brothers and my mom held a separate *shivah*. A short time later, Steve taught me the trope (musical incantations) that enabled me to become a frequent Torah reader during Shabbat morning services. More recently, he was the only person who responded to my e-mail inquiry about the Hebrew wedding *piyyut* that Josh would sing at his wedding.

The vibrancy of my Jewish identity had wavered after we moved to Colorado. None of the Boulder or Denver synagogues that we attended was welcoming. The slippery slope of ambivalence took control. Being an active participant in a Jewish community became a distant and cherished memory. Our home celebrations took on more significance as my Jewishness shifted to our family celebrations. In New Delhi, I was further disenfranchised, empty, and unconnected to the congregation of diverse worshippers. At least I had Josh by my side, but I longed for Ira's presence and the added closeness of my other children.

The conclusion of the service resembled an auction, as Ezekiel sought to grab everyone's attention by moving around the sanctuary selling the coveted ten spots for the next day's minyan. According to Jewish tradition, ten individuals (Orthodox communities restrict this practice to men) are required to be in attendance for certain communal prayers to be recited. Although I raised my hand, I wasn't included.

The remainder of the day continued quite differently from my past experiences. Rachael's family's ties to the organized Jewish community had diminished over years of alienation from the synagogue. Jewish celebrations were distant memories as her family carried on without any acknowledgement of the holiday season. I spent most of my time daydreaming and worrying about Josh's future in India.

My curiosity was aroused as our driver approached the synagogue on the second day of Rosh Hashanah. Only a few cars were parked in front. *Would there be a minyan?*

All eyes looked upon us as we entered the sanctuary. Josh was the magical tenth person. *Ah, our presence made a difference. Would this ignite a spark to enliven my worshipping or would it remain flat like a black-and-white photo yellowing with age?* I read along in Hebrew and mumbled a few verses here and there. The alien melodies were distracting and made it almost impossible to focus on the words because in my head I heard my own version of the prayers.

I wondered how Ira and Jordan were faring. After no effort was made to reach out to our family in the wake of Ira's accident, I regretted not looking for another rabbi and congregation. Yet I realized that such a search before I left for India would have been impractical, since Ira was avoiding crowded places after the accident and surgery. Ira had no choice but to return to our regular place of worship.

In August, I surreptitiously contacted the synagogue's executive director to see if he could connect Ira and Jordan with another Jewish family. My first e-mail went unanswered. I was disappointed. The response to my second e-mail provided a single opportunity. I felt helpless when I learned that Ira and Jordan would be forced to fend for themselves and that the congregation had once again turned its back on us.

41

I had the luxury of spending two additional days with Rachael and Josh before I had to fly to Bangalore on Sunday afternoon. This was indeed a bonus. If I had remained in the United States, my time getting to know Rachael would have been nonexistent. One day we wandered from store to store as Josh looked at various batts of fabric, different types of ornamental stitching, and various styles for his custom-made Indian wedding outfits. It would take several more weeks of shopping before Josh would methodically make his choices to match the fabric that Rachael would be wearing at all of their events. Rachael vacillated over her color choices. Although Jewish women traditionally wear a shade of white on their wedding day, Indian women normally wear red. In India, white is considered a sign of mourning. Rachael eventually chose a cream-colored wedding sari and stunning, colorful fabrics for the other parties she'd be attending.

Early Sunday morning, I awoke to an all-too-familiar cramping in my lower abdomen. *What did I eat or drink this time?* My abdominal cavity was under attack as I made my way to the toilet. My body was warm to the touch and occasional chills were running up and down my spine.

As soon as I took a few sips of water, I immediately had to bolt to the bathroom. By the time Josh and Rachael awoke, I could barely raise my head off the pillow. My head was vibrating to its own beat. In just a few hours, I was scheduled to take a flight to Bangalore followed by an hour-and-a-half ride back to campus.

Shit. How was I going to pull this off without a potentially embarrassing accident? I chose to eat nothing and consumed a minimal amount of water. I preferred dehydration to the specter of uncontrollable diarrhea. I made it back to my guest room at the school without any devastating consequences. As soon as I was rehydrated, the unrelenting cramping and diarrhea returned.

"Yuck" was the first word I uttered when I awoke and tasted the metallic taste in my parched mouth. My torso felt like it had been turned inside out. I turned on the Carole King YouTube video "Beautiful." I walked around the room singing along with the lyrics at the top of my lungs with a huge smile on my face. I continued to hum the melody as I bathed and dressed. I was mentally prepared to meet the physical challenges of the day. I had missed only two days of class, but I couldn't wait to see my students' faces or read their letters.

I entered the room and immediately went to my yellow box to collect my mail. "That's strange," I whispered. I looked at the bulletin board and none of the kids' boxes had mail, either. My stomach was cramping. I decided not to meet the children at lineup, but instead waited in the classroom. Soon, a large pack of kids pranced into the room followed by several smaller bunches.

"Miss…Miss…Miss Mahi told us that we can't write letters anymore," Pankaj whined. "Yeah, Miss Sandra, we're punished," Neha said.

"What happened?" I questioned.

"Miss Mahi read some of our notes and said that *no one* could write letters anymore," Arjun said.

With one quick blow, Mahi had wreaked havoc on my writing program and the wonderful exchanges that were occurring between the students. Instead of dealing directly with the students she believed had written inappropriate messages, Mahi had terminated the letter writing in its entirety. I chose not to confront Mahi. For the time being, I suppressed my anger and put the writing campaign on hold. I was disappointed that she had prematurely severed this avenue to learn more about my students.

Later in the week, we had a dress rehearsal in the auditorium for the Jewish assembly. Pavan, the IT specialist, supposedly had downloaded the slide presentation and music onto the stage computer. The folder couldn't be found. Mahi glared at me. I tried reaching Pavan on the phone. There was no answer. I tracked him down in the secondary school. Sweaty and out of breath, I returned to the auditorium with him.

"Anyone who has their part memorized will get five extra merit points," Mahi said as I walked into the cavernous room.

I walked back several yards to hear how well the voices were projecting. Most of the kids were rushing through their lines out of fear of forgetting. The sound man at the back of the auditorium walked toward me. "Miss Sandra, they need to slow down," he said.

I walked toward the stage and asked for the class's attention.

"Everyone is talking too fast. Slooow down. Please use your lines."

"Miss Mahi told us to memorize our parts."

"It's better to be heard. I'll mount your lines on colored paper."

Mahi stomped back to the computer station and didn't say anything to me.

As the class was lining up to leave the auditorium, I told them how proud I was of their accomplishment and wished them good luck. I was disappointed that I would miss the production.

42

In order to ensure our timely arrival in New Delhi before sundown, Josh and I left bright and early on Friday morning. Still wiping the sleep from my eyes, I heard Josh's gentle reminder. "Mom, buckle up. Early morning drivers have been up all night. It's not safe." No sooner had I fastened my seatbelt than I saw a large bus on the verge of broadsiding our vehicle.

"Phew! We're damn lucky! That bus came within inches. Seat belt or no seat belt, we would've been toast." After that incident, I went into preservation mode. I closed my eyes until Josh let me know we had reached the airport.

By the time the Kol Nidre service eventually began in New Delhi that evening, the sanctuary was almost full, with close to a hundred people. Additional reinforcements augmented the security force outside this tiny

Jewish haven. The numbers may have changed inside and outside, but the feeling inside the synagogue remained the same. Familiar tunes were missing and the service was in disarray, as several members found themselves in a disagreement. Without a rabbi or cantor, it was natural for the lay leadership to squabble.

The next day, I awoke early with another round of intense stomach cramps, and I cried in my room. It just did not feel like Yom Kippur, especially without Ira. I was betrayed by a company that purposely kept my husband away from me. Being together for Jewish holidays was one of the negotiated points of his employment. Now I was in the untenable position of living on my own while celebrating sacred moments without my husband. It all seemed so unfair, but I could do nothing to change Ira's situation. If the legal community was faring better or Ira was fully recovered from his surgery, he may have started looking for a new position. But with the limited use of his arm and less than a year of employment with IST, it seemed prudent not to consider any hasty changes. Making the best of my predicament took center stage.

I reluctantly returned to the synagogue the next morning for Yom Kippur services. My thoughts wandered. My attention was drawn to a recurring fantasy. In the dream, I packed my bags and disappeared from the campus in the middle of the night. The guards at the front gate attempted to stop me. I laughed out loud as I cruised away in a waiting vehicle that miraculously transported me back to the States. This vision was troubling. It contradicted what I believed. But then again, daydreams usually are surreal and only partially connected to reality. Even if I were to disregard the terms of my contract and try to leave the country, I might be barred from returning for Josh's wedding because I would need to reapply for a new visa.

Harboring such fanciful ideas was ridiculous. My style was not to kvetch or linger on unproductive thoughts. Taking control of my life, being the best teacher possible, and enjoying my time with Josh and Rachael were my goals.

By 1:30 p.m., my blood sugar level had begun to drop and my customary Yom Kippur migraine headache appeared on schedule. Josh accommodated my wishes and we returned to Rachael's apartment to rest. As we drove, I envisioned my Jewish soul fluttering around like a kite that had been let go by its flier. I hoped my kite wasn't lost forever.

But we did return later and Sara, a New Yorker working in India for a Fortune 500 company, caught sight of my vulnerability and reached out to me after the service. I hadn't seen her or her family on Rosh Hashanah, but they were present for Yom Kippur. Her husband, Amnon, a robust Israeli with an outgoing smile, played a prominent role in leading the service and chanting Torah, while three of their four sons, dressed in suits and ties, sat next to Sara. I envied her ability to share the holiday with most of her children. That was one of the perks of working for an American company that extended a lucrative expat package encouraging families to stay intact. We exchanged brief greetings in the sanctuary and renewed our acquaintance in the social hall after the service.

We exchanged stories of our travails in India. Instead of reaching their intended destination on the first day of Rosh Hashanah, her family had been hijacked by a driver who didn't understand their words. They ended up on a wild adventure that took them to the Humayun's Tomb instead of to Humayun Road, the location of the synagogue. Then, when they tried to convey that they wanted to go to the synagogue since they were "Jews," they ended up at the "zoo."

Oh how I wished that Sara and I weren't separated by a two-and-a-half-hour flight. At the very least, I had her contact information for my next trip to New Delhi in a few weeks. Our brief friendship gave me the strength to reach for the kite's string before it disappeared.

On Sunday morning I prepared homemade pancakes for Josh and Rachael in Rachael's kitchen as a torrential downpour flooded the streets. Later, huddled under umbrellas, we trudged through the swamped neighborhood streets to visit bookstores. I was looking for additional resources for my barebones classroom.

When I said good-bye to Rachael at the airport, I hugged her tightly. My emotions matched the streets drenched by the afternoon downpour as I plodded to the gate with Josh.

43

The next morning, I was walking down the hallway toward my classroom and one of the fourth-grade teachers stopped me and said, "Miss Sandra, Shaa…oh, I can't remember."

"*Shana tova?*"

"Yeah, that's it. What does that mean again?"

I smiled and said, "It means Happy New Year in Hebrew."

"Your class did such a wonderful job." As I walked away, my cheeks became warm to the touch and the delightful sensation quickly spread throughout my body. I was proud of my students and looked forward to hearing their version of what happened.

The students would be at lineup for another five minutes, so I hastily rearranged the daily schedule and wrote reminders on the board. As I looked around the room, my eyes stopped at Jonathan's desk. Jonathan's soccer shoes, stuffed with his mud-crusted socks, were lying next to his backpack, which was bursting with creased papers. My head jiggled slightly.

Sounds of children talking and laughing could be heard down the hallway. Neha approached me first. "Miss, Miss…look at my diary."

I looked down at her mother's short note.

"You weren't able to do your homework again?"

Neha didn't answer as I jotted a quick note back to her mother. Then I spotted Jonathan when he entered the room. "Hi Jonathan. Did you drop off your bag early or has it been parked next to your desk all weekend?"

"Miss, I've been looking for it."

"You live on campus. Why didn't you ask one of the guards to let you into the classroom?"

Jonathan just shrugged his shoulders.

"Didn't you have homework?"

"Oh," he replied.

Most of the kids were back in class and I wished everyone a good morning. Somewhere within the throng of students, Mahi had walked in. She remained smug and aloof. She said absolutely nothing and didn't share anything about the assembly or what had happened in my absence. It didn't even occur to her to take any pictures. Luckily, I had had the foresight to ask someone else to take some.

Later, during social studies class, I was forced to punt. The audio feed in the AV room was distorted. So we returned to our regular classroom and I began reading an Indian short story from *The Bird with Golden Wings*, one of the books I had just purchased. As I read the story, the students drew pictures that illustrated the moral of the story. This unexpected lesson produced vibrant pictures (I mounted them on the hallway bulletin board) and an engaging dialogue with the class. Sometimes spur-of-the-moment lessons end up being more successful than well-thought-out ones.

After school, I followed my maid into my guest room. While she cleaned, I sat on my bed reading one of the Newberry Award-winning books I had purchased for my class's library. Something crossed the path of my peripheral vision. I looked up. Less than two yards away was a monkey, just a tad smaller than me, sitting on top of the round table and rummaging through my food supply. I shrieked.

The cleaning lady came out of the bathroom with her mop just as the monkey grabbed my newly purchased package of dried fruit and a box of crackers. He bolted out the patio door before either one of us could do anything. The cleaning lady laughed as my chest tightened with anger and fear.

One of my frequent guests, a monkey sits on my balcony.

I would frequently lie awake at night with mild abdominal cramps and discomforts. I started eating less and less. My meager portions were now like Emily and Kamala's lunches. Oftentimes my menu consisted of a scoop or two of rice, a roll, and possibly fruit. Most of the school's food was prepared in sauces that were too oily or too spicy for me. The homemade pizza was fairly good, but the kitchen staff usually failed to prepare enough. I limited the number of slices I took so that my students would have a sufficient amount.

One day, Elizabeth requested that I cover the afternoon primary prep session afternoon for the boarders. I didn't mind spending time with the students, even though it prevented me from swimming that day. I often supervised this study hall and occasionally assisted the students with their homework. I also provided a small dose of tender loving care. I especially concentrated on the second-language students and the students with learning issues who were given the same assignments that the rest of their class received. Usually they were frustrated because the work was too difficult for them. The hour-and-a-half study session far exceeded the amount of time needed to complete the assigned homework. Other than reading a library book to them, I could not provide a secondary activity. I wasn't given access to any of the outside resources that would have been available in an American school.

The following day, knifelike pains shot back and forth in my midsection like a ball bouncing around in an old-fashioned pinball machine. I was alone in my room, feeling helpless and vulnerable, so I sent a text message to Josh in the middle of that October night.

I was reluctant to return to the school nurse. When the sun had peeked through my blinds, I was doubled over in pain and dripping in sweat. I walked deliberately to the medical center and collapsed on the sofa there. The nurse gave me four different medications and told me to return to my room. She ordered toast and tea to be delivered. A few hours of sleep were all that I could garner before the trips to the bathroom began anew.

Despite my precarious condition, I felt obligated to teach my afternoon classes. I had no desire to draw attention to further days off. Like a mother hen, the principal's secretary was keeping tabs on me and reporting to the principal and the primary unit directors each time she saw me return to my room for medicine or additional beverages. Some of the teachers made passing comments about how *lucky* I was to have Jewish holidays when everyone else worked.

I showered and put on a black jumper that allowed my distended stomach to hang loosely without any constraints. I looked at Tuffy Tiger. Once again, I forced out an artificial smile and gave myself a pep talk. I could do it.

When the next morning arrived, there was little improvement.

Josh texted me and was concerned. "If you're still sick, see a doctor."

See a doctor. Was Josh kidding? I didn't want to take another trip to the hospital.

Midway through the day, the librarian came into the classroom to let me know that Josh had called. He was picking me up in an hour and taking me to Kiran Hospital, the same hospital I had visited for my leg. I made my way to Elizabeth's office so that I could start gathering the mandatory three signatures. Elizabeth was deeply concerned about my condition. "I'll take care of this," she said sympathetically as she took the form out of my hand. *Maybe the key to passing through the main gate was to ask someone from the outside to rescue you.*

Going to the hospital ended up being a wise choice. The mature doctor with deep lines running across his forehead rolled his eyes at the medicines that the school nurse had prescribed.

"Throw all these drugs away. These drugs will make you sicker."

"Okay, what should I do?"

"Rest, eat a very simple diet, and drink, drink, and drink."

He wrote prescriptions on his pad and said, "Take this one for a blood test and this for a stool culture."

I thanked the pleasant doctor and walked into the lab area, which was littered with cotton balls dotted with splashes of dried blood. I was handed a specimen container the size of a small medicine bottle. Nothing else was provided—no gloves, collection container, or scoop. Oh how gross, considering that the hospital bathroom lacked toilet paper and paper towels and was slimy and smelly due to the murky liquid covering the bathroom floor.

It was a major hassle. A driver took me across town to Josh's apartment and then I returned to the hospital to drop off the specimen. After that, I had the driver return me to the school. When I got back to my room, I took off my damp clothes and went to sleep shivering.

In anticipation of an upcoming court ruling on the Ayodhya case, a hotly contested land dispute between Muslims and Hindus, the local government of Karnataka directed KIS to close for safety reasons on September 24 and 25. The Ayodhya court case revolved around the traditional birthplace of a Hindu god and the location of a Muslim mosque. For decades, tensions had been rising as extremists and terrorists caused thousands of deaths. Many Indian municipalities were on high alert in anticipation of the long-awaited verdict. Bangalore was nowhere near the Nepal border where the contested land was located, but the local government still felt the threat of mass unrest. They wouldn't take any chances that students would be the unintended victims of potential riots, and mandated that *all* schools be closed. The staff kindly warned me to remain on the campus and to avoid going anywhere near Josh's Muslim neighborhood. Without a television, I had no idea what was happening.

When I informed my class of the unexpected school holiday, the normal, anticipated response of cheers was replaced by cries of "Oh no, does this affect our class trip?" The Kabini trip had been cancelled, and it fell on my shoulders to convey the disappointing news. Mahi cowered in the corner and refused to be the harbinger of unpleasant news. Although I wasn't certain that the trip would be rescheduled, I provided the optimistic perspective that we would go during a cooler and drier period.

But then, after the parents, students, and teachers had been informed of the KIS closing, the Allahabad High Court postponed its verdict. This meant that school was now back in session. But it was too late to reschedule the Kabini trip, and telling the students this revised news was a hard sell.

With the pending verdict temporarily averted, I was able to communicate with my family on my birthday using Josh's phone. And I was free to make my way to the city. Sitting in the middle of the bus was now my preferred spot. A wide, brimming smile and a hearty "hello" led me to take a seat across from Varsha, a sparkly eyed woman in her late twenties wearing slimming khaki pants and a bright, flowered top. She was a third-grade English and social studies teacher who, at one point, had taken a free period to observe one of my writing lessons.

Our friendly conversation distracted me from the hustle and bustle of the crowded street and the jerking movements of the bus. Our conversations centered on school-related matters, but we also talked about the upcoming Commonwealth Games in Delhi. She was deeply disturbed by the negative press focusing on the inadequacies of the city's infrastructure and the backwardness of life in India. No doubt, she waved the flag for India and wore rose-colored glasses that prevented her from seeing the country's deficiencies in a clear light.

Without any reservation, Varsha said boldly, "What's the fuss about?

A few construction issues and the pollution shouldn't make the press go wild."

I glanced out the window as we passed an open sewer that resembled a polluted river and empty lots brimming with debris. I was thinking, *Oh my God, doesn't she see what's outside?* I smiled and politely said, "You definitely have a good point."

I enjoyed her company and had no intention of offending her. Nevertheless, as an American, I sided with the foreign correspondents who were obligated to compare India with Western countries where enforceable laws controlled pollution and new construction. Our friendly dialogue ended when she exited the bus and wished me a good weekend.

Being alone on my birthday was devastating. I could commiserate with Ira's experience the previous month. After this, I never, ever planned to repeat such a dreary and depressing scenario. Just as religious holidays are meant to be shared with others, birthdays should be, too. I hibernated in Josh's apartment as the afternoon rains splashed on the pavement.

In between periods of no power, I listened to Internet music from the '70s that reinvigorated me and allowed me to relive past moments with Ira. "A Time for Us," the theme from *Romeo and Juliet* and the song that was played during our first wedding dance, was my preference. I played it over and over again and focused intently on the line that encouraged people to stand up to adversity.

44

With the social studies textbook still on back order, I created innovative ways to engage my class in the study of rivers. While my colleagues made cumbersome and lengthy PowerPoint presentations and filled the period by lecturing in front of the class, I exposed my students to the wonders of rivers by showing a collage of videos downloaded from the Internet. Like so many other aspects of teaching at KIS, I needed to be flexible and have backup plans. On any given day, we had no guarantee that the computer or audiovisual equipment would be working. This, of course, can be a universal problem, but in India it happened way too frequently.

One of my memorable moments was when the kids' eyes grew enormous and they squealed watching experienced kayakers navigating down a raging river.

"Wow, is that what Colorado looks like?" Arjun asked.

"Yep. The mountains are amazing," I responded.

"Miss, do you live near there?" Neha inquired.

"Not too far."

To enhance their video experience, I drew five columns on the board and then said, "In your social studies notebook, create five columns that correspond to your five senses. Let's work together to fill in the chart. Who can tell me what you might smell?"

After collaborating on two of the senses, I left a few minutes for the students to complete the remaining columns. Next, I asked them to write about the experience.

Without a textbook, I had to think out of the box so I could draw my students into the topic and I decided to use more group activities. I probably wouldn't have acted any differently in an American school, except the school would have been more forthright with printed information and better-equipped from the onset. I would have been able to plan by using curriculum guidelines, classroom materials, designated time frames for units, and guidelines for assessments provided before the start of school. In India, I was constantly engaged in a treasure hunt, trying to garner whatever information I could from my evasive team members. Most troubling was the fact that neither Asha nor I was provided *all* of the information regarding assessments. It was handed out to us in dribs and drabs, at the discretion of the other team members.

During orientation, I was led to believe that there were very few tests. I was absolutely astounded that midway through the social studies unit on rivers, I was handed four assessments that were a total regurgitation of facts and almost identical. There were no assessments that addressed the needs of students who were working above or below grade level. American teachers usually begin their unit of study knowing where they are headed and then tailor the lessons accordingly. I was miffed.

At the very beginning of the school year, I witnessed how the students struggled when they took the International Assessment for Indian Schools created by the University of New South Wales in Australia. This test included many complex questions that required advanced analytical skills. Test results graded by a third party revealed that the *top 3 percent* of the class *averaged only twenty-eight correct answers out of a possible fifty*. This score should have been a giant red flag pinpointing major shortcomings in the curriculum.

Equally troubling was the cumulative test that the fifth-grade students would be taking later in the year. Large gaps existed between what I was being asked to teach and what was eventually being tested. If there was an underlying premise that assessments were unimportant, why would they be giving a cumulative test at the end of the school year? Usually comprehensive exams were graded by an outside party but this one was graded by the teachers themselves, who obviously had a vested interest in the final scores.

Then, for the second time, the local government responded to a pending court decision on Ayodhya by enacting a mandatory two-day holiday for all schools and colleges in Karnataka. This announcement was made during the weekly primary-unit faculty meeting, where the principal made a rare appearance. I giggled softly as everyone rose up like robots and sang out in unison, "Good morning, Dr. Robert." After he made his token announcement, it was business as usual.

The two unexpected days off were a welcome respite. I took down my defunct "You've Got Mail" bulletin board and replaced it with an ice cream scoop motif. Each student was awarded a colored scoop after he or she successfully fulfilled the requirements for a written book report. I created colored charts tracking performance and decided to award prizes to the first boy and girl who read five books. I also got Elizabeth's approval to have classroom treats—a pizza party and an ice cream party—when different benchmarks were attained.

When I stepped away from the newly finished board, I was pleased with the overall design but disappointed by the lack of vibrant colors. Our supply of poster board was limited to bleak and boring black, gray, and tan.

When class resumed the following week, the students congregated around the bulletin board. I overheard students talking.

"Look at this," Kabir exclaimed.

"What happened to the mailboxes?" Jonathan inquired.

"We'll talk about the reading challenge after you come back from PE," I told them.

While the girls were swimming and the boys were at PE, I placed their colorful mailboxes on their desks together with the new forms for book reports—one for fiction and the other for nonfiction. The three second-language learners were given a simpler format. After the students returned, I introduced the ice cream scoop challenge and was met by questions.

"Miss, can we write a report tonight?" Kabir asked.

"Yes, if you've just finished a book."

"What's the prize?" Jonathan blurted.

"You'll see."

"Will we have pizza parties and ice cream, too?" Neha inquired.

"Yes, if the class reads."

As the students did their work, I wrote their English homework assignment on the board. "Prepare a book chat on one of your favorite books." This would kick off the reading challenge.

By the end of the week, all of the students had presented book chats. Only a few reported on American literature; most read books written by either British or Indian authors. I made a modified assignment for the second-language learners. Emily chose to go first. I was delighted to see her willingness to take chances.

I introduced the reading challenge to my class as a way to stir more interest in outside reading. Maintaining a reading log was a weak approach to encouraging reading. I sincerely hoped my fellow teachers would see the merits of having their students write about the books they read rather than merely keeping track of pages read.

The following week, Elizabeth and Pari gave me the distinct honor of teaching at one of the weekly primary-unit faculty meetings. I had no shortage of viable subjects, since the school did *not* have a school-wide literacy program. Each grade did its own thing based on personal preferences and the team's interpretation of the mandated textbooks. To link all of the primary grades with a common vocabulary, I opted to introduce a writing program as well as the reading challenge.

A lack of resources stymied my ability to do a presentation. The library had no books on the subject. I hadn't brought any of the pertinent books from home because I erroneously assumed that the school would have a writing program in place. Websites provided various ideas and I was undecided on which one I preferred.

With less than a week remaining before the presentation, I took a gamble and e-mailed Ruth Culham, a noted expert on a program called 6 Traits plus 1. I am indebted to her quick and friendly response. She graciously sent me attachments that I could copy. Due to her assistance, I was able to give the primary-unit staff a comprehensive overview of an internationally accepted program.

I walked confidently up to the whiteboard and wrote, "If you can assess, you can revise." Words flowed smoothly and easily as I highlighted the importance of agreeing to implement a school-wide literacy program and explained briefly the underlying goals of Culham's attachments. My audience listened respectfully. I was eager to hear its response.

"I've done a lot of talking. Now it's your turn. Does anyone have any questions?"

I looked around the room and not one hand was raised. I squinted. The silence was disappointing.

"I'm surprised you have no comments or questions," I blurted.

Several teachers raised their hands.

I called on the first one and she said, "Just because we don't use *this* method doesn't mean we aren't *good* teachers."

I took a few steps toward the teachers and said, "I'm not talking about capabilities. I'm highlighting the importance of continuity and common language."

This was followed by another comment. "We do the same thing. We just don't have anything in writing."

"Yes, many of you may be doing bits and pieces. But a school should adopt the same script, whether it's this program or another."

There was a lull, so I continued. "I'm curious. Do you give your students a rubric before they begin writing?"

No one raised a hand. Most of the teachers just looked at one another.

I called on one of the early primary teachers, who asked, "Why do the students need a rubric? Isn't the rubric for the teacher?"

"It is actually for both. The students should know what is expected before they start writing." I looked around the room and a few teachers nodded their heads.

I was uplifted by this opportunity to share my expertise. I received praise from the primary-unit directors and some of my fellow teachers, in contrast to the negative feedback that my team members gave. I was empowered by this experience. *Maybe my purpose for being at the school was what I could offer its staff. Could I be the beacon that awakened them to Western teaching methods?*

Taking Detours

45

T he following Saturday morning, a private minivan whisked me away. I was on my way to joining Josh and his partners, Neill and Linda, at Shreyas Yoga Retreat on the outskirts of Bangalore. After a two-hour drive, I reached my destination.

A gracious barefoot man greeted me and delicately placed an aromatic necklace of tropical flowers around my sweaty neck. The colorful, dainty flowers exuded an intense fragrance that easily could have doubled for an expensive French perfume. I breathed in deeply to capture the essence of the floral arrangement, which bounced lightly against my chest as I trekked barefoot on the designated pathway to Josh's cottage. I was comforted by the chirping birds and a canopy of trees and foliage that shielded me from the intense rays of the sun. After passing through a trestled archway adorned with magnificent purple and pink flowers, I reached the accommodation I was sharing with Josh.

The porter slowly opened the door to the garden cottage. Josh was curled up into a ball and partially buried under a beige comforter. I knew instantly that what Josh had described as a minor fever was something much more serious. On the phone, he simply complained of a lingering fever with no other symptoms other than the expected headache. I stroked his forehead with the back of my hand and sensed the immense amount of heat radiating off his lethargic body. His eyes blinked open and shut a couple of times as I peeked at his dark brown eyes.

I strode to the adjacent bathroom, drew cold water onto a washcloth, and twisted the cloth back and forth to extract the water. I gently placed the cool compress on his forehead. Within seconds, the heat from his head had warmed the cloth. Meanwhile, I grabbed several more cold compresses and laid them on his sizzling-hot back.

Josh was far too weak to join me for lunch so I reluctantly left him sleeping. I was famished. I hadn't eaten anything since breakfast. I was wined and dined by the attentive staff as they served the vegetarian selections for the day. As I followed the meandering path back to our cottage, a jarring sound made me jump. It was similar to the sound of the cannons that are fired for avalanche control in the Colorado Rockies. With trepidation, I scurried back to Josh.

Josh had followed my suggestion that he take a cold shower to bring down his alarming temperature. He was sitting up in bed and I saw that his eyes were a bit clearer and that he was lucid. He guzzled coconut water and nibbled on a few pieces of bread that had been delivered to our room.

I sat next to him and said, "I'm glad to see you're up. How're you feeling?"

"Mom, don't worry. I'll be all right."

"Why didn't you tell me about the fever? Do you have any other symptoms?" I questioned.

Josh started to rub the back of his neck and said, "My head is throbbing and I just feel crappy. Can you ask them to bring more coconut water?"

"I'll call for the coconut water. Hey, did you hear that loud noise?"

"Oh, that. Did it startle you?"

"It sounded like the place was under attack."

Josh responded, "There's a quarry nearby where they blast dynamite throughout the day."

"Huh? Doesn't that take away from the serenity and the ambience of this yoga spa?"

Josh just shrugged. Who builds an exclusive spa that charges well over $400 a day near an active quarry and busy railroad tracks? The rumbling of passing trains was a mild irritation compared with the abrasive and inhospitable sound of the nearby explosions.

Shreyas Yoga Retreat

Josh suggested that I explore the property before dark. I headed to the secluded area that was in the opposite direction from the pool and the dining hall. The foliage, an array of different shades of green, was dotted here and there with splashes of color from the fall-blooming flowers. A horde of monkeys the size of preschoolers had overtaken the field and adjoining path.

"Oh no, not again!" I whispered as I stopped in my tracks.

"Let me see…two, four, six…eighteen, twenty, twenty-one…uh, twenty-two." My count didn't include any monkeys in the neighboring trees.

I convinced myself to keep walking. My heart was thumping so hard that I felt the reverberations throughout my body. I held my breath as I bolted to the driveway.

That evening, I shared dinner with Josh's partners, Neill and Linda, in an exquisite garden setting that was romantically lit with candles meticulously placed in bags on top of reflecting mirrors. As I stared at one of the candles, I visualized Ira sitting alone at our round, glass, kitchen table, eating dinner while watching television. I also remembered Adam's recent proposal to

Rachel. I once again wished that we were all together.

When I eventually returned to the room, it smelled like the beach. Josh had sweated to such an extreme that the sheets were totally wet and his clothing was saturated with saltwater. He took another shower to cleanse his body of the salty film.

It was a long night. I periodically rose to check on Josh and replenish his liquids. I was worried as he shivered on and off during the night. By daybreak, I was sleep deprived but too wired to rest. I found my way to the wellness center for a massage and a trip to the eucalyptus-scented steam room. I was rejuvenated by this welcomed perk and merrily went back to the room to check on Josh. My upbeat attitude dissipated as soon as I saw Josh's face. His fever was over 102 degrees Fahrenheit. After I had a quick lunch, we were on our way to Kiran Hospital.

When we reached the entrance to the emergency room, Josh was beginning to show signs of disorientation and was complaining of nausea, tingling in his extremities, tightness in his chest, and a bad headache. The entryway was jammed with people and, from my low perspective, it was impossible to see the location of the check-in desk. As we pushed our way into the main room, I passed two bloodied bodies lying on gurneys. I approached several hospital personnel who brusquely ignored me. Frantically, I interrupted two nurses who were conversing with one another in a foreign language.

They escorted Josh and me into a small room with a dozen hospital beds lined up in two cramped rows. They instructed Josh to lie on the last available bed, which was covered with a worn-out sheet dotted with small holes. Splotches of brown, yellow, and blood stains caught my eye. I was fixated by the unsanitary conditions.

Oh my God, how do you avoid becoming sicker in a place like this? This was unlike any ER that I had ever visited in the United States. The room reeked with a foul odor that couldn't be masked by disinfectants. I was nauseous as I breathed the tainted air. I peeked around the filthy curtain that separated Josh from the others, and was overwhelmed by the sheer number of people stuffed into this small ER ward. Patients occupied every square inch of the place. There was almost no room to walk.

A nurse appeared and thrust a thermometer under Josh's arm. A few seconds later, she smiled and claimed that his temperature was normal.

"Excuse me. That thermometer isn't accurate." I reached inside my purse and pulled out Josh's thermometer. "His temperature is 103.2 degrees Fahrenheit. Can we see a doctor?" She smiled and bobbled her head. Next, a heavyset young Indian doctor with waist-length black hair came to examine Josh. Josh explained that he had visited the ER a few days earlier with a high temperature. She immediately ordered blood tests and an IV. We waited another four hours for his fluids to be replenished and the test results to come back. The doctor dismissed his abnormally high platelet count and discharged Josh from the hospital. Our waiting driver dropped Josh back at his apartment and then drove me back to campus.

I worried about Josh managing in his apartment. He could barely raise his head off the mattress. Without a car, I was of little assistance. To soothe myself, I listened to Simon and Garfunkel's "If You Need a Friend" and placed a call to Ira.

46

Elizabeth and Marissa had approached me a few weeks before to see if I had any travel plans for the Dussehra break, which coincided with the beginning of the winter season. Dussehra is an Indian festival that highlights the concept of good versus evil by marking the triumph of Lord Ram over the demon King Ravana. Most of the Indian faculty intended to spend the festival with family. The expats were all taking advantage of the time off to explore different parts of India. I couldn't resist the opportunity to travel with two of my colleagues.

We eventually reached a consensus—round trip by air to Cochin, a private car, three nights' accommodations at a bed-and-breakfast in Munnar, and a half-day tour of Cochin. I was content.

We were off to a good start when the taxi arrived on time. It was smooth sailing to the airport in the wee hours of the morning. Hours later, the small propeller plane landed in Cochin, where ominous rain clouds hung over us. Huge puddles and a damp tarmac let us know that the monsoon season still lingered in Kerala, an Indian state located on the Malabar coast of southwest India. A torrential downpour pelted our car. This minimized our view of the lush landscape that surrounded us and the breathtaking, cascading waterfalls that we passed as we wound our way up to an altitude of approximately 6,000 feet above sea level. Anytime we attempted to open a window to take a photograph, we immediately regretted the deluge invading our space.

The pitter-patter of raindrops decreased as we gained altitude. Had it not been for the occasional cows strolling down the roadway or the periodic piles of garbage, I could have imagined we were on another continent. Marissa candidly remarked that the rolling countryside reminded her of the Caribbean. Signs reminding people to pick up their litter were ubiquitous.

It was close to dinnertime when our vehicle made the steep climb up the rocky driveway to our accommodations, which reminded me of an American bed-and-breakfast. As we climbed out of the car, our congenial hosts, Anil and Jeeva, greeted us. At the Royal Mist we had a bird's-eye view of the surrounding peaks, which were partially covered by low-level clouds. The cool, unsullied air had me inhaling deeply and marveling at an outstanding example of God's paintbrush. I was relaxed and calm.

Soon thereafter, our waiter delivered a simple, piping-hot Indian dinner with a meat entrée, a vegetable entrée, and chapatis. Our table sat on a wooden deck outside our bedroom doors. The dampness and chilly temperature caused Elizabeth and Marissa to bury themselves in layers of clothing topped off with heavyweight pashmina shawls. I reveled in the crispness of the evening air and managed comfortably with my hooded, black, waffle shirt embroidered with a University of Colorado logo.

Each of us, in our own way, needed this time away from campus.

We clung to our memories of home and family, and we connected with one another. Because our school obligations and responsibilities normally limited our time for socialization, we soaked up this opportunity. We deliberately chose to avoid all mention of KIS. After all, we were on vacation.

Although coming from diverse backgrounds, we shared commonalities. Elizabeth randomly asked if either one of us ever heard music playing in our brains. Marissa crinkled up her nose and shook her head. She didn't understand. I, on the other hand, could relate to what she said. For weeks, songs had become part of my daily life. We happily shared our belief that loneliness was the cause of this melodious reliance.

Our first destination at the retreat was one of the scenic hill stations. The tea fields' patchwork shades of green lost their vibrancy as clouds started to hide the sun. And the winding roads became increasingly dangerous as we encountered more and more motor coaches filled with vacationers taking advantage of the days off from work. At certain points, the road narrowed to such a degree that only one vehicle could pass at a time.

"Gridlock" and "rural sanctuary" are words that usually conjure up contrasting images. In Munnar, these images became one, much like the scenes you see during the peak summer months in US national parks. Our driver casually asked us if we were interested in seeing elephants. The previous day, our planned stop at an elephant sanctuary had been rained out and now he was offering us a second chance to ride elephants.

Marissa responded, "Please, can we stop there? I'd do anything to ride an elephant. Please, please."

While not high on my list of must-dos, I certainly didn't want to dampen Marissa's excitement. "Sure, let's go," I said.

Lush tea fields and mountains in Munnar

"I had my fill of elephant rides in Thailand. But we can stop," Elizabeth chimed in.

"Are you sure?" Marissa and I said in unison.

"Go and enjoy. I'll wait," Elizabeth responded.

Without delay, Elizabeth instructed the driver to take us to the elephants.

Marissa and I climbed the wooden two-story structure to board the elephant. It had short tusks and was considerably smaller than the African species. Marissa took the front position and I slid in behind her. We were off.

Thirty minutes became the ride of a lifetime. The elephant trainer took us up and down a pathway that led us in a giant, meandering circle through a lush tropical forest with an earthy fragrance. Each step made us sway from side to side and we laughed unreservedly. After the ride, I thanked Marissa for her insistence. Months had passed since I had laughed so deeply at something so hilarious. The pictures taken by the trainer captured a wonderful moment in my life—simple moments can be truly exceptional.

Later, we hiked up a path in a forested area and came to an unexpected sign. If we wanted to view the scenic overlook, we needed to pay a few rupees for the privilege of trekking on private property. We paid. Although we needed to climb some carved steps and the vertical rise on them was higher than normal, I bounced from one to the next. After years of living in pain and being inactive, I was able to endure a challenging trek pain-free. I was ecstatic. Looking out at the horizon, I realized that there was so much to be gained from my adventure in India.

The next morning, our hostess, Jeeva, treated us to her all-time favorite. It was a Kerala specialty called *appam*. I was so intrigued by this food that Jeeva provided a private cooking lesson later in the day. The secret of this delicacy was the mixture of rice, coconut milk, and yeast fermented over-night. It was cooked in a special pan that allowed the center to rise up to the depth and size of a hockey puck while the outer edges became lacy, like the dainty pattern on a doily.

After another day of sightseeing, we were eager to have Anil provide a walking tour of the surrounding area. We were joined by a young European couple who had just checked in. Upon reaching a clearing, Anil stopped to issue a stern warning about leeches. "They're everywhere. Stay on the trail and let me know if you feel anything." I looked at the young couple dressed in short shorts and short-sleeved T-shirts. If anyone was a likely candidate, it was one of them. The three of us had on long-sleeved shirts and pants.

We had walked only a small distance when Marissa began jumping up and down. "Look! Look! Is this a leech?" she screeched. It seemed highly unlikely. But sure enough, one had attached itself to her ankle. Within sec-onds, Anil had removed it and we were on our way.

Our brief stay came to an end the following morning. My share of the accommodations and breakfast came to 5,150 rupees (approximately $114), my dinners came to 150 rupees (a little more than $3), and my share of the car and driver came to 2,000 rupees (a little more than $44). Our good-bye hugs were sincere because not one of us anticipated a return visit.

We had been exceptionally lucky. The comments on Trip Advisor were totally accurate. A home stay could be a chancy encounter, especially in a rural part of Asia, where acceptable standards tended to fall far short of

Western standards.

Our car headed to Jew Town, where the notable Paradesi Cochin Synagogue, or "foreigners' synagogue," was constructed in 1568. This amazing synagogue was adorned with hand-painted, willow-patterned, blue-and-white imported Chinese floor tiles, and had become a must-see after I noted it on a Jewish calendar that featured famous synagogues around the world.

Our driver parked the car within a few blocks of Jew Town Road. As we walked, I wondered about the Jews who once lived and worked here. I was eager to locate Sarah Cohen, the owner of Sarah's Embroidery Shop. According to postings online, she was the sole Jewish entrepreneur left in Jew Town. The once-vibrant Jewish community had dwindled over time to fewer than ten.

Above the doorway to her store was a simple, rectangular, white sign with black Hebrew letters. But this "shalom" sign was not nearly as obvious as the colorful hanging sign that read "Sarah's Embroidery Shop" or the blue Stars of David adorning the shop's windows. An older Muslim gentleman approached us and said that he was taking care of Sarah since she was all alone. Her husband and brother were deceased and she'd never had any children. Though I really didn't need any embroidered goods, a memento from this historic shop was a necessity.

In a nearby fabric store, Elizabeth and Marissa bargained over a selection of shawls. The skies darkened unexpectedly and a deluge pelted the doorway. The storm was so intense that the storekeeper hastily closed the open door. After the purchases were made, one of the merchants said, "You'd better hurry—the synagogue is closing."

"What! Are you kidding?" I said under my breath as we darted out the door and ran toward the synagogue.

We jogged down the cobblestone street, but as we came close to the synagogue, we saw a sentry in a khaki uniform posted outside a storefront police station just a few steps from the synagogue door. The man yelled, "The synagogue is closed."

"No, no," I whined.

We each took turns pounding on the faded, blue, wooden door. Elizabeth and Marissa left me standing by the door as they approached the guard.

"She's a Jew...She's a Jew...Jew...Jew...," Elizabeth yelled as she pointed in my direction.

"She's come from America to see the synagogue," Marissa announced.

Under most circumstances, those words—"She's a Jew...She's a Jew"—would be offensive. In this scenario, I was hoping that they would be magic words, like "open sesame." We heard the bolt start to move on the old door. An older Indian man dressed in dark slacks and a white, button-down shirt appeared. He motioned with his hand to come closer.

"Quick, quick, I'll let you in. No cameras or videos are allowed."

It was just like the picture in the calendar and online. This ancient synagogue had a centralized *bimah*, a second-floor women's section, glistening blue-and-white floor tiles, and antique colored lights. Looking at all of this made me reflect on a lost community that relied on visitors to maintain its vitality.

If only the walls could retell the stories of this dying community. It reminded me of other notable synagogues that I had visited—like the Caribbean-style synagogue in St. Thomas with the sand floor and the Choral Synagogue in St. Petersburg, Russia, with the KGB office across the street.

After we left the synagogue, a group of four goats, who strolled along with a couple of stray cats in tow, escorted us to the nearby cemetery, which was located down a side street. Like most old cemeteries, it was locked behind a rusted gate. We located the enclosed structure by the faded dedication sign that was written in Hebrew, English, and Hindi. It bore a date of 1898 for the erection of the tall compound wall and shed.

On Jew Town Road with the synagogue in the background

As long as we were in Kerala, I was curious to see if I could locate a recommended book, *The Last Jews of Kerala*. We entered a quaint bookstore
near the cemetery, where I found the book and two additional books on the
history of Indian Jews. As I thumbed through the smaller of the two, my eyes
came upon the author's name, Rachael Rukmini Israel. My jaw dropped. I
quickly turned to the back cover and saw that it was published by my future
daughter-in-law when she was in law school. I let out a giant yelp and let

everyone in the store know that my son's future bride had authored the book.

Our holiday getaway ended when we returned safe and sound after a harrowing ride from the airport with a driver who had not slept in over twenty-four hours.

47

The next morning, I was recounting the highlights of my glorious vacation to my mother on Skype when I heard the familiar scratching sound of Velcro strips being pulled apart. I turned to see a monkey's arm disengaging the Velcro that held my window screen in place. I clapped my hands. No response. More of the oversized monkey's head and torso penetrated the room. I screamed louder and louder and louder.

Faintly, I could hear my mother calling to me, "Sandy, is everything okay?"

My initial protests went unheeded. I jumped up and down and made as much noise as I could until the monkey retreated.

I had had cable TV installed during my time away, and the cable had lured him. I disconnected it from my TV and pushed the wire out my window and secured the screen. Now the cable ended on my deck instead of in my room. I saw a whole family of monkeys scaling down the TV cable, which was dangling like a vine from the roof onto my patio. I recalled the game A Barrel of Monkeys, in which a group of monkeys forms a long, continuous chain. I stared at this large entourage of assorted monkeys gathering outside.

Faintly, I heard, "Sandy, Sandy, what's happening?"

I was still shaking when I sat down at my desk.

"My God, you look dreadful."

"Aaah, l-let me shh-show you something," I stammered.

I disengaged the power cord from the back of my computer and took the laptop toward the window. I opened the blinds. The deck was filled with a multigenerational group of monkeys that were showing their wide teeth. The monkeys had taken my socks off the drying rack and were parading around with my garments. My mother was rolling to and fro in her chair, laughing hysterically. It wasn't funny. Didn't she realize that I could become deathly ill if one of them bit or scratched me?

The two oversized vertical windows were still propped open, and the only thing that separated the band of monkeys from me was the flimsily attached screen. I was not going outside to close the windows until the monkeys were long gone. After logging off Skype, I ventured down to the reception area.

"Can you help me, Deven?"

Half-jokingly he responded, "I heard you screaming. What's the problem?"

"Why didn't you come to my rescue?"

"Uh…uh, I thought you were yelling at someone on the phone."

What a brave one. He ordered the cleaning man on the next floor to fix the problem. Alone in my room, I paced back and forth. It had taken weeks for them to run the cable and now the monkeys sabotaged my new connection to civilization. And were my socks lost forever?

My first stop on the way to class was Mohan's office. A profoundly stern disposition replaced his usually friendly demeanor as I relayed my fears about the monkeys coming into my room and taking my clothing. Out of the blue, Mohan now considered my residency on campus to be short-term and started questioning my intentions. I was dumbfounded.

I could only surmise that I was expected not to make any waves. This attitude made me think back to my colleague's warnings during orientation about avoiding any confrontations. By raising an issue about the monkeys and my lost possessions, and by asking for the cable to be run another way, I was making myself too visible. I sat silently as waves of renewed fears stroked my body. My concerns about my personal safety were becoming a catalyst for future eviction. *Was I an unwanted guest who might be told without notice to pack her bags?*

I headed to Elizabeth's office with the hope that I could talk with her before the buses arrived. Fortunately, she was still there. I summarized my conversation with Mohan and asked for her advice. She calmly assured me that she would do everything in her power to intercede on my behalf.

This incident only heightened my sensitivity as to how I should act on campus. And it made me realize that I needed to make more frequent visits to Josh's apartment. Although I never ventured out by myself at night, I was able to handle the Bangalore streets by myself during the daylight hours and used rickshaws and taxis without any reservations.

The subsequent Friday afternoon bus journeys to Josh's apartment afforded me the opportunity to converse with colleagues or just simply space out. On my next bus ride into town, I sat with Rohan, a charming, middle-aged man whom I'd met during one of the orientation meetings for new faculty. Before working as a college guidance counselor at KIS, he was a college instructor in the States. We occasionally exchanged small talk on campus whenever we passed one another.

As the bus left the school parking lot, he leaned toward me and started talking. "Have you seen Stefan or Jade lately?"

I shook my head and replied, "It's been awhile. Why?"

"Well, neither one is on the campus."

"I didn't know they were missing. What happened?" I asked.

"I tried contacting Stefan on Facebook. He never responded."

There was a long pause. I didn't know what to say. Then I asked, "Were they fired or did they quit?"

"I'm not sure. Probably fired. Please be careful," he warned sternly.

My stomach became knotted as I wondered about their whereabouts. *How strange that two expats would disappear within a few days of one another. Was Rohan's paranoia warranted?* In order to lessen my anxiety, I switched the topic.

"Hey, how's your job going? Do you miss being on a college campus?"

"I came to Bangalore to spend time with my family. But I'd rather be working in the United States. I'm not getting much cooperation."

"I hope things improve. Let me know if you hear from Stefan or Jade."

When I entered Josh's apartment, he was relaxing on his sofa, watching TV. Since our trip to the ER, he still complained that he didn't feel well. Follow-up blood tests showed a steady increase in platelets. I was hoping that an upcoming doctor visit would shed some light on his condition.

After the weekend, I returned to campus. I discreetly asked Elizabeth if she knew the whereabouts of Jade or Stefan. She nervously blinked her eyes and then rolled them.

"Come on, why can't you tell me?"

"I can't say too much. Both caused waves and said things they shouldn't have."

"Okay, then they were fired."

"I can't say anymore. Be careful. The walls have ears."

48

By the end of October, I'd earned two thumbs-up with regard to my blooming friendships around the campus, but was scoring a dismal two thumbs-down when it came to my relationships with Mahi and the English/social studies team. Oftentimes when I was dealing with the fifth-grade team, I heard lines from a Sesame Street song from my sons' youth. I instinctively wanted to insert the words, "me, me, me" whenever I heard the reoccurring question from "One of These Things (Is Not Like the Others)."

I was becoming increasingly self-conscious and spent large amounts of time by myself. Socially, I sensed an invisible barrier that limited my interaction with some of the Indian primary-unit staff. A few outgoing souls included me in the rehearsals for the faculty dances and conversed with me, but the vast majority kept their distance. I willingly danced on the auditorium stage in two different primary assemblies. This was the first time I'd ever participated in an organized dance performance. When I watched the videos, I couldn't believe I had summoned the gumption.

Elizabeth and Pari recognized the shortcomings of the team and scheduled one meeting after another, hoping to create cohesiveness and collaboration. Thankfully, they understood my plight and didn't frown upon the conflict, as Mohan had done. Elizabeth skillfully led these discussions like a tightrope walker stepping gingerly on a narrow-gauge wire. I remained optimistic that change was on the horizon. Over time, the dialogue became more open and forthright. My optimism faded when Kavya attacked my use of supplementary materials.

If I was following the curriculum objectives, why was she concerned with the materials I used? How did she know specifics about my class?

The truth slowly oozed out like the pus in Kavya's pimples. Without asking, Kavya took one of my student's English and social studies notebooks home over the weekend to review the student's work. Kavya was annoyed that my teaching didn't conform to *her* ideas of what I should be teaching. Ironically, most of the additional materials with which she took issue had been selected by Elizabeth during one of our many trips to the supply room during orientation. Kavya may have been annoyed by my reluctance to follow *her* Indian approach to teaching. But I was outright furious with her antics. *I felt dejected and marginalized.*

In her attempt to mollify the situation, Kavya handed me a student's creative writing notebook from the prior year. "Here, this is what we did last year."

I politely smiled and accepted her peace offering. "Thanks," I curtly replied.

I looked at the positive side. I had more pieces to the puzzle.

During my next free period, I reluctantly returned to Mohan's office. I couldn't avoid seeing him again. Mohan had agreed to reroute my TV cable by running it through the ventilation flaps in my bathroom and then over my bathroom door to a table. It wasn't the most ideal place, but at least I could finally watch TV. The luxury of a TV quickly became a substitute for companionship, as I often turned the set on just to hear voices in my room.

The topic of eviction magically disappeared. Instead, I was advised that it wasn't possible to move across the hall to a less sunny room because all of the rooms were occupied. This was not true. All of the rooms except for one, Deven's room, were empty.

That evening, I opened the student's journal that Kavya had given me and flipped through it. In the opening pages were the following simple directions that were organized under two headings: 1. Qualities of a good paragraph: a. Order; b. Unity—some idea; c. Variety of sentences. 2. How to write a paragraph: a. Think out points you wish to write; b. Arrange the points in proper order; c. Make the first and last sentence the most interesting or attractive; d. All points must deal with the same theme; e. Make sentences varied in length; f. Revise what you have written—spelling, punctuation, and grammar.

Now I could see why my students struggled with writing paragraphs. The team's approach was watered down compared with an American game plan. Very few pages contained the student's actual work. In fifth grade, teachers asked the students to do almost *no* writing. No wonder the sixth-grade teachers had hit the panic button during the orientation meeting. The class's work wasn't being graded correctly. Poor-quality work was praised with smiley faces and extra merit points, and notable mechanical errors went uncorrected.

Not until I was near the end did I come upon any evidence of a grading system, which relied on only eight points: opening of the story, ending of the story, appropriate paragraph breaks, spelling, vocabulary, sentence structure/grammar, neatness, and rough notes.

How could I not be discouraged? If it weren't for the children's faces I visualized at night as I graded their papers, I would have escaped in the black of night. The inner voice that propelled me to India was now calling again.

I was determined to find a way to meet my students' needs while also maintaining a working relationship with my peers.

When I turned the calendar to November, I began the countdown for Josh and Rachael's wedding. At the end of the first week, I was traveling to New Delhi for the Diwali break. Soon after I'd be going on the previously postponed outdoor experience with my fifth-grade class to the jungle terrain at Kabini, which was located approximately 220 kilometers (roughly 137 miles) southeast of Bangalore. A few days later, I would be jetting back to New Delhi to meet up with family and friends for our adventure to the Golden Triangle and a visit to the Taj Mahal.

Days later, Josh and Rachael were to be married at the Judah Hyam Synagogue, and that evening, Ira and I would return to KIS. Ira planned to spend an additional week with me. I was happy that Josh suggested that Ira travel on a personal Mileage Plus ticket. Suraj and Vinay continued to prevent Ira from visiting his team, so Ira planned to continue communicating with his managers by telephone and e-mail when he came to India. But he didn't intend to visit the IST campus. I was eager to spend Diwali break with Josh and Rachael.

Just about everyone I saw on the streets of New Delhi had a stash of fireworks. It was as if the entire population had become pyromaniacs, and I witnessed fireworks for several days in a row. Rachael was noticeably ill at ease as she veered this way and that to avoid being ambushed by rockets launched from every vantage point possible. Falling ash residue daintily swirled through the atmosphere and littered our moving vehicle. By the second day, the air quality was abysmal. A low ceiling of dark, gray dust, thick smoke, and small particles of debris made breathing laborious. I'd never experienced an asthma attack or a significant breathing disorder, but I was struggling to breathe and a burning sensation lingered in my throat and nose.

I learned that in one respect, Diwali is similar to the Jewish holiday, Chanukah. Both are referred to as the Festival of Lights and both represent a battle between good and evil. Thousands of small oil lamps and candles decorated homes, courtyards, verandas, rooftops, and side-walks. Strings of lights, similar to Christmas lights, were a focal point for homes and commercial buildings. The fireworks extended the light theme. Hindus believe that they need to spread light in order to destroy the reign of darkness.

I found the Hindu beliefs to be fascinating, but my comfort level with my Jewish identity made the experience more like a museum outing than a cultural immersion. The mere mention of idols and multiple gods made me shudder. One thing I didn't anticipate was the way that Rachael's family had become assimilated into Indian culture by adapting some aspects of Hindu traditions. Similar to some secular American Jews and interfaith couples who display Christmas trees in their homes, Rachael's parents deco-rated their flat with indoor and outdoor lights for the Hindu holiday. They celebrated a modified *pooja* ceremony in front of a small idol while listening to a taped version of chanting.

Decades ago, I taught religious school in suburban Chicago. The famous *Midrash* found in the Talmud—of Abraham smashing the idols in his father's idol shop—immediately flashed before my eyes. As they stood before the idol chanting in Hindi, I could hear Abraham telling his father that the biggest idol smashed the other ones. It was an awkward moment.

I wondered whether this Hindu practice would become a part of my grandchildren's legacy. The future was up to Josh and Rachael to decide. It wasn't my place to intervene. I hoped that the Jewish customs and traditions that Ira and I had passed down to our sons would continue to remain vibrant and live on long after we died.

Ongoing concerns for Josh's health remained. His blood tests were con-tinuing to show elevated platelet counts, although there were no red flags in any of the other blood tests that had been ordered. This wasn't the first time our family faced an undiagnosed disorder. Years of experience gave me the strength to deal with each of our medical conditions as rationally as possible. We had taken a circuitous path from one specialist to the next when Josh, a precocious eight year old, had suffered unbearable headaches. It wasn't until we visited the fifth doctor, a notable neurologist at the University of Chicago, that anyone could pinpoint a potential source of Josh's pain. A complex operation removed the culprit and restored Josh to his happy-go-lucky self. That experience, along with others, had made me leery of the medical profession.

I was reluctant to leave New Delhi. I was developing a rich relationship with Rachael. A part of me yearned for the day when my time with her would be more than a few days here and there.

Back in Bangalore, the days were moderate and the nights were cool. I was comfortable wearing a long-sleeved, cotton top. Not having to deal with the oppressive heat did wonders to improve my disposition.

The day set aside for parent-teacher conferences was a little less than two weeks away. To accommodate the parents who were teachers at the school or who had conflicts with the assigned date, we arranged meetings during our free periods.

Our first conference was with Arjun's parents. I was discussing his English performance when a small monkey, about two-and-a-half-feet tall, climbed through the widely spaced bars of the open window. The monkey grabbed a student's plastic food container and exited the window. I regained my composure. "As I was saying…" I was not going to let the monkey interrupt me.

"Are you pleased with Arjun's progress?" the father inquired.

"His class writing is a different style from his homework writing."

"We do help him," the mother said.

"You can guide him, but please let him make mistakes. I need to see his errors."

The mother leaned forward slightly and said, "We're only trying to help."

"I understand. I'm a parent, too. Helping him too much might affect his confidence."

"How so?" the father asked quizzically.

"He might become reluctant to write in class."

This first conference gave me an inkling of what to expect at the others.

On the way to lunch, I passed Jade and did a double take. It had been at least two weeks since Rohan informed me of her mysterious departure. Putting her thoughts in a letter had been the cause of her dismissal. With a little more than six months left on her contract, Jade didn't want to be unemployed and barred from living in India. She had apologized and was reinstated.

She heard that Stefan had likewise voiced opinions that were contrary to the administration's wishes. He wasn't returning. Jade reinforced Rohan's advice to be careful.

After lunch, the students huddled around the bulletin board where I had posted the reading challenge.

"We've almost earned an extra recess. Just five more scoops," Kabir said.

"Isn't Sanjay reading *Harry Potter*?" Jonathan asked.

"Yeah, that's worth two scoops," Kabir stated.

"Hey, Amit, you need to start reading," Jonathan prodded.

Amit blushed and chirped, "I will."

I loved seeing the kids' growing excitement about reading. Such a simple interactive display created positive peer pressure—a rarity. I was pleased.

Within a few minutes, everyone else returned to class and it was time to line up for their weekly computer lab class. Neha led the students down the corridor. Pankaj was lagging behind.

I leaned toward him and asked, "Everything all right?"

"Fine, Miss."

"Are you sure?"

"Yes, Miss."

"Go catch up with the other boys."

For weeks, Pankaj's behavior had worried me. He spent too much time by himself or lingering alone in the classroom. Perhaps being so far away from his parents was causing him to withdraw.

49

After months of hype and the disappointing postponement, fifty-four fifth-graders loaded onto two buses an hour or so before dawn for our trip to Kabini. Seven other teachers joined me on the journey—two men and five women. The destination for our Sunday-to-Tuesday mini-trip was the Kabini River Lodge, a former hunting lodge for the maharaja of Mysore. Located in the southern part of the Rajiv Gandhi National Park, the lodge stands on the bank of the Kabini River, a tributary of the Cauvery River. The driver advised us that our arrival time would be mid afternoon.

We were still within the city limits of Bangalore when Kabir and his twin brother took turns vomiting in tandem. There were no bathrooms inside the vehicle. The kids adapted well to this inconvenience while the staff was a bit harried as we cleaned one place after another while the boys played a game of musical chairs.

Anxieties over Josh's medical issue gave me *shpilkes*. I had spent the previous day at several medical institutions looking for answers to Josh's lingering, high platelet-count issue. I roamed the bus and viewed the ride from different vantage points as the bus driver continuously used his shrill horn.

Part of the time I sat near Shane, a newly hired Canadian teacher, who was positioned in the middle of the bus near the two barfing brothers. Like all expats, he struggled with many of the inadequacies of living in a Third World country. He talked endlessly about the recent flooding of his apartment, an inattentive landlord, and his subpar living conditions. I could relate to his frustrations over flooding because just the week before I had stepped onto a submerged floor in the late evening. I sloshed my way next door to Pavan's room, only to be told that nothing would be done until the next day. The normal urgency to avoid water damage was missing. There was no one to call at night.

Occasionally I shifted to the back of the bus to sit near Elizabeth. She preferred to have the bird's-eye view of everything happening on the bus. We talked about her options for next year. The school was willing to extend her contract if she wanted, but her future was dependent on where her husband was planning to teach. He was currently teaching in Oman and they had been living in different countries during the school year for the past two years. I could sympathize with her being separated and the state of uncertainty. I recently went through such a phase and was happy that I didn't need to look for another job for over a year.

After a few hours, my ants-in-the-pants status settled down and I was parked in my own seat staring out the window. I figured it was best to rest because I anticipated being up late supervising the boys. The bus eventually lulled me into a quiet state until I heard some of the kids say that they had seen a sign for the resort.

As we exited the air-conditioned buses, we were enveloped by bright sunny weather and intense heat. Refreshing cold beverages in paper cups were handed out. Asha, Natasha (a fourth-grade teacher), and I would be sharing a room in the middle of a block of rooms with outside entrances. The six boys under my charge were assigned adjacent rooms.

Everyone in our block was pleased with the rustic rooms, which were appointed with cathedral, wooden ceilings; fireplaces; cozy beds; and bathrooms with full-sized bath/showers. This was the first time I'd laid eyes on a bathtub since arriving in India.

Our time at Kabini was divided between Jeep safari tours, a boat safari ride, a trip to a nearby dam, and free time in the play areas; fresh-cooked meals and snacks, nightly bonfires, and a trip to the small resort gift shop completed our days. By far, the best parts of the excursion were the safari trips.

Once we entered the animal preserve, it was a hit-or-miss adventure. We drove on dirt roads that led deep into the jungle. Some groups saw more wildlife than others did, and some guides were better at explaining the habitat and pointing out wildlife. Spotted deer, or *chital,* were the predominant animal and had few predators. Their natural enemies, the big cats—leopards, panthers, and tigers—were rarely seen this time of year, so the children were disappointed. Nevertheless, we did come upon langur monkeys, India's largest deer (*sambar*), wild boar, Indian bison (*gaur*), wild dogs (*dhole*), herds of Asiatic elephants, mongooses, peacocks, parakeets, eagles, and an assortment of owls.

When we stepped off the Jeep, Kabir said, "I'm feeling sick again." I looked at his glassy eyes and touched his forehead. I was certain he had a fever. I let the other teachers know that he was still sick. There were no contingency plans for sick kids, so Kabir stayed with the group.

The bus trip to the dam took about an hour each way. The buses dropped us at one end of the dam and would pick us up at the other end. We had a minimal explanation of the facility. Initially, there was some confusion over whether it was possible to view the hydroelectric plant, located down a set of steps, which students had visited in the past. As a consequence of increased security, this wasn't possible, although a couple of the teachers tried to persuade the guards to bend the rules. The students and teachers wandered aimlessly to the other side, many of them whining along the way. It was hot and sunny. Few were carrying any water. It was a welcome relief to climb aboard the air-conditioned motor coaches and return to the resort for lunch.

On the buffet table was a delectable assortment of Indian and Western foods. The barbeque chicken was noteworthy. I watched Kabir pile an enormous amount of food on his plate. "Hey, slow down there. I know you might be hungry, but save some for the rest of us."

He looked up at me and said, "Yeah, I guess I took a lot."

I chuckled and said, "After throwing up all morning, you shouldn't eat too much."

He blushed and said, "Um, I'll try."

I was standing near the buffet eating a banana. Several people were forming a line to get cups of chocolate ice cream. One of the Indian chaperones extended her hand out to me and offered me some ice cream.

"No thanks. I'm fine with my banana."

"You do eat ice cream?"

"Of course."

"What about during the winter?" she asked.

I paused and wondered why she was asking this and then responded, "Sure, I eat ice cream year-round."

"It doesn't make you sick?"

"Why should it?"

"I don't eat ice cream when it's cold outside. It makes me sick."

"Okay, I'll keep that in mind."

Climbing the ropes at Kabini

While the chaperones were waiting for everyone to finish lunch, I supervised a group of kids climbing on an oversized net that was anchored to several thick tree branches and the ground. The kids and I frolicked about as a few teachers watched from below and an audience of monkeys sat perched on the adjacent rooftop and nearby tree limbs. Without much notice, the monkeys started prancing toward us. They were coming to reclaim their territory. We departed in a flash.

For the afternoon activity, Asha and I were paired to chaperone twelve boys on a boat safari.

"Everyone please grab a lifejacket and take a seat," I said as the boys hopped aboard.

The boys were horsing around with their lifejackets and the boat driver was growing annoyed.

I clapped my hands once. Then I paused. Then I clapped three more times and paused. Finally, I clapped twice. The boys responded in kind and found their seats. The boat sped off.

"Kabir, how are you feeling?" I asked.

"Miss, I wish I felt better."

"If you feel the need to throw up, please let us know," I added.

"Okay."

"I'll see if you can rest after dinner and not go to the bonfire."

When we arrived at our destination, the boat driver turned off the engine and we floated close to the shore.

"Is that a crocodile over there?" one of Asha's students asked.

The driver looked through his binoculars and replied, "No, just a log."

"Look Miss, are those tortoises?" Kabir asked.

Asha responded, "No!"

Asha pointed to branches of wood that sprung forth from the water and said, "Look at the egrets and herons."

"This is so boring," a boy with glasses whined.

Seconds later, we spotted a small elephant. It was in the clearing directly in front of us. The waves were pulling our small craft closer to the shoreline. The elephant turned in our direction and stared directly at our boat as it used one leg to paw at the ground. The driver started the engine and we sped away from the land.

"Why was the elephant staring at us?" Arjun asked loudly.

"If we came any closer, the elephant might have charged our boat," the driver responded.

After hearing the driver's response, I was relieved that he'd acted promptly.

We didn't see any crocodiles, tortoises, monitors, or snakes, which disappointed the boys, but we saw an overabundance of river terns, kingfishers, ducks, herons, egrets, storks, and swallows.

During dinner, Asha, Shane, and Natasha reaffirmed my concern that the Kabini trip was not tied to the social studies curriculum. We were all led to believe that the river would be the focus. This was not true. The emphasis was on wildlife and the resort's ecosystem. The river and the dam were secondary focuses.

Elephant on Kabini River shoreline

That night, Kabir was still feverish. He spent the night sleeping on a mattress placed on our floor. I used my mobile phone flashlight to avoid stepping on him when I went to the bathroom in the middle of the night. Sleeping in a strange place always leads to a restless night. This was compounded by the fact that I wasn't used to sharing my room with two other ladies. It had been almost ten years since I'd slept in a room with someone other than my husband. Now I was adjusting to the presence of two women and self-conscious that my snoring might keep them awake. Sleep came slowly.

The calf cramps that I had been experiencing periodically returned in the middle of the night. Standing and applying pressure returned the muscle to its normal state. By then I was wide awake and found myself staring at the vaulted ceiling.

Our last Jeep safari was on Tuesday morning at the crack of dawn. I climbed aboard one of the open-sided vehicles, which had three rows of passenger seats and a cloth roof. A driver and a guide sat in the front, while three boys sat in each of the rows. As we headed toward the sanctuary, we saw an elephant standing just a few feet from the road with his trunk curled upward. I jokingly told the boys that this was a good omen. Minutes later, our guide instructed the driver to stop abruptly. In the mucky path was an enormous paw print cast in the mud. He reached down and placed his watch next to the print so that the boys could judge the size of the print.

Due to the freshness of the print, the guide hypothesized that a tiger was somewhere in the vicinity. The boys' dilated eyes were scanning the horizon. Everyone was speechless as we waited and waited. The guide received a call that a tiger was sighted a kilometer away. The driver put the Jeep into gear and there was a loud clanking sound. The gears malfunctioned and we were stuck in the middle of the jungle. My first thought: *I hope there's a gun aboard.*

"Miss, are we safe?" Arjun questioned in a serious voice.

"Of course we are. Do you see those big men in the front seat? They wouldn't let anything happen to you," I said confidently. The guide turned toward me and smiled.

"But Miss, this is the jungle and we're in an open Jeep," Jonathan said.

"Where's your sense of adventure? Didn't you come here to see the big cats?" I chirped back.

"How long will it take for us to get another vehicle?" Pankaj asked.

"We'll just have to wait and see."

"Maybe we should start walking back?" a blond-haired European boy from 5B suggested.

"That's not a great idea. The guide just told us another vehicle was coming."

I asked the guide if he would share some of his pictures with the boys as we waited. He turned on his Nikon camera and the boys huddled around him.

"Wow. Why couldn't we see those cats?" Jonathan said.

"Look at the next picture, it's even better," Pankaj said.

"Some things in life are purely luck. I thought we'd be lucky today, but it wasn't meant to be," I said.

I breathed an enormous sigh of relief when the replacement vehicle pulled up beside us. The boys handled a potentially dangerous situation with maturity and expressed a minimal amount of disappointment over their abbreviated safari. I awarded them special certificates at the next primary unit assembly.

The bus ride back to Bangalore was slowed down by a driving rainstorm. Part of the time, I sat near three of the boys as they played an American question-and-answer game. The American history and geography questions were mostly beyond their reach, since none had ever lived in the United States. Their reasoning was occasionally comical. One student proudly told me that he knew Los Angeles was near Hollywood because he learned that fact watching a *Tom and Jerry* cartoon.

Many of the students opted not to use the bathroom facilities when we made a stop after lunch. Some of the kids expressed their displeasure with the bathrooms by saying, "It's gross," or "I'd rather wait until I get home." Not surprisingly, we had to make two emergency stops so that a handful of kids could relieve themselves before we reached Bangalore. The places we stopped at looked grungier than the original choice. When we eventually reached the school, several kids bolted for the nearby restrooms.

I returned to my room and ate a simple meal of cereal, soy milk, and a piece of chocolate, which satisfied my tired and worn-out body.

The phone rang.

"Hi Josh."

"I wanted to make sure you got back all right. Did you like Kabini?"

"Yep, it was awesome. How many American teachers can say they chaperoned a fifth-grade trip to the jungle?"

"I'm looking forward to seeing you."

"Me too. I can't wait. Are you still considering the bone marrow biopsy?"

"I'm still thinking about it. I'll let you know."

"Please keep in touch and take care. Love you and Rachael."

"Love you, too."

I turned on the TV and waited for Ira's nightly call. I faded off to sleep listening to the voices on the TV.

50

I lay in my bed Wednesday morning wishing I didn't have to move. The long hours of the Kabini trip and sleeping in a strange place had made me weary. I looked over the long to-do list taped to my desk and shuddered. I was relieved that Elizabeth and Pari had extended my report-card deadline—that was a huge stress reducer.

I spent most of the remaining week preparing for the upcoming parent-teacher conferences and preparing the class for my week off. On Sunday afternoon, I would be traveling back to New Delhi for Josh and Rachael's wedding week and my *first* opportunity to see Ira since I left Colorado the end of July. I was eagerly counting the hours until my departure, much as a child anticipates Christmas.

After Friday's lunch, the 5C class was scheduled to visit the sandpit for a long-awaited river project. The previous week, I divided the class into four groups. Each group had two planning periods to decide how they would build their river model and what materials they needed to bring from home. This was the most exhilarating, hands-on, authentic, social studies class of the term. I was just as enthusiastic as the kids to spend time in the sandpit and see which team would win the competition.

Before going to lunch, I reminded the students that they needed to return promptly after recess. I waited patiently. Five...ten...fifteen minutes passed before they arrived. I was annoyed. Scurrying about, everyone gathered the supplies and lined up at the door. We rushed over to the long, rectangular sandpit that was on the other side of the secondary building, not too far from the auditorium. Each group was assigned one of the four corners.

"One person should be responsible for checking the directions. Good luck," I bellowed.

"Oh no! Miss Sandra, I forgot my instructions," Kabir whined.

"Me too!" Arjun echoed.

"We did, too," Jonathan added.

"Does each group have at least one set of instructions?" I yelled.

Before anyone answered, Sanjay spoke in a panicky voice, "Miss Sandra, where are the shovels and buckets?"

"Did anyone bring any sand tools?" I inquired.

Only one group had instructions and another group had a bucket and one shovel. I allowed some of the students to return to the classroom for their missing papers and dispatched two students to the preschool for the sand tools.

The chaotic start to this activity was driving me crazy. I had depended on others to make sure the class was dismissed on time and that the sand toys were in place. I was annoyed.

Meanwhile, I told the students to look at their drawings and to start planning how they were going to lay out their models. They would be graded for their creativity, the model's proportions, the river features, the team's spirit, the group's time management, and their efforts at cleaning up.

I walked over to Neha. She had taken charge of her group and was delegating responsibilities. She designated certain spots in the sand for different parts of the river. Kabir was creating the border for their model, but chose not to follow the stipulated dimensions for the perimeter. The space he made was substantially larger.

I stepped to the next corner to see what Arjun and Emily's group was doing. Like the previous group, they didn't use the metric sticks to measure a perimeter. One of the students just used his heel to create an arbitrary border. No one stepped forward to be the leader. Emily and another girl worked side by side designing the lower part of the river, while Arjun and the two others focused on the source of the river and the mountain peaks.

Next, I went to the third group. They were sitting in the sand being unproductive. I asked the group why nothing was happening. Sanjay said, "Miss, we left our sketch in the classroom."

"Just create a new idea," I encouraged.

I then took a few steps to the side and watched the last group. This group had only four students because one of the members was recovering from dengue fever. Two of the three boys had wandered off and were standing under a tree. I asked the boys to rejoin their group.

By the time I made it back to the first group, they had made substantial progress. The students worked together to create a large mountain range and also made all of the parts of the river that led to the mouth. Neha and another girl were adding the final touches by putting the plastic buildings in the city while the boys added cotton balls to the mountaintops and blue plastic paper to the river bed.

"Miss, it's harder than I thought to show all the stages of the river," Kabir commented.

"Look at all the props we're adding," Neha bragged.

"Keep up the great teamwork," I said enthusiastically.

Jonathan and Pankaj wandered over. "Why didn't we bring props?" Jonathan whispered.

I asked the two boys to return to their station and followed behind them to see their group's progress. By following the perimeter directions, they had less space to fill in so their task was easier to accomplish. They created mountains that covered almost two-thirds of their plot. The other features of the river were not as well defined. One of the girls was putting plastic wrap in the grooved area that corresponded to the river.

"Oops, we should have left it as one piece. Water is going to leak through," the girl said. I turned around when I heard Arjun saying, "Miss, Miss, come quick." I walked over and he said, "Look at what we did." He poured water into their source and I watched as the water flowed downhill. "Cool. What an amazing job you're doing."

Amit's group was constructing large mountains by using buckets full of wet sand. Amit stood up and motioned for me to come closer. He picked up the plastic bag and murmured, "Look what we're going to add to the water."

In the plastic bag was a small container of blue ink and large sheets of plastic wrap.

"Awesome idea," I said.

I clapped several times. "Fifteen minutes left. Look at your checklists."

The students put the finishing touches on their masterpieces. Amit had a giant grin on his face and said, "Miss, look at the blue water. The plastic wrap is working. The water is going through the meanders and the delta."

I walked over to Arjun's group. "Miss, I wish we had brought plastic like the others. The water won't stay in the river or the lake. It's absorbed into the sand."

"That's okay. What did you learn?"

"We should have planned more?"

After that I headed to the other side to see Sanjay's group. "How are things going?"

"We got off to a slow start, but in the end everything worked out."

I was speechless as I followed the class back to the room. Despite all the mishaps, everything had fallen into place and the kids' smiles matched mine. I couldn't wait to explore more child-friendly activities for the next term.

51

Parent-teacher conferences started at 9:00 a.m. on Saturday and didn't conclude until close to 4:00 p.m. We allotted parents fifteen-minute blocks of time. Mahi and I sat at the two desks positioned in the front of the room, and the parents selected chairs facing us. The large, round clock ticked softly behind our heads, as waiting parents clustered in the hallway and entered through a doorway behind us.

Kabir's father had flown from Mumbai to attend the conference. He was older than I anticipated, perhaps close to my age. His whitish hair covered only part of his head. He listened intently to our comments.

Toward the end, he said, "Kabir is a sensitive child. He's upset that his dorm room was changed and wants to leave."

"I've been off campus the last few weekends and didn't know. What can I do?"

"Please encourage him to stay."

I was surprised that no one had let me know about Kabir's unhappiness. It provided a partial explanation for his inconsistent work.

One mother came to the conference irritated with her son's performance. For weeks, I had written detailed suggestions and comments on his papers. When he wrote his final drafts, he copied the rough draft and disregarded my remarks. "Can't you do something?" she asked.

"What are you suggesting?"

"Um, can't you punish him?"

"If your child refuses to rewrite his papers, I can't make him do it."

"Why don't you stand next to his desk during recess?"

"Your son needs to take responsibility for his work."

She didn't respond. After a long pause, I said, "We could try positive reinforcement instead."

The mother was interested only in negative consequences and was convinced that I should coerce her son.

Emily's parents were content with the progress she was making in English. She was putting forth tremendous effort to master her English assignments. Emily received the prize for being the first girl to read five books and was becoming more comfortable in class.

For weeks, I had been concerned about Pankaj's behavior and was eager to speak with his father, a thirtyish man with fine features and thin, dark hair.

"I'm glad that you could make the journey. Do you have any concerns?" I asked.

He looked directly at me and said, "How's Pankaj's social life? Does he have any friends?"

"I don't see him mingling that often. He tends to stay aloof."

"Is there anything you can do?" the father asked.

"I've tried pairing him with different kids, but sometimes he creates his own problems."

Wrinkle lines formed between his eyes when he asked, "What do you mean?"

I hesitated and then stated, "He oftentimes doesn't do his share in group projects."

"I'll talk with him."

"Likewise. I'll keep an eye on him."

Some of the conferences went longer than the allotted time. The break time evaporated.

In the afternoon, Jonathan's mother came to the conference. She was a tall woman with a fair complexion and blue eyes. Mahi and I had sent her frequent messages in Jonathan's diary. Although we both agreed that Jonathan had organizational issues, Mahi was reluctant to say anything because his father worked at the school. It was in the child's interest to be frank and honest. Each time I made a diary entry, Jonathan came close to tears. He feared negative consequences. Jonathan's learning required a proactive approach, I felt.

I calmly asked, "Can we work together to create a positive-reinforcement system?"

"I'll have to talk with my husband."

"If I were teaching in the United States, I would also recommend that Jonathan be screened by an educational psychologist. He has many focus and organizational issues that may or may not be related to his hearing loss."

"That's out of the question," she responded emphatically.

Later, I voiced my concerns to Elizabeth. Having witnessed the frustrations of one of my own children, I knew the value of psychological testing. Pinpointing causes for certain behaviors empowers a child because he is given tools to combat deficits. Without an understanding of the undesirable behavior, the child is left feeling helpless. If we could find a reason for Jonathan's poor work habits and behavior, a qualified psychologist would hopefully rule out forms of punishment.

Late in the afternoon, a tall, broad man wearing a polo shirt and khaki slacks strutted into the classroom with a woman with deeply set eyes. Their son was a quiet boy who never caused any trouble in class. But recently he had developed a bad habit of being delinquent on assignments.

"Have you looked at your son's notebooks?" I asked.

The father and the mother just stared and remained unresponsive.

"Are you checking his homework diary?" I continued to prod.

The parents moved their heads.

I took a small breath and said, "Your son is missing two major assignments."

"Something must be wrong with this class. My son's always *number one*. What is his ranking?" the father bellowed.

I shook my head and said, "I don't rank the kids."

"He's in the hallway. I'm going to get him."

The father opened the door and called his son's name. The boy walked in with his head drooping.

"You're an embarrassment. I can't stand a son who is a failure. You're going home and not doing anything until all of your work is done," the father roared.

The boy was trembling as he left the room with his parents. For the first time since I'd met Mahi, we shared something in common. We were both appalled by the father's behavior.

The last conference was with a young Korean couple. Their daughter was quiet and respectful, but she needed significant assignment modifications in order to be successful.

Her father asked, "Can she drop the special English class?"

"I wouldn't recommend it. Her reading and writing skills are two years behind the class."

"The class isn't helping," the mother said.

"I don't teach that class. But introducing either Hindi or French at this time would be a bad idea."

The mother looked toward her husband for support and said, "Her English seems okay."

"I recommend that you talk with Ms. Elizabeth."

They listened to my recommendations and then left.

Mahi and I met with everyone's parents except for Kamala's. It wasn't possible for her parents to travel from Thailand. Instead, her older sister dropped in. Kamala's writings illustrated her loneliness and her strong desire to return to Thailand. In her dorm room, she had a calendar with a countdown of the term's remaining days.

I, on the other hand, had been counting down for the next day. I was flying to Delhi the following afternoon. If all went as expected, I would be reunited with my family by the middle of Sunday night.

Reaching a Crossroad

52

I leaped out of the hotel bed and sprinted down the stone steps in my bare feet. The chill of the New Delhi night air caused goose bumps to form on my limbs, even though I was partially clad in a stretch tank top and black Capri leggings. I felt like a teenager in love for the first time as I reflected back to the magnificent sunsets Ira and I had shared on the beaches of Maui during our honeymoon. I was overjoyed when I saw Ira, my three sons, and Rachel walking toward the hotel lobby.

Those first few moments of being reunited made me realize that precious time had been lost. I didn't want to let go of Ira and proceeded to cling dearly to each of my sons with all my strength, hoping somehow to recapture the missed minutes, hours, and days. Oh, how I wished that I could put time in a bottle, as Jim Croce had sung in the seventies.

"I missed everyone so much," I said with tears streaming down my cheeks.

"We missed you, too," the boys said in unison.

"Rachel, you're a trouper. How's your back?"

Instead of answering my question, Adam and Rachel merely blurted, "India sucks!"

"What happened?" I asked.

"The guard wouldn't let the bus through the gate. We schlepped our luggage here," Adam complained.

"Mom, why are so many people out in the middle of the night. What's that about?" Jordan asked.

"Guys, it's India. There're lots and lots of people all the time."

"But Mom, the garbage. How can you stand it?" Aaron asked.

"Just close your eyes."

"Close our eyes. You've got to be kidding. It's disgusting!" Jordan responded.

"My luggage is lost," Aaron chimed in.

"Your clothes? Your medicine?"

"I have my medicine. No extra clothes. How stupid was it to wear dress shoes?" Aaron replied.

The boys lugged their suitcases up the curved staircase to their respective rooms.

Ira and I spent the next few hours caressing one another and hugging intensely. Our forced separation had caused a severe sensual deprivation. I had an unquenchable desire to be touched. Ira responded, but seemed a bit distracted. I feared that if I let go, even for a second, Ira would sail away like an unsecured helium balloon. Ira eventually drifted off to sleep. I stared at him. It had been less than five months, but he looked like he had aged more than that. I quietly prepared to meet Josh and Rachael for an appointment at a cancer specialty hospital and crept out the door.

The hospital's outdated appearance made me wince with apprehension as we walked through the hallways, which needed a fresh coat of paint. Josh kept insisting that the competency of the doctors outweighed the physical attributes of the structure. To a certain extent I agreed. However, cleanliness and hygiene in a hospital were crucial, especially when undergoing an invasive procedure.

I sat patiently waiting with Rachael and her mom while Josh underwent a painful bone marrow biopsy. I kept telling myself that I had to be positive. Everything had to be all right. Tears dotted my face. I swiped them inconspicuously, hoping no one noticed. I couldn't erase the word "cancer" from my thoughts.

Ira arrived. The skin around his eyes was puffy and darkened, and his face was paler than normal. I clung to Ira as the doctor described possible catastrophic diagnoses. Ira sat stoically through most of the conversation. Once, he forced the doctor to actually say the word "cancer" instead of using euphemisms to describe the dreaded diagnosis.

Hoping that the worst-case scenario wasn't the case, we left the hospital with frightful visions but no definite opinion. Ira's recent face-to-face encounter with his own mortality put the doctor's preliminary appraisal of Josh's condition into a troubling perspective. *I shuddered at the thought that a terrible disease had invaded Josh's body during the prime of his life.*

We caught up with the boys and Rachel at a restaurant. They had been wandering around as they waited for us to return from the hospital. They didn't have a cell phone that functioned in India. We communicated with them by calling their driver, and as Rachael and Josh parked the car, we talked.

"How's Josh doing?" Adam asked.

"The biopsy results won't be back until Wednesday or Thursday. We're a bit shaken. It might be cancer."

"You've always told us to wait for test results. Follow your own advice," Aaron calmly said.

"I know. But being in India just makes me more on edge."

"That's why Josh should see an American doctor," Adam responded.

"We've been through this already. It's his decision," Ira said.

"Mom, does everyone look through you all the time?" Adam asked.

"Yes, people do stare at me."

"Mom, Dad, the garbage…it's pathetic. Why doesn't anyone clean up?" Aaron asked.

"Do you ever feel safe? Crazy maniac drivers," Jordan said.

"Take it easy, guys," Ira said.

"Mom, do you wear goggles or a mask when you shower? I'm closing my eyes and my mouth when I shower so that none of the water gets in," Jordan said with a smirk on his face.

That got a rise out of everyone and we all laughed. "Jordan, that's pretty funny. But guys, you know the answer to all these questions. Please don't harp in front of Rachael or her family," I said.

The boys were careful not to insult Rachael and Josh, but were far from reticent when they were alone with me.

I had waited months to be reunited with my family, all the while believing this monumental event would be a panacea that put aside all of my troubles. Yes, I was ecstatic that we were all together, but my expectations were now overshadowed by so many unpredictable factors. I considered myself a pro at handling unusual family health issues. Yet there was something about the word- cancer. It caused an imaginary dagger to pierce my belly. I was defenseless. In order to overcome our anxieties, Ira and I realized that we needed to put our emotions aside until we had diagnostic information.

How was I going to balance the needs of one son whose health was at issue and was soon to marry an Indian woman with the reactions of our three other sons, who absolutely detested just about everything India had to offer? The three boys wanted Josh to return to the United States after his wedding so that he could receive the best medical treatment possible. I took on the role of a referee in a hotly contested battle between rival teams. I stood in the middle, trying to be impartial and fair, but my human weaknesses made me occasionally side with one team over the other.

53

As streams of pale yellow light pierced the cloudy morning sky, we prepared for our journey. Delhi, Jaipur, and Agra, three cities in the northwest part of the country, formed a triangle with a distance of approximately 200 to 250 kilometers between each.

From our New Delhi hotel, we would be traveling southwest to Jaipur until early afternoon. Upon arriving in Jaipur, we would check into the world-renowned Hotel Raj Palace. After lunch, our tour guide was to take us past Hawa Mahal and then provide a guided tour at the City Palace and Jantar Mantar. After spending the night in the exquisite hotel, we were planning to ride elephants up the hill to the Amer Fort. After touring this site, our driver would take us east to Agra, with a stop at Fatehpur Sikri. The following day would start at the Taj Mahal, one of the Seven Wonders of the World. Additional stops at the Agra Fort and Sikandra would conclude our tour. The bus would then head northwest back to New Delhi, just in time for a Thanksgiving feast.

Since the gate to the hotel grounds remained locked, we hiked the short distance to the main road. There we met up with Josh and three of his American friends, Vic, Diana, and Dominique, and our longtime friends Kay and Cary. Josh's friends had arrived the day before from California, while Kay and Cary had flown in several days earlier from Texas. Ira had met Kay when they were students at the University of Colorado in the early 1970s. She was a little older than Ira and was married to Cary, a Dallas attorney.

Unseasonal rain was an unwelcome guest that morning. Josh obsessively checked his phone for updated weather reports. Sloshing around in ankle-deep water was not an appealing way to tour. Josh's plans for an outdoor wedding reception were in jeopardy. But unexpected weather, like unantici-pated medical issues, was part of the human condition. And each made you come to grips with the fact that certain things in life were way beyond your control.

The persistent rain and cool temperatures caused condensation on the windows of the bus as it drove into the countryside. Josh was reclining, doing his best to nurse his wound from the bone-marrow procedure. The jostling to and fro not only affected Josh but also had deleterious effects on Rachel, who had recently fractured her tailbone, and Ira, whose shoulder was still recovering from surgery. Ira was unusually quiet. I assumed that he wanted to rest or was in pain. He spent the entire bus ride in one place. I was worried. It was best to let him nap.

I went to the rear of the bus to talk with Kay. Although we kept abreast of one another's lives through phone conversations and e-mails, we hadn't seen each other since Jordan's bar mitzvah more than five years ago. Like my family, her four children were now grown and taking their separate paths. I listened as she provided an abbreviated version of their lives.

At mid afternoon, we pulled into a long driveway. A large, creamy-lemon structure stood before us, and we parked just a few feet away from an ornate silver-and-gold doorway with elephant appliqués on the lower portion. An Indian man, dressed in a patterned shirt; baggy, off-white slacks; and a bright red turban stepped forward to play a tarnished brass instrument. We were treated to a royal welcome to the Hotel Raj Palace, one of the maharajah's former residences.

In the hotel, glasses of freshly squeezed juice and some warm, damp towels to remove the dust and grime of the road instantly refreshed the weary travelers among us. We had entered a magical place that immediately intrigued us with its rich history. Everyone was assigned to a distinctive suite fit for princes and princesses. The boys and I couldn't help but gawk into every nook and cranny we passed in this fairy-tale location. Ira rarely smiled and said very little.

After a quick lunch, we climbed onto the bus to begin our guided tour. The chatter and poor acoustics made the guide's voice partly indecipherable, while fogged-up windows continued to obscure our vision. Jantar Mantar, a historical site filled with astronomy instruments dating back to medieval times, stood out as the most notable site. We could only imagine what our guide was trying to describe about the ability to measure time, predict eclipses, and plot other astronomical events as the clouds overhead continued shedding rain.

All night long, the repetitive sound of enormous raindrops pounded the adjacent pavement. I sat up several times and stared down at Ira. He insisted that nothing was wrong, yet his detached behavior told me otherwise. I became anxious. *Was it a delayed ramification of his head trauma? Was it months of being separated? Was it his work situation? Was it Josh's illness? Was it a paradoxical reaction to the upcoming wedding or perhaps something else? I didn't know.*

The next morning, the bus took detours to avoid streets that had become swiftly moving rivers filled with debris. None of us was prepared, especially Josh, who was wearing Birkenstock sandals. Kay and Cary improvised by using plastic shower caps to line their gym shoes. With only one umbrella among the seven of us and no raincoats, I worried.

Adam and Rachel retold their US travel doctor's warning: "Whatever you do, don't walk in a flooded street. You're bound to end up with a terrible disease."

As we approached the Amer Fort, a rugged sixteenth-century structure of red sandstone and white marble, our group vacillated between taking an enclosed Jeep ride or the open-air elephant ride. None of us was planning to return, so we unanimously agreed to the enticing elephant rides. As we disembarked, we stepped in ankle-deep, brown water swirling with debris. We collectively joked about the maladies associated with toxic water.

I bargained with a street urchin for two umbrellas while Josh commented that I was wasting my money. The captive market at any tourist attraction was prey for hawkers, even more so in a driving rainstorm. I didn't care. We had a long day ahead with the potential of being soaked. The flimsy mini-umbrellas partially warded off the ravages of the storm as we huddled like a football team waiting for the quarterback's play call.

My second elephant ride in as many months was once again an uplifting moment, as Ira and I jostled back and forth in a sidesaddle carriage. As our elephant plodded up the steeply inclined pathway to the fort, we could see the strategic advantage of the elevation and admired the craftsmanship that went into building such a secure place. Drenched through and through, we explored the fort. We hiked down a manure-covered pathway similar to an alleyway, with buildings and vacant land on either side. Stray dogs, goats, cows, and pigs shared the litter-strewn dirt trail with us.

Our Jaipur guide's poor time management caused us to arrive at Fatehpur Sikri, a UNESCO World Heritage landmark site, less than two hours before closing time. The Agra-based guide didn't even bother to provide much of an explanation as he encouraged us to scurry through the grounds.

The sixteenth century structures had resisted the wear and tear of nature and were in remarkable condition. The massive perimeter walls, with towers and arched gateways, provided a foreboding atmosphere to a city that barely ever existed. This complex had been abandoned shortly after completion and had been hardly occupied thereafter. *Could people be as resistant to adversity? How much stress could individuals endure before their natural defenses crumbled their inner strength?*

The next day, the sky turned a pale shade of blue and the lingering clouds were chased away. It was a glorious day to tour the Taj Mahal. I was eager to see this magnificent piece of history. The excitement of the day temporarily put aside my worries and concerns. After breakfast, I experienced an incredible amount of pressure inside my abdomen. It was as if I had drunk a gallon of liquid instead of a small glass of juice and cup of tea. I wiggled back and forth and tried diverting my attention. By the time we reached the main gate, however, I was ready to explode. I raced to the restroom.

Although the impressive structure was visible to the naked eye, the lingering cloud cover obscured the clarity of the initial pictures we took. It was if a magician had waved a magic wand and made the structure partially disappear. Fortunately, we took pictures from a variety of angles and at different sun angles. The marble color took on different characteristics as the morning progressed. *This experience ran parallel to life itself. Events could always be viewed from opposing angles and oftentimes, the participants' perspective was tainted by the time and place in which they found themselves. At any given moment, my ability to cope with my Indian adventure fluctuated, as outside forces either masked or revealed my vantage point.*

Our next stop, the Agra Fort, provided a different view of the Taj Mahal. Once again, I was struck by the sheer size of the buildings and palaces. Without any direction, we wandered from one building to the next, admiring the art of a lost breed of craftsmen. When I glanced in the direction of the Taj Mahal, the structure appeared muted and subdued by a low ceiling of dull clouds.

Jordan, Adam, Ira, Aaron, Josh, Rachel and me at the Taj Mahal

Our last tour site was Sikandra, another imposing structure that illustrated how the Mughal rulers chose to memorialize their existence. Wildlife roamed freely in this parklike setting and added to the monument's serenity. We moseyed along at a controlled pace until the tour guide motioned us to return to the bus. I was grateful that Josh had taken the time to arrange this condensed tour to share with our family.

I was the last to board because I had to make an urgent run to the restroom. In the rear, Adam appeared to be falling asleep on his fiancée's shoulder while my two younger boys were listening to their iPods. Every ounce of liquid I consumed continued to run through me in record time. *Was I nervous about the wedding?*

I took the window seat next to Ira. He affectionately embraced my torso as I squeezed past him. My stomach was grumbling and my mouth was parched. I quickly munched on some trail mix. As I swallowed the last morsel, a random pain shot through my lower right side. The sensation was unpleasant.

Although the pain was growing, I didn't want to disturb Ira, who was now dozing next to me. I scooted past him and stood in the aisle adjacent to our youngest son. To grab his attention away from his iPod, I gently tapped him on the shoulder.

"Wasn't today awesome?" I asked.

Jordan took off his earphones and said, "I can't look out the window anymore. Masses of people are living in garbage piles."

"You've been to Mexico. Didn't you see poor people and pollution there?"

"Of course. But this...this is different. Mexico looks a thousand times better."

"Come on, weren't the Taj and Agra Fort fascinating? Until Josh moved to India, I never imagined that I'd visit India's Wonder of the World."

"Neither did I. But the beggars, the filth, and the men pissing in the street."

I leaned over Ira and pulled my water bottle out. I took mini sips of water as I walked up and down the aisle. Midway through my second lap, I sat next to Aaron so that I could spend some time with him.

"Holy shit!" Aaron screamed.

Everyone was now awake and looking out the window. A truck had flipped over in the middle of the road, and to avoid the accident our driver had crossed the median and was speeding toward oncoming traffic. It was now a massive game of chicken with the oncoming cars. A line of cars was following our driver's audacious move. Our driver weaved through the oncoming traffic, and then without warning, he crossed back over the median and into the correct lane.

I returned to my seat next to Ira and stared out the window. The outskirts of the city had been replaced by open space. The sparse farmland was infrequently interrupted by groupings of dilapidated structures that appeared in strips and small villages with masses of people. Jabbing pains were intermittently shooting through my lower core. Pressing on my skin, I located a tender spot near my right pelvic bone. I shifted from one hip to the other, desperately trying to find a comfort zone.

"Sandy, you're uneasy. Is something wrong with your hip?" Ira asked.

"It's not my hip. It's my lower abdomen. It feels like a sizzling hot poker is turning inside me."

"How long have you felt this way?"

"You were sleeping. I didn't want to bother you. The pain is almost as bad as when I needed the incisional hernia repaired."

Ira looked at his watch. "We're hours from Delhi."

Tears built up in my eyes when I started to respond. "The bumpy ride and the constant lurching are driving me crazy."

Ira leaned across the aisle and asked Josh to talk with the bus driver. Having lived in India for over seven years, Josh knew some basic Hindi. I hoped the bus driver could find a place to stop.

54

Hours later, I lay suspended between sleep and wakefulness. I sensed an oddly shaped garment draped loosely over my torso while the lower half of my body was haphazardly covered by a coarse bed covering. As I tried to move the irritating blanket with my left arm, I sensed a burning sensation on the outside of my wrist. My eyes flickered while adjusting to the streams of sunshine filtering through the worn-out drapes. Within seconds, I saw the plastic tubing leading to my hand from two glass bottles positioned on a metal stand.

It seemed like a dreadful dream. Suddenly, I remembered. It was not a dream. Slowly, frame by frame, I recalled flying to Delhi, being reunited with my family, a long bus ride, rain and more rain, touring several structures including the Taj Mahal, and riding again on a bus.

What happened next? Unrelenting pain and agony. Ah, there was an emergency stop at a restaurant. I vaguely remembered our cramped hotel room. But how did I get there? I was in such terrible pain. Then, somehow, I was in Rachael's car and ended up in an emergency room. It was so hazy. It seemed real, but was it? Why was I in this room?

Now I remembered. In the middle of the night, the on-call urologist had admitted me. Oh no! I was scheduled for surgery. I breathed a sigh of relief. At least I was not parked in a filthy ward with dozens of other people. Then I remembered my fears.

Did doctors perform this procedure in the United States? Would the operating room be clean? What type of anesthesia would I be given? Would I be all right afterward?

To the left, I saw Ira lying motionless on a makeshift fold-out bed. My head pulsated as I moved carefully to my side while trying to avoid trapping the plastic line under my body.

"I can't believe my *mazel.* Josh is about to be married and I'm stuck in this hospital room," I cried out.

"Just calm down. One way or another, we'll see Rachael and Josh get married," I heard Ira say.

"Calm down? It's impossible to relax. Look at this intravenous. If the bottles are glass, they're probably reusable. I can't afford an infection with my hip replacement."

"I'm not comfortable, either. I wasn't happy when the nurse drew your blood without wearing gloves," Ira said.

Ira turned the wall-mounted television on manually. I pressed the call button for the nurse. A young woman in a beige uniform entered the room.

"When is the surgery?" I asked

"Ah, um," she uttered and bobbled her head.

"Will the doctor be coming?"

"Doctor…soon," she replied, and then left the room.

Shortly thereafter, technicians administered a follow-up ultrasound. The kidney stone had moved a smidgeon, but it was still lodged.

I faced Ira and pleaded, "Promise me you'll stay with me."

Ira sat on the edge of my bed. Holding my hand, he tenderly said, "Take it easy. You can't become too frazzled."

"How can I not be crazed?"

"At least you're not alone. If it wasn't for the wedding, you'd be in Bangalore by yourself," Ira responded.

He was right. The timing was not ideal, but I couldn't even think about the alternative. There was a faint knock. Adam slowly entered with Aaron.

"Where are Jordan and Rachel?" Ira asked.

"This place is a fortress. You're allowed only two visitors at a time. A guard is at the elevator and he actually checks for passes," Adam responded.

"You've got to be kidding," I replied.

"We'll figure out a way to bypass the system," Aaron said.

The door opened and the surgeon strolled in; he immediately wanted to know my decision. I raised a few questions and concerns, but once again my inquiries and doubts were dismissed as unimportant.

With Josh's wedding less than forty-eight hours away, time was not on my side. Even though the profuse vomiting and intense pain had temporarily ceased, my dark red urine worried me. I reluctantly agreed to the procedure. The doctor left the room.

"Mom, are you comfortable with this?" Adam asked, his voice barely controlling his anger. "That doctor is an asshole. I don't want you having surgery."

"Yeah, what a douche bag," Aaron added.

I sat up and said, "Sometimes you have no choice."

"Dad, do you agree?" Adam asked.

"Under the circumstances, yes. With the wedding in less than two days, Mom can't wait."

Aaron walked out of the room just as a nurse entered. She handed me the consent form. Many of the handwritten parts were not legible or there were just letters rather than complete words. I pointed to several places that needed to be explained. She casually mentioned that a stent would be inserted to keep the passageway open so that my kidney could drain properly. My heart began to beat quickly and my back and neck became as damp as a fresh bed of moss. *Was the stent necessary?*

Shortly thereafter, Aaron, Jordan, and Rachel tiptoed into the room. Rachel immediately faded into the background as she politely sat next to Ira on the sofa. Adam took center stage, standing just a foot away from the side of the bed while my two youngest sons, Aaron and Jordan, positioned themselves at the foot of my bed like towering bookends.

Adam wasted no time in going on the offensive. "None of us are little kids anymore. We don't like you in India and now look what happened."

"I could get kidney stones anywhere."

"That's the entire point. Yes, you could, but you never did," Aaron replied.

Adam raised his voice, drew closer, and added, "Who knows what will happen to you today or after Dad returns to the United States."

"I'm glad you didn't need one of those quirky ambulances parked outside. That'd be a disaster," Jordan added.

"This is not Avista Adventist Hospital in Louisville, Colorado, but it's cleaner and more modern than the Bangalore hospital."

"After the wedding, you're flying home," Adam insisted.

"Let's just get past the next two days. Remember, the focus is on your brother and Rachael, not me."

A nursing assistant with coarse skin and a forced smile walked into the room carrying a small stack of newspapers and a white plastic box. She motioned for Ira and the kids to leave as she made a simple command in broken English. Ira insisted on staying. She pointed to the door. After everyone left, she locked it.

I shook my head as she spread dirty newspapers under my body. She proceeded to open the box, revealing a small shaving kit. Having undergone four C-sections, an incisional hernia repair, and numerous orthopedic surgeries, I was well aware of pre-op routines. This was the only time that I was *not* placed on a sterile pad. After she finished, the door was unlocked and my family returned.

One by one I hugged and kissed the kids. I insisted that they attend Friday night services at the synagogue with Josh and Rachael. I remained composed until they left. Without any pre-op medication to reduce my apprehensions, I dreaded being put to sleep in a place where sterile conditions were questionable and my words were not fully understood.

The nurses placed me on a narrow, antiquated gurney. Tears washed my face. I quivered as I kissed Ira and we exchanged our final "I love you" and "See you after the surgery." While I was wheeled down the hallway, the fear of the unknown inspired me to whisper the Shema prayer: *Shema Yisrael Adonai Elohanu Adonai Echad* (Hear O Israel, the Lord our God, the Lord is One).

At the end of the corridor, I entered a stark operating room with bright lights. I counted heads. One, two, three…eight, nine. The young nurse standing closest to me interrupted my counting.

She gently caressed my forehead and inquired, "Do you have tension?"

I vociferously responded, "Tension? What do you think I feel, lying on this cart?" Meanwhile I drifted back to my counting. *How many people are needed for this procedure? Why are there so many men?*

After a momentary pause, I continued talking. "Everyone in this room is speaking a language I do *not* understand. Why can't everyone in this room speak English?"

My question was never answered. A mask was gently placed over my face and the anesthesia had me drifting off into another place and time.

55

My eyes were closed. I was out of touch with my brain. *Had I taken a Zyrtec before I went to sleep?* My eyes flickered open. The brightness of the fluorescent lights caused me to blink several times. I stared at the ceiling. *Where was I?*

I looked at my body and scanned whatever was in my line of sight. I was in a large hospital ward with cloth partitions. *Oh my God, it's all real. I had a surgical procedure in India!*

A large clock was mounted on the wall to the right. I watched the second hand go round and round. The vague image of an older woman in a uniform now obstructed my view of the clock.

"How're you feeling?"

"I'm very thirsty. Can I have water or ice chips?"

The nurse raised four fingers and said, "Nothing for four hours."

"Please."

"No."

I closed my eyes and drifted off to sleep. Eventually, I was wheeled back into my room and reunited with Ira.

"Ira, I'm a bit fuzzy. What day is it?"

"It's Friday night. We're in Delhi for Josh and Rachael's wedding."

"Yeah, I know that. I just couldn't remember the day."

"Are you feeling okay?" Ira asked.

"All things considered, yes. I just can't believe that I'm here."

"Neither can I."

"Please come closer and hold my hand."

Ira stood by my side and clutched my hand, caressed my head, and said, "Remember Tuffy Tiger in your room. You've always handled tough situations."

"I know. But I didn't want to be in a hospital right before Josh and Rachael's wedding."

"I'll get you out of here as soon as I can."

Early the next morning, I summoned the nurse.

"Where's the doctor?" I asked.

She shook her head and quietly mumbled a few words that neither Ira nor I could understand.

"When is breakfast?" I asked.

"Breakfast?" she repeated.

"Yes. Food." I used hand motions to describe eating. "When can I eat?"

"Later."

The nurse shuffled out of the room.

I turned to Ira and said, "I'm starving."

"Should I try the cafeteria?"

"Don't bother. I'd prefer that you stay."

A few minute later, a short Indian man with yellow teeth and gray hair appeared with a carafe and some crackers. He handed Ira a bill for twenty-two rupees.

Ira shrugged his shoulders as he handed over the money.

As the morning hours waned, the likelihood of my immediate discharge was uncertain, and the nurse became the unlucky recipient of Ira's wrath. A security guard was posted outside my room. I was made to feel like a prisoner until we paid the bill.

A supervisor eventually interceded. Ira was given permission to pay downstairs. A straightforward credit card payment soon became a complex procedure requiring numerous forms. Ira was still negotiating with the cashier on the first floor when the doctor finally entered the room.

"I've been waiting and waiting. Didn't you tell me first thing in the morning?" I blurted.

"You aren't my only patient."

"I realize that. But I'm the only one with a son getting married tomorrow."

The doctor shook his head and said, "Are you ready to leave?"

"I'm more than ready. I'll be lucky to attend my son and future daughter-in-law's luncheon that started an hour ago."

"The biopsy results will be ready to be picked up on Wednesday. Call me if you have any problems."

The doctor left without sharing any information about the recovery process. Under my breath, I mumbled, *what a jerk.*

Time lagged until Ira returned. The security guard continued peering in at regular intervals. A discharge slip became our pass to freedom. I hobbled through the hospital and into the parking lot. My insides were pulling with every tiny step.

Back at the hotel, I laboriously climbed the stairs. I was swearing under my breath. The pulling sensation felt like I had undergone abdominal surgery instead of an endoscopic procedure. Then again, I did have a stent inside of me.

The *mehndi* luncheon was at its tail end by the time we arrived at the Lodi Garden Restaurant. I couldn't wait to hug all of my children. I then sat on one of the wicker chairs placed at the tables. The chairs had red sashes tied in bows and bright red cloths covered the tables.

Rachael and Josh, who was dressed in a cornflower-blue *churidar kurta* with a hand-embroidered, baby-blue collar and cuffs, sailed from one group of guests to the next. Rachael was radiant in her plum and sky-blue *anarkali*, her shiny black hair hanging straight with a slight curl at her waistline. Traditional red-and-white bangles cuffed the lower part of her arm. I couldn't imagine how she was coping with the events of the past few days. Earlier in the week, she was left dangling with the possibility that Josh had a catastrophic disorder and then a few days later she was driving me to the ER. Despite one doctor's insistence that the wedding be delayed because Josh's future was uncertain, Rachael was not deterred. What an extraordinary introduction to the Bornstein family.

I looked at Josh. My eyes watered. Did he look thinner or was it just the narrow cut of his long kurta that accentuated his tall stature? He still had a healthy appetite whenever I dined with him. Could I rely on outward appearances to assess his health? He had undergone extensive testing and an overabundance of Indian specialists had seen him. Despite it all, the cause of his high platelet count remained elusive. I just wished that Ira and I could convince him to have an American evaluation. After all, he was an American living in a foreign environment. But my hospitalization had curtailed any chance of having a heart-to-heart talk. We needed to wait until after he came back from his honeymoon.

Jordan handed me a tall glass of water while Aaron brought me a smorgasbord of Indian food. I guzzled down the first glass and without hesitation asked for another. These tender gestures reminded me that I had raised caring and compassionate men. All of Josh's brothers worried about his lingering platelet issue and expressed their wish that he return to the States. Despite our persistence, Josh remained adamant that he could handle his medical concerns in India. All of us thought that he was making a giant mistake.

I glanced over toward Adam, who was watching Rachel as a traditional *mehndi* pattern was being painted on her hand. Adam seemed more relaxed now that I was out of the hospital. I saw a tiny smile on his somber face. I anticipated a barrage of caustic remarks before he returned to the States. My three younger sons were all against my remaining in India by myself, but Adam was the most vociferous. I couldn't discount their general concern for my welfare, especially in light of my current medical issue, but there was no way that they could comprehend all of the factors that were driving me to teach in India.

Person after person asked how I was doing. I kept a perpetual smile on my face as I tried camouflaging my true feelings. The Sandy that was released from the hospital needed to be resting, but the mother of Josh needed to remain as energetic as possible. My emotional high temporarily lessened the throbbing and the persistent sensation that I needed to pee.

We had a small hiatus between the conclusion of the afternoon party and the party we were hosting that evening. Resting in our hotel room, on a horizontal plane, did wonders for me. I napped peacefully until it was time to leave.

Once inside the Veda Lounge and Bar, I found a chair that acted as my throne as I greeted all of our guests. Other than foraging for food at the nearby buffet table, I remained seated as I watched everyone pulsate to the deafening music played by the DJ. I was disappointed that I couldn't dance at my own son's wedding party, but accepted my sideline position. Ira stood next to me and didn't socialize much. *Was he being protective or was something bothering him?*

Josh and Rachael were beaming and my other sons were dancing among the bouncing bodies. I was fortunate to witness two joyous occasions that as recently as Thursday I had feared I would know only from pictures. Josh and Rachael's love for one another glowed as magnificently as the diamond she wore on her hand. I had to derive pleasure from their intense joy and be relieved that my medical emergency was behind me.

Back in our hotel room, Ira and I sat next to one another in the bed. I gazed into Ira's sad eyes. "What's wrong?" I asked.

"I'm not sure. The accident…the job…your being in India…Josh's platelets…your operation, and the thought of being separated again. Take your pick."

I inched closer to Ira and countered, "Yes, it's overwhelming, but you're detached."

"I hate being without you. I've lost control over my life."

"We're both control freaks, but we need to go with the flow," I said as I put my arm around him.

"After surviving the accident, I want more out of my life. Being separated isn't what I want."

"I agree. We need to live under the same roof."

After Ira turned off the lights, I stared up at the ceiling. Being separated had caused both of us to reevaluate our lives. We realized that something needed to change.

56

On Sunday morning, our family arrived at the synagogue more than an hour before the scheduled ceremony. Long bands of colorful flowers hung between the vertical metal bars of the fence and gate that separated the synagogue property from the street. Inside the sanctuary, narrow silver poles at the four corners of the *bimah* supported a chuppah made of blue velvet with scalloped, gold-fringed edges. On the vertical face of the chuppah were written the words "Judah Hyam Synagogue, New Delhi" in both English and Hebrew. On the far wall was the ark housing the Holy Scriptures.

Ezekiel, a short man wearing a dark suit and a red *kippah* with gold trim, greeted us at the doorway and wished us mazel tov. Ira and I had met Ezekiel during our first trip to New Delhi in February, when we came to meet Rachael's parents. Ezekiel and I had become reacquainted during the Jewish High Holidays. As both the designated leader of the synagogue and the wedding officiant, he was running back and forth directing the custodian to perform last-minute chores. As guests trickled into the tiny sanctuary, Neill and Linda poured the kosher wine that they had brought from Israel.

Ira and I left our younger sons and Rachel in the sanctuary and joined Josh in the courtyard near the front gate. I gripped Ira's hand and tingling sensations raced through my fingers and up my arm. Next, I reached over to Josh and embraced him. He tilted his body so that I could kiss him on the cheek. Minutes before the ceremony was scheduled to begin, Rachael was helped out of a car by her mom and dad. The sun caused all the golden stitching on her ivory sari to glimmer. Her thick black hair was pulled tightly away from her face into a carefully constructed bun at the back of her head. This accentuated her wide smile, the gold choker necklace that hung just below her neckline, and the intricate gold earrings covering her earlobes. I marveled at her striking beauty.

As Josh's parents, Ira and I were to walk him to the chuppah, also known as the marriage canopy. This is a moment that all Jewish parents await from the time of a child's birth. I looked up at Josh and then Ira. The boy who had kindergarten dreams of being a paleontologist, and as an adolescent had insisted on having a bar mitzvah in Israel, was now a successful venture capitalist in India on the verge of being married in the only synagogue in New Delhi. My eyes started to water and tingling sensations flittered inside me.

Ezekiel, holding a leather-bound book titled *Guide to Bene Israel Ceremonies*, began serenading us in Hebrew. With Ira to Josh's right and me to his left, we followed Ezekiel into the synagogue, where a handful of knowledgeable Indian Jews supplemented his singing. Josh was wearing his bar mitzvah kippah and holding his *tallit* bag and the script for the ceremony. As we approached the bimah, I heard the melodious chanting, "*Torat moshe emet oonvooato. Baruch adie ad shame t'helato.*" I led Josh and Ira onto the small stage. The three of us stood under the chuppah, the symbolic home of the bride and the groom, while Ezekiel went back outside.

I gazed at my handsome son, who was dressed in a cream-colored *sherwani* highlighted with gold embroidery, cream-colored pants, and specially made shoes called *jootis*, which resembled those worn by medieval court jesters. Reaching behind Josh, I squeezed Ira's hand and smiled. Flashbacks from Josh's childhood invaded my thoughts until I faintly heard Ezekiel singing the same words as before. I dabbed my eyes gently, trying not to smear my mascara.

Everyone turned to the doorway. Rachael's radiance and immense beauty captured the crowd's attention. Rachael's parents stood by her side and walked toward the bimah as Josh sang his version of "Yonati Ziv Yifatech" ("My Beloved Is a Dove.") This sixteenth-century, four-stanza Hebrew *piyyut* was composed by Rabbi Yisrael Najara, a noted Sephardic poet, Lurianic Kabbalist, and scholar. Ira and I had been told that for many generations, the singing of this *piyyut* had been an integral part of Sephardic Indian wedding ceremonies for the Bene Israel community in India.

This ritual stood in sharp contrast to the staid procession of a typical American Jewish wedding, where the groom has a passive role. Not only did Josh sing the *piyyut*, but he also led parts of the marriage ceremony. In America, few would consider making any jovial comments during a solemn wedding ceremony. But the atmosphere inside the Judah Hyam Synagogue was cheerful and lighthearted as Ezekiel made a series of humorous remarks. Josh and Rachael appeared at ease and natural as the culturally diverse crowd laughed freely. Droplets splashed on my face, not out of sadness but from pure joy. I was genuinely content with Josh's choice and knew that their union was indeed meant to be.

Rachael, in her flowing, cream-colored sari with the outer edge draped over her head, stood under the chuppah next to Josh. Their hands were interlocked. Ezekiel then asked Josh to circle his bride seven times. In America, a Jewish bride traditionally circles her groom seven times. It is unclear where this deviation in custom came from.

As Josh put on the multicolored Joseph's coat *tallit* that his Grandpa Buddy and Grandma Shirley had given him for his bar mitzvah almost seventeen years earlier, my face glowed. Oh, how I wished that my in-laws and the extended family could share this moment with us. Some couldn't attend for health reasons, while others couldn't afford to devote time or money to overseas travel. These were reasonable explanations. Yet there remained a sense of emptiness. I swallowed hard as I remembered my father and sister, who for irrational reasons had chosen not to celebrate my wedding over three decades ago.

Our good friends Kay and Cary were called to the chuppah to be the designated witnesses. Ezekiel, however, preferred having two males. Josh's Jewish friend, Mark Kahn, was thus asked to replace Kay at the last moment. The traditional *ketubah* signing, which usually occurs prior to the ceremony, actually occurred a little later under the chuppah. Josh and Rachael had selected a gold leaf *ketubah* that was handcrafted in Israel and purchased at Hamakor in Skokie, Illinois.

Josh and Rachael signing the ketubah

Small strings were tied to each of the two wedding rings, which were then gently dipped into a glass goblet filled with red kosher wine. Josh recited a series of scripted Hebrew blessings as Ezekiel and two Indian men responded in Hebrew to Josh's words by chanting additional words at designated points. Josh and Rachael then shared the sweet kosher wine. This was followed by some Hebrew words and the traditional breaking of the glass. Rather than using his foot, Josh stooped down and used a rock. Since Indian Jewish grooms were traditionally either barefoot or wearing soft-soled shoes, a rock was more practical than a foot. I looked down at his unusual shoes and giggled. I never ever imagined Josh getting married in India.

Each placed their specially made platinum bands on the other's right forefinger with the appropriate blessings in Hebrew and English—"Behold you are consecrated to me with this ring according to the Law of Moses and Israel." I looked down at my ring and then at Ira's and then up to his face. Ira was the happiest I had seen him since he had arrived in India.

The *ketubah* was then taken out of its protective container and Rachael's father read the English. Following the *ketubah* reading, Josh and Ezekiel recited another series of prayers. Ezekiel poured two glasses of wine and held one while Josh and Rachael jointly held the other. Ezekiel proceeded to sing the traditional Seven Blessings in Hebrew. Upon the completion of the blessings, Josh and Rachael shared the wine.

Ezekiel first blessed Josh and then Rachael by placing his hand on their foreheads and reciting the traditional prayer. Tears were welling up in my eyes and I anticipated a flood. Neill, Linda, and Reuben (Rachael's father), added an impromptu choral version of a Hebrew prayer called *Y'varechacha*. Ezekiel instructed Josh and Rachael to go to the Holy Ark and kiss the Torah. I looked toward the Ark with unsurpassed happiness. Before departing for the reception, Ezekiel asked the guests to partake in a small cup of kosher wine.

With an estimated population of fewer than 5,000 Jews in a country of 1.21 billion, I was in awe over the chance of Josh and Rachael meeting one another. Only two other weddings had taken place in this New Delhi sanctuary since the 1970s. Ira and I are indebted to the mutual friends who had brought Rachael and Josh together when a two-and-a-half-hour flight physically separated them.

When Josh accepted an Indian position in 2004, I never dreamed he would marry a Jewish woman whose family was part of the largest group of Indian Jews, the Bene Israel. The exact origin of these Jews remains open to speculation among historians. Rachael's family believes they are descendants of the fourteen Jews who were shipwrecked at Nowgaon on the Konkan coast, approximately twenty miles south of Mumbai, just prior to the Maccabean revolt in 175 BCE. Today, two other distinct groups of Jews, the Cochin Jews and the Baghdadi Jews, comprise a minuscule percentage of the total number of remaining Jews in India.

Bountiful rays of sunshine fell upon the guests, who were scattered all over the gardenlike setting at the India International Centre. While I would have preferred mingling with the reception guests, nagging pain prevented me from doing what a mother of the groom would typically do. I resembled a wallflower at a teenage dance sitting by the refreshments instead of a gregarious teenager openly socializing with her peers.

I spotted my friend, Sara, and her family sitting at one of the round tables. The last time I had seen her was when Josh, Rachael, and I dined at her New Delhi apartment in October. I sat down next to her and talked.

After hearing my hospital tale, she frankly said, "Maybe you should have run away in the middle of the night."

Her glib remark took me back to our Yom Kippur conversation, when I expressed my concerns about living apart from Ira. Now, months later, my predicament had become more complicated with my recent medical issues and IST's intransigence. I wasn't going to dwell on my impending decision— I wanted to enjoy the festivities as much as possible.

For the remainder of the reception, I sat at a table resting my weary body. The adrenaline rush of the past two days was waning and the impact of the surgical procedure was taking its toll. I asked one of Josh's friends, who had a full command of Hindi, to help us rebook our evening flight. I was too weak to maneuver through the airport. I was exhausted and unsettled. I could barely keep my eyes open.

Many of Josh and Rachael's friends came by to chat. I had met many of them previously during my dinners with Josh in Bangalore. One of Josh's physicians, a guest at the wedding, had asked us to convince Josh and Rachael to delay their departure to New Zealand. Without a firm diagnosis, neither Ira nor I considered interfering with their honeymoon plans. We simply nodded our heads as the woman spoke.

Were her concerns warranted? We didn't know.

Like all special occasions, the time flew by. The photographer took our customary family pictures with two additions to our family—Rachael-India and Rachel-USA. The once-vibrant crowd began to dissipate as the sun shifted in the sky. The fountain area lost its luster as deep shadows encased it.

Bornstein family at the wedding reception

"Can you believe Josh is married?" Aaron exclaimed as we strolled back to our car.

"Rachel and Adam, we'll be celebrating your *simcha* next," Ira said.

"Something was missing without the hora," Adam remarked.

"Josh wanted the reception outside. Only later did they find out music wasn't allowed," Ira responded.

"Rach, aren't you looking forward to the chair thing?" Adam asked.

"Yep, can't wait," Rachel replied.

In the middle of the night, our three younger sons and Rachel were in the process of starting their return journey to the States while Kay and Cary were taking a train to a town near the Ganges River to explore Hindu culture. All of Josh's out-of-town friends were scattering as well. Before Kay and Cary departed, I hobbled down to their room.

As I entered, I hugged Kay and said, "Thanks for coming. I'm glad that you shared this simcha with us."

"We didn't want to miss a once-in-a-lifetime experience."

I sat down on the desk chair. "I'm sorry you had to see me out-of-control. The pain was close to being unbearable."

Kay stood next to me and said, "Friends need to be around for both the good and the bad."

"I know, but I wasn't myself."

Kay reached for my hand and said, "You and Ira need to take care of one another."

"Yeah, I agree." My eyes began to water. "It's been one challenge after another."

"Please consider staying in the United States," she pleaded.

"Why?"

"It's not good to be apart. Ira needs you."

We embraced tightly as we said good-bye. As I walked up to my room, I knew that I was heading toward another crossroad.

Ira and I left for Bangalore the following afternoon. Not until the morning did Josh and Rachael choose to disregard the doctor's recommendation about canceling their honeymoon. Ira and I took off for Bangalore at the same time that Josh and Rachael left for New Zealand.

57

W hen I opened the door to my room back at school, I saw a brown, wooden table against the far wall, a clean bathroom, and a nongritty floor. Elizabeth obviously had arranged to have my room cleaned and had convinced Mohan to add the table. After months and months of eating my meals either standing or at my computer desk, I finally had a designated place to eat.

Ira and I sat on my unforgiving mattress.

"You said your bed was hard, but this is worse than Adarsh Gardens."

"I told you. But look how I've customized my room with my handmade Cochin coverlet, my Delhi candle, and this lovely Diwali gift from Asha. I just need some framed artwork."

"Don't get carried away."

"Other than Elizabeth and Marissa, no one has a clue about my Colorado life. I miss everything I left behind."

"Left behind—I can't believe you've survived. Honestly, I couldn't have done it."

"So many times, I've visualized different rooms in our houses or remembered the smells of my favorite recipes."

"Talking about food, what's there to eat?"

We ate one of my daily specials—cold cereal with soy milk, dried fruit with nuts, and some Australian cookies that we had bought at the airport.

It was comforting to have Ira sleeping next to me, but the negative effects of the hard bed, the occasional leg cramps and night sweats, the biting bugs, and the horrendous street noise remained. Neither of us slept soundly.

"Be careful. The floor is exceptionally slippery after showering," I cried out as Ira went into the bathroom.

"I'm almost done with physical therapy. I don't need any more problems," Ira yelled back.

"Do you want to eat in the cafeteria or are you ready for another daily special?"

Ira sighed. "Whatever."

"We'll try the cafeteria and then you can always come back and eat more."

On the way to breakfast, we saw Elizabeth with her right arm cradled in a sling.

After introducing Ira, I said, "Are we in competition for medical sympathy? What happened?"

"After you called on Saturday, I was in a hit-and-run accident."

"What?"

"I was crossing the street and a motorcyclist knocked me over."

"Was anyone with you?" I prodded.

"Nope. I had to pick myself off the street."

"How did you get to the hospital?"

"I took the city bus back to campus and then the school nurse took me to the hospital."

I shook my head. *How did she manage an hour-long bus ride followed by another hour in a car.* "What's the prognosis?"

"The doctor is recommending surgery."

"Maybe you should seek a second opinion," I offered.

"I can't afford surgery. Right now, I'm more concerned about proofreading all of the PY report cards."

"Can't Pari do that?" I questioned.

"No, I'm the only one who can check the English."

As we parted company, I said, "Thanks for fixing my room. I really appreciate it."

It was typical of Elizabeth to minimize her plight. I assumed that she

would work more and more hours in an attempt to lessen her pain and suffering. She fit the stereotype of a stoic Brit.

After breakfast, we walked to my classroom. I asked Ira to contact the
boys. Adam picked up the phone after just a few rings.

"Hi Mom," Adam answered in lackluster voice. "Don't worry. Rach and
I are sitting in a police car."

"What happened?"

"It's a long story. We missed our connection to Philadelphia. Instead, we
took a flight to DC and then rented a car."

"Okay, then why didn't you wait for the next flight to Philadelphia?"

"We needed to get back to work and didn't anticipate a deer hitting us."

"A deer?"

"Yep."

"Are you sure you're all right?"

"Yeah. The airbags deployed, the front of the car was demolished, and
Rach's door jammed. The engine is still smoking. The deer is a different
story."

"Why?"

"It was shot."

I was shaking as I retold the story to Ira. Their accident was like a scene
out of a movie. Being halfway around the world made mishaps like this more
foreboding, since our ability to be useful parents was totally diminished.

Ira's cell phone rang. We assumed it was Adam calling back. Instead, it
was Aaron. He was running a high fever and had spent most of his time in
the airplane's bathroom vomiting and experiencing diarrhea. A doctor on
board the plane had insisted that Aaron be taken to an ER when the international flight made a stop in Chicago. He was in an ambulance heading to
a nearby hospital. This second unexpected event increased my anxiety level
tenfold.

We quickly placed a call to Jordan's cell phone. We were thankful to hear
that he was back safe and sound in Colorado. Ira and I had no intention of
talking to the newlyweds unless they contacted us.

My excitement over returning to my students was dampened by my sons' distressing news. I took a few moments to rebound before my students found their way to their seats. Several of the kids asked me to grade their book reports. They were patiently waiting for additional scoops so the class could reach the next award level. After everyone found his or her respective place, I started with my routine. "Good morning."

Their programmed response followed: "Good morning, Miss Sandra."

I briefly introduced Ira before he retreated to my guest room to make follow-up calls to Aaron and Adam.

I apologized to the class for not returning the previous day. I knew it must have been disruptive to have both of their teachers gone at the same time. Mahi had left to attend her brother's wedding two days after I left, and she would return tomorrow.

Jonathan raised his hand and asked, "How can you be here if you had an operation?"

"I had a simple operation to remove a kidney stone."

I called on Emily. She innocently asked, "You swallowed a rock?"

There were snickers and jeers from several of the boys.

I reprimanded the boys. Then I paused as I tried to choose my words carefully. I couldn't leave anyone thinking that I had eaten a rock. I did my best to explain in a simple way that unwanted stones can form in the body when you eat certain foods and don't drink enough water. I went on to explain that sometimes doctors have to remove these undesirable objects. By the end of the discussion, the students understood what had happened and the class had received an added bonus—a lesson on how to avoid kidney stones.

Later that day, I initiated a discussion on the writing process. I invited the students to tell me why they sometimes ignored my suggestions.

Arjun interrupted before I could call on anyone. "Miss, Miss, sometimes I can be lazy."

After that I called on Kabir. "Miss, I forget or I have too much maths and science work."

"Are these good excuses?" I questioned. I scanned the class and saw most of the kids shaking their heads no.

I motioned next to Amit, who added, "I don't always understand what you want."

I queried further, "If you don't understand, why don't you ask questions?" He shrugged his shoulders.

Neha caught me off guard when she boasted, "Gee, your corrections aren't always right. My sentences are better."

I heard muffled giggles coming from all four corners of the room.

I responded simply, "The final draft is always your choice. To improve your writing, revisions should be made."

Asha was especially thoughtful. She couldn't believe the calamities that had befallen my family. The next day, she brought me an assortment of fresh fruit, cheese, and multigrain bread. Her kindness made it possible for Ira and me to eat in my room.

Coming back to campus had shed new light on my situation. My family's words, Kay and Cary's concerns, and Sara's comment had convinced me that I should resign. But now that I was back in the classroom with the kids, I had second thoughts. There were so many things that I was planning. How could I simply pick up and leave? I couldn't just quit. Yet I couldn't disregard my medical issues. If there was any possibility of staying, the living conditions at the school would have to change. The urologist in Delhi had ardently insisted that I talk to the school about providing a diet that included more fruits and steamed vegetables and fewer spicy sauces. I also had to be more conscious of my hydration.

While I was teaching, Ira tried doing some IST work. He chose to work from the school rather than commute to the Electronic City office. After all, he had paid for his international ticket because Vinay and Suraj believed his presence in India was not warranted. After his stellar American legal career, Ira was disheartened to be so marginalized by an Indian company. He had never fully appreciated my daily doses of Internet hassle until he attempted to use the school's wireless connection.

Mahi returned on Wednesday from her brother's wedding. Coincidentally, her brother was married on the same day that Josh and Rachael had been. I was sitting at my desk when she strutted into the room during the morning break.

"Have you finished your report cards?" she queried.

"Remember, mine aren't due until next week."

"Can we talk about your comments?"

I raised my eyebrows and responded, "I haven't written them yet."

"I just want to talk."

"Okay."

Our meeting was contentious. Mahi wanted to avoid controversy with the parents. Since the parents were accustomed to seeing high marks, she asked me to inflate my grades. In her opinion, it was better to be dishonest and avoid complaints than to be frank and possibly incur the wrath of disappointed parents. We had already seen that during the parent-teacher conferences.

My integrity as a teacher was at stake. I wasn't going to fabricate grades simply to appease the parents' egos. Several years before, I had been asked by a school director to lie about ethical issues. I had flatly refused to be a pawn. No way was I going to purposely mislead parents now.

That evening, in my guest room, Ira and I celebrated the first night of Chanukah. This was the first time in thirty years that we were not joined by at least one of our children and weren't feasting on potato latkes or *sufganiyot*. We were overwhelmed with a sense of emptiness as we sang "Maoz Tzur," a song dating back to the thirteenth century.

The following night, we took Marissa and Elizabeth out for dinner in nearby Whitefield. This outing gave Ira the chance to become acquainted with my Kerala companions. Ira finally had an opportunity to eat a filling meal, and we later stopped at a grocery store for more perishable foods.

On Friday, Ira and I went to see a Bangalore urologist for my post-op visit. He was a friendly chap whose bedside manner was diametrically opposite to that of the New Delhi urologist. He was genuinely concerned about my well-being and asked numerous questions about my living conditions. If

I had any doubt that KIS would change my diet and accommodations, he suggested that I stay in the United States after winter break.

He recommended that I undergo an extracorporeal shock-wave lithotripsy to pulverize the kidney stones in my left kidney before taking my transatlantic flight. His logic seemed rational. I was surprised that the New Delhi urologist hadn't discussed any future treatment for the remaining stones even though the stones were the same size as the one that was removed surgically. As long as Ira would be with me for this noninvasive treatment, I hesitantly agreed.

We had missed the cafeteria lunch period. Upon returning to my room, I apologized for the limited food options and heated up water in my hot pot for tea.

"Sandy, I'm happy we missed lunch. The food sucks."

"The cafeteria offers more choices."

"Most of that food looks like diarrhea. It's disgusting," Ira responded.

"That's Southern Indian cuisine. I don't care for it, either."

"Between the water and the food, no wonder you lost weight."

I grabbed a few crackers with cheese and headed toward my classroom.

My afternoon classes went by quickly. After school, we shifted to Josh's apartment and then joined Asha for dinner. The restaurant that Asha chose was located on a main street in a well-known part of Bangalore. Despite this, our inept driver ended up stopping five times on the ten-mile journey to ask others for help—in addition to asking Asha three times if she knew the way. It was a treat to meet Asha's husband and some of their friends. She and her husband commiserated with my predicament and agreed that the administration lacked warmth and hospitality. Asha was the only Indian faculty member who ever made an effort to meet me off campus.

The following morning, the driver arrived on time and took us promptly to the hospital. I was asked to lie on a specially designed table. Under my hip area was a retractable, worn-out cushion. The technician rolled an ultrasound wand with a gooey, cold substance over my flesh so he could visually observe the kidney stones. He then calibrated something on the adjacent machine, using old-fashioned dials that brought on a hammering sound and a pulsating sensation. *Why am I doing this? Maybe I should have waited until I returned to the States.*

I had only a small amount of discomfort. But as the frequency of the sound waves increased, the thumping sounds intensified and the pain level skyrocketed. The man told me to expect additional throbbing because one of the stones was near a bone. I clenched my teeth and made fists with my hands while my forehead and backside grew increasingly damp. The technician gently asked how I was doing. I nodded, thinking, *Please stop this machine!*

I breathed deeply and soon recalled the view from our Summit County home, looking out on Buffalo Mountain and Lake Dillon. Unfortunately, this Lamaze technique had no effect. I waited for the machine's maddening sound to cease. Another ultrasound confirmed that the stones had disintegrated. I was escorted to an adjacent room, where I was directed to lie on a soiled sheet. I vowed that I would do whatever was necessary to avoid developing any more kidney stones. I later learned that painkillers or sedatives are usually prescribed to patients who undergo this same procedure in the US.

I eventually joined Ira in the waiting room and hugged him tightly. We then went across the street for lunch. The hotel was swarming with police and army personnel. Everywhere we turned, we saw armed men and women in uniform, as well as a handful of undercover agents with earpieces. Ira and I played a game trying to guess what type of person required such a display of weaponry and tactical support. The following day, we read in Josh's newspaper that French President Sarkozy was a guest in the hotel. We rolled on the ground in laughter when we read that Sarkozy had brought his own food and chefs for his stay in India.

Sunday was my last day with Ira. Just as our boys had wanted to kidnap me and put me in their luggage, I fantasized about taking Ira hostage and forcing him to stay. I didn't want to be alone again.

I phoned Margot, who was one of Josh's Jewish friends, to see if she was going to attend the Chanukah party that evening at the Chabad House.

She answered the phone while she was riding in a taxi in Indonesia. She promised to see me before I returned to the United States and recommended that I call our mutual friend, Rohan. Ever since this guidance counselor had abruptly left KIS, I had wondered about him.

Rohan was delighted to hear from me. He was still unemployed. I bluntly asked why he left. Without any reservation, Rohan stated that he had butted heads too many times over his sense of right and wrong. In a nutshell, Rohan had a sound reputation that he was unwilling to tarnish. The administration had expected him to edit and proofread the students' college essays and the teachers' recommendation letters for college admittance. In too many cases, the quality of the work was so poor that it had become a question of ethics, inasmuch as his credibility would be at stake if he made all the requisite corrections. One of the administrators had even insisted that every essay be letter perfect without even a comma out of place. Rohan didn't want to mislead highly acclaimed American, Canadian, and British colleges into thinking that the recommendations were written by teachers with a complete command of the English language or that the students were proficient writers. As someone who valued integrity, I fully understood his unwavering position.

In all fairness, I have never heard the administration's side of the story. When I candidly asked Elizabeth about Rohan, she flippantly said, "Don't worry about him. He's an odd guy." Rohan's side of the story was believable. I had observed firsthand some of the secondary teachers' limited command of the English language. Ira and I witnessed the extraordinary amounts of time that Elizabeth had taken to rewrite the primary unit report card comments. Mahi had previously asked me to correct her comments because she lacked confidence in her writing. Equally relevant was the fact that the fifth-grade English teachers had exhibited a lack of proficiency in grading essays and simple spelling tests. This was a serious reflection on the subpar capabilities of the teaching staff.

Ira joined me on another excursion to UB City. We went to my favorite Sunday brunch restaurant, Café Noir. After eating brunch, we purchased sandwiches for dinner and my usual goody bag of French bread and pastries,

"Near Whitefield."

"That's far. We'll come to you."

I hesitated. "It's too far. I'll manage."

"We're responsible for the Jews in Bangalore. Candles shouldn't be lit alone."

I provided directions and then walked to Dr. Wilson's office. *Was my request going to create an issue?* I knocked on the principal's door. "Do you have a couple of minutes?"

"No! I'm too busy. Please make an appointment."

"Um, this can't wait. I promise it'll be less than a minute."

"Okay."

"The Bangalore rabbi is coming to light Chanukah candles. Where can I meet with him?"

"Does it have to be tonight?"

"Yes, he's on his way."

"I'll get back to you."

I was perplexed as I tiptoed out of his office. *Would he actually consider denying me the opportunity to celebrate Chanukah with other people? What would I say to Ariel and Shira if the principal said no?* I walked down the steps and Mohan approached me. I could use my classroom. He would contact the front gate to let the guards know that guests would be arriving.

The rabbi, his wife, and their two small children arrived two hours later. I escorted them to my classroom. After lighting the chanukiah, we sang a medley of Chanukah songs and ate the sufganiyot they had brought. I, in turn, gave them a couple of packages of chocolate *gelt* for their children. I spent time getting to know Ariel and Shira. They were worried about how thin I looked and that I didn't have facilities to cook my own food. At times, language was a barrier as they struggled to find the appropriate word in English.

"Ariel, I respect your orthodoxy so I won't hug you. I'm just so happy you came."

Shira extended her arms and said, "You can hug me."

I gently embraced her slender body and said, "Lighting candles alone was awful. You answered my prayers by coming tonight."

The next morning, I passed one of my teaching colleagues and we started to converse. She looked down and spotted my royal blue socks with colorfully embroidered Jewish symbols—dreidels, Stars of David, and menorahs.

She asked, "How can you wear religious symbols on your feet?"

I replied, "Why not?"

"Why would you step on holy symbols?"

"The embroidered symbols are just decorations. They're not considered holy."

She politely said, "I understand." Her expression, though, didn't match her words.

In order to understand her viewpoint, I tried looking through her Hindu eyes—the eyes of someone who worshipped idols and symbols. Our respective traditions attributed different meanings to symbols.

Later that day, I introduced the two fourth-grade classes to Chanukah using a multimedia approach. I used a charming, animated YouTube video to provide the historical meaning. To show different ways that Jews celebrate the holiday, I taught a few Chanukah songs with the lyrics projected on slides and chanted the blessings while lighting the candles on my portable chanukiah. I then read *The Christmas Menorahs: How a Town Fought Hate*. I was able to provide the teachers with a selection of colorful plastic dreidels.

To my disappointment, logistics prevented me from making latkes for these students, as well as for my class. KIS was missing the true essence of education, which I believe is the ability to connect ideas with practical and authentic applications. What better way for the students to learn about Chanukah than to see how Jews actually celebrate the holiday.

The students were attentive when I read *The Christmas Menorahs: How a Town Fought Hate*. We then discussed the universal message gleaned from the people's response in Billings, Montana. Religious intolerance was unacceptable everywhere, and people needed to take action against bigotry and hate. We discussed the actions of the non-Jewish people in Billings who had rallied to support the city's small Jewish population in the 1990s. I briefly mentioned other points in history at which intolerance had resulted in mass killings of Jews, and I provided examples of righteous Gentiles who had risked their lives protecting Jews.

I called on a girl sitting with her legs crossed. She said, "Miss, why have so many people tried to murder the Jewish people?"

"That's a great question. I don't have time for a complete explanation. The simple answer is that some people can't accept others who are different."

A boy with glasses who was rocking back and forth asked, "Aren't there other groups that kill one another?"

"Of course. Wars and controversies are never ending. Just look at the ongoing problems between India and Pakistan."

Next, I called on a tall, lanky boy sitting near the back wall.

"What about the Jews in India?"

"Jews have lived peacefully in India. After 26/11 (November 26, 2008)— the date of terrorist assaults in Mumbai—the Indian government made additional efforts to protect their Jews. Every synagogue I have visited is guarded."

After fielding a few more general questions, I brought the discussion back to the story. I asked the students a hypothetical question. "If you were a child living in Billings, would you display a menorah in your window?"

An Asian girl said, "No Miss, I would be afraid that something bad would happen."

Another girl answered, "Miss, I'm not sure. I'd have to ask my mom and dad."

A few replied, "Miss, I'd want to do the right thing and help the family."

My time for teaching this topic was far too short. I had exposed the children to positive ways that people had responded to hatred and animosity. I hoped that my message was heard. Everyone has the choice to either stand up for others or to remain silent.

By the middle of the week, I had become frustrated by the school's intransigence. Apprehensively, I went to visit Mohan. Finally, I reiterated the list of items that were still on my agenda—steamed vegetables at lunch and dinner, relocation to a cooler room, and the class overhead projector. Mohan told me to visit the cafeteria manager.

On the way back from the cafeteria, I saw Pankaj and Kabir. They were disappointed that I had missed the prep class the previous day. I apologized and told them about my visit with the rabbi and his family. They understood my desire to celebrate Chanukah with other people. Kindheartedly, they offered to join me in lighting the candles. That evening, they listened respectfully as I chanted the blessings and sang a few songs. It was a warmhearted exchange as we talked about the Chanukah books that I had shared with the class. They lingered in the classroom for awhile before returning to the dorm.

Christmas was in the air. The team had decided to allot several periods to developing the Christmas theme in the fifth-grade corridor. Hours were spent decorating the bulletin boards and making assorted ornaments and cards. The Hindu teachers weren't averse to adapting some of the customs of their Christian neighbors. These teachers were puzzled by my refusal to follow any Christian traditions.

Instead of having a holiday program, as is customary in the United States, the primary school devoted many weeks to practicing and preparing for an all-school play. Hours and hours of instructional time were used for this cultural-arts event. American schools wouldn't forgo so much classroom time for a simple performance. Students walked in and out of class on a continual basis, sometimes following the practice schedule and other times spontaneously being removed without notice. As a result, I needed to water down what I was teaching. Tailors were hired to make colorful custom costumes.

Due to Elizabeth's extraordinary efforts, all of the children from kindergarten through fifth grade came together in a magical musical adaption of *A Thousand and One Nights*. Her musical expertise and patience guided this spectacular production, which required a tremendous amount of cooperation in the primary unit. The show's only performance took place on a Friday night.

There was one week left in the term. Everyone—except for Ira, Josh, and Rachael—believed I should pack all my possessions and return home. As the months passed, the likelihood of Ira traveling to India had diminished. If I was healthy, I could cope. Now I was unsure.

But I simply couldn't walk away. I had committed to teaching these students and had developed many ideas for the next term. And I couldn't disregard the possibility that I might be paired with Asha.

A new round of headaches, stomach cramps, and diarrhea, with an additional burning and gnawing feeling in my upper abdomen had begun shortly after the painful shattering of my kidney stones. Once again, the school nurse arranged for me to return to the urologist. He diagnosed gastritis and prescribed an antacid and an antispasmodic drug. He assumed that my stomach was producing too much acid for the amount that I was eating. I was instructed to call him back if I wasn't better in two days.

The final day of the term had arrived. It was a low-key day filled with a Christmas assembly, arts and crafts work, an all-school movie, a party that included a wide array of snack foods brought from home, and an extended recess period.

After lunch, I saw Pari in the hallway. The administration had agreed to the classroom change. I hugged her and said, "Thanks so much. I appreciate your going to bat for me."

"It was a team effort. Elizabeth was also in your corner."

I smiled and gleefully said, "You've made my day."

"Go home and take it easy. If you're still not well, let us know."

"I'm sure that I'll be better soon."

"If not, we'll understand. Your health is your priority."

I embraced Pari one more time and told her to enjoy her vacation time. It wasn't until the kids were immersed in an extended recess that I touched base with Asha. Her blasé attitude and halting speech gave me concern. She showed little interest in talking about our future classroom. I searched for Mahi, but couldn't find her.

Pankaj and Kabir were dismissed early so they could take a bus to the airport.

Both approached and wished me a safe journey. All of the other fifth-graders were released from the field and scattered all over the place. I yelled, "Good-bye and have a great vacation." I walked up to Kamala and said, "Day Zero. You can go home." She put her arms on my shoulders and said, "Thank you." I followed the swarms of students and teachers toward the parking lot. From a distance, Mahi and I exchanged waves. Emily ran up to me and wrapped her arms around my waist. With a big smile she said, "See ya next year."

I went to Elizabeth's office to say good-bye. She confirmed that Dr. Diya and Dr. Wilson saw the merits of a change in the fifth-grade teams. I expressed my concerns over Asha's initial reaction. Elizabeth reminded me that Asha would be the one to start over with a new group of students in midyear. *Was this asking too much of Asha? Would this affect our working relationship? I hoped not.*

Back in my room, I repacked my possessions for the umpteenth time. Being paired with Asha made a huge difference, but was it enough? If Ira never returned to India, what would happen to my marriage? I was in a quandary. My final decision had yet to be made, so I opted to leave about half of my possessions in the guest room. Josh could always retrieve these things if I didn't return. At the last minute, I grabbed Tuffy off the shelf and packed him in my large, rolling suitcase. I pulled my suitcases out of my guest room and stood at the open doorway. I wondered whether I would return.

I spent the next two days in Josh's apartment waiting for my return trip to the States. Just hours before my departure, I entered the Kabini grades into my grade book, typed the students' Kabini poems into a Word document, and took digital pictures of Emily and Kamala's Kabini artwork. While I worked, Christmas songs, such as "I Want to Wish You a Merry Christmas" and "Silent Night" blared from a neighbor's window.

I took my last trek to Café Noir. Now, instead of singing Rogers and Hammerstein's "You'll Never Walk Alone" as I walked toward UB City, I sang Simon and Garfunkel's "Homeward Bound."

The owner of Café Noir, who had previously befriended me, came by to schmooze as I slowly ate a delicious, thin, blueberry waffle and sipped a steamy hot cappuccino. He shared how he missed his wife and three sons, who were living in France. Our experiences overlapped due to the fact that his sons were close in age to Aaron and Jordan. He had a distinct advantage because he periodically traveled back to France to see his family. Neither his wife nor his sons had any desire to leave the culture or the sophistication of France.

My last stop before reaching the airport was dinner with Ariel and Shira. I asked Ariel why my family had encountered so many unfortunate events. He looked to the mystical nature of Hebrew letters losing their potency due to age. Ariel pointed to a possible set of aging *Tefillin* sitting in our Colorado home. I found it unlikely that Hebrew letters could alter the course of nature, but his comments made me continue contemplating what other factors might be controlling my future.

I drew the rabbi further into my life when I inquired about my destiny in Bangalore. *Was there a reason that I ended up living in Bangalore for all these months without my husband? Or was it just a fluke?* Although not mentioning Martin Buber by name, I asked if the idea that "All journeys have secret destinations of which the traveler is unaware" was valid. Ariel was not comfortable with my questions.

Like so many others, Ariel and Shira believed it was a dreadful idea for me to come back to Bangalore. Sanctity of marriage and the home were prime Jewish values, especially for observant Orthodox Jews. Their hearts and souls reached out to me as they expressed their fears that my marriage, my family life, and my health were hanging precipitously over a cliff, awaiting a future disaster.

Their message was simple: I needed to stop living among people who *did not* respect me enough to safeguard my health and well-being. As Ariel talked, I remembered a passage from *Ethics of the Fathers* that my former professor, Rabbi Harold Stern, had discussed. He advised my graduate-level Jewish ethics class to distance ourselves from bad neighbors.

Ariel and Shira did reassure me that they would take care of me if I chose to return. They would continue to deliver weekly challah loaves to the campus. They also offered to prepare kosher meals. I was comforted by their hospitality.

Prior to meeting Ariel and Shira, I had been ill at ease around Orthodox Jews. They oftentimes ignited unnecessary friction because of our differing views on the subject of adhering to rigid religious standards. Sometimes I could see Ariel and Shira's disapproving looks as I talked about my Conservative Jewish traditions or Josh and Rachael's wedding. Despite our differences, they never made me feel that I was at all inferior. They opened their hearts and their home to me without any reservation. My view of Chabad rabbis and their wives was forever altered. Fleeting thoughts that my prayers had mystically caused our pathways to cross remained with me during my long journey from Bangalore to Denver.

Finding My True North

59

"Ladies and gentlemen, welcome to Denver, where the local time is 8:05 p.m. Mountain Standard Time."

The announcement could be heard over the chatter of the passengers gathering their possessions. I hastily unbuckled my seatbelt before the plane was parked at the gate and catapulted myself into the aisle as soon as the captain turned off the "Fasten Seat Belt" sign.

I unlatched the overhead compartment and tried to remove my backpack, tugging at the shoulder strap, but it was stuck. My small stature prevented me from getting the necessary leverage to dislodge it from the compartment. Before I could even look around for assistance, a young man—who could easily have been a linebacker on the University of Colorado football team— came to my rescue and freed my bag. I didn't care if he was trying to be a gentleman. I assumed he was just as eager to be set free. I was grateful that I had made it home, since most of the flights throughout Europe had been cancelled that day. Once inside the airport, my naturally slow pace increased to slightly longer strides. The lingering tugging sensation in my lower abdomen restricted my full range of movement.

Other than my first visit to Israel, I cannot remember another instance when I became so emotional upon entering a country. As I gently blotted away the droplets on my face, I thought of Ira. Our love for one another was responsible for over three decades of incredible memories, yet the past year had brought a chain of events that created an unpredictable life. We had faced each event, sometimes together and sometimes as individuals. Somehow an impregnable bond kept us together, despite the adversity we encountered.

My blissful memories were interrupted by the reality of standing in a line zigzagging to the customs agents' booths. I recalled a medley of patriotic songs that I had not sung since my elementary school days at Lincoln School in Highland Park, Illinois.

"This land is your land…"

I shifted my weight from one leg to the other as I analyzed the number of people ahead of me. How many would go to the booth as couples or as families? Who looked suspicious, causing possible further interrogation by the agent? Only the single man dressed in a red T-shirt, faded blue jeans, and a beanie cap projected the appearance of a potential terrorist. My awareness was heightened after having lived in a country where my purse was checked every time I entered a mall.

I shifted back to the songs.

"God Bless America…"

"Next." The word tore me away from my daydreams. The Asian-American agent was looking my way and motioning slightly with his hand. I skipped like a small child over to the booth with my US passport and immigration paper in hand.

"Hmmm…where are you coming from?"

"India," I replied, as the agent searched for my visa. "I've been working there."

"India?"

"I've been counting the minutes until I could come home. Until I lived and worked in India, I had only a vague idea…"

"I was in the military," the agent quickly countered, cutting me off mid sentence. "I had my share of long stretches away from home. What were you doing in India?"

"I was teaching. It's been a rewarding experience, but the *monkeys* are a bit much."

He chuckled and mumbled, "Monkeys…monkeys."

As soon as I exited the immigration/customs area, I unzipped my purse to retrieve my Blackberry. For months it had been safely tucked away in

Josh's closet. I didn't want to incur excessive international roaming charges. Instead, I had made do with my inexpensive Indian phone and prepaid sim card.

I dialed Ira.

Ira had been parked at the airport for over an hour-and-a-half. This was a rarity, since he is not someone who typically sits around waiting, especially during the winter holiday season. But this was different. I was coming home.

The airport doors opened like a magical entryway into another world. The air was breathable and clean-smelling. Streets and sidewalks were pristine and all of the voices spoke English. The cool, crisp air hit my body full force. The lightweight, quilted, beige jacket I had on did little to protect me from the first blast of Colorado's refreshing climate. Goose bumps formed quickly on my arms and my teeth chattered softly.

I sat on a nearby bench. Finally, I saw our car. My heart began beating rapidly as my palms came alive with unexpected warmth. Ira leaped out of the car like a young boy running to catch an ice cream truck. He embraced me and lifted me off my feet, which accentuated the floating feeling that had already transformed me. Our mouths drew closer as we passionately kissed one another. We were in our own world, unaware of our surroundings.

As we merged onto I-70, the majestic Rocky Mountains captured my soul. I was on my home turf and within minutes would be in my comfort zone.

Although it had been just a few weeks since I had seen Jordan in India, there was an extraordinary feeling as our eyes met when I walked through the door. When he said, "You're finally home. I've been worried about you since the day you left," a shiver ran down my spine.

While embracing his slender body I replied, "I missed you so much. I'll always love you."

After a light dinner of eggs, I retreated to my room. I lit several aromatherapy candles and soothed my body in a warm bath. What a delight to have hot water flowing freely without having to wait ten to fifteen minutes for a water tank to heat up. As I draped myself in a clean, fluffy, oversized towel, I watched the water swirling down the drain, carrying the residue of a day of traveling and the everyday dirt that clings to a sweaty body. This bath magically removed the trappings of living in India from the outer layers of my skin. My inner turmoil remained, though.

Sleeping became my favorite pastime as my body attempted to overcome the cumulative effects of months of sleep deprivation. Ten or more hours a night, plus a nap during the day, became the norm. Like a flower leaning toward sunlight for its sustenance, my body sought the comfort and security of my thick mattress, clean soft sheets, down comforter, and my specially configured—and dirt-free!—pillow.

Doctors' visits became the focus of my daily schedule. My internist was genuinely concerned and advised me to consider not returning to India. He prescribed a new medication to counteract the over-production of acid, which was the continuing assumption.

The next day, a middle-aged Denver urologist hobbled into the examination room with one shin resting on a movable trolley. He was recovering from an Achilles heel operation and one leg couldn't bear weight. He placed the monitor alongside my head so that I could watch his scope salvage the stent from my body. Local anesthesia did little to offset the sharp pain when the appliance was pulled swiftly but gently from my body. Before leaving the office, the doctor reiterated what I had been told by the two Indian urologists. It was unwise to put myself in a position that would increase the likelihood of more kidney-stone attacks.

Finding a gastrointestinal doctor during the holidays was not going to be easy. Luckily, I managed to get an appointment with one who recommended that an upper endoscopy be performed as soon as possible. The scope detected symptoms pointing to GERD—gastroesophageal reflux disease. My medications were changed once again. Upon learning about my lifestyle in India, the gastroenterologist also recommended that I consider staying home so that my stress level would return to normal.

I was overdue for a dental checkup. Dr. Harwood, a towering man with a compassionate disposition, had been our family dentist since we moved to Colorado. As he lumbered into the cubicle, he greeted me.

"I see that living in India agreed with you."

"You know the Bornstein luck. Can you believe that I needed an operation in India? There were two things I didn't want there—an operation or dental work."

"You're lucky on the second point. The crown on one of your back molars needs to be replaced." He pointed to the X-ray screen and said, "See this darkened area under the crown?"

"I see. How long can I wait?"

"Not more than a month or two."

I squinted as I opened the door leading out of the dentist's office and the bright sunlight hit my face. I turned to my left and gazed at the Flatirons that are Boulder's pride and glory. I was thrilled to be home and happy that my initial round of doctor appointments was behind me.

60

No matter how many times Ira and I drive I-70 to our home in Summit County, I always manage to observe something that revitalizes my appreciation of nature. Like a downpour that momentarily cleanses the smog above a major city, looking at the majesty of the Rocky Mountains refreshed my spirit and cleared away layers of confusion.

The exhilaration of skiing down one slope after another at Keystone Resort a few days later made me cognizant of the natural rhythm of shifting my weight from one ski to the other as I methodically carved my turns. My skier's high was somewhat dampened by the lingering memories of Ira's unforeseeable accident at the same mountain. My insides tightened whenever he was out of view. The trauma from last spring was too fresh. More time needed to pass before the horrific recollections could be stored in a place that didn't allow easy panic and fear. I remained on high alert—an overanxious, doting wife at best.

On one of our ski adventures, we rode the chairlift with a ski patroller. Our conversation reverted back to Ira's terrible accident. I applauded the work done by the men who came to Ira's aid, but regretted that no one had listened to Aaron or Jordan's words. We were delighted to hear that the ski patrol had made Ira's case the subject of much discussion and that they were no longer tying peoples' arms above their heads, as had been done to Ira.

I was on vacation but frequently remembered my students and hoped that they were enjoying their break. I looked through my pictures and recalled all of the incredible moments I had shared with them. I decided to create a slide presentation highlighting the students' artwork and poetry and to make a Smilebox collage of over a hundred pictures. I sent the end product to the parents.

I spent endless hours catching up with family and friends. My conversations with my mother became increasingly more futile. Her barrage of negativity toward my family was divisive and unsettling. I couldn't accept her premise that Ira and our sons had abandoned me in India and were responsible for my declining health. That simply was not true.

Ira and I laughed and cried as we reminisced about the past year. The start of the New Year, 2011, closed the 2010 chapter and engendered a new sense of optimism. I remained ambivalent about returning to India. My procrastination stoked my emotions. The longer I waited to commit, the more my insides burned. Just a handful of days remained until my scheduled flight.

Months before, I had signed a contract to teach at KIS and was then forced to go above and beyond in order to obtain my employment visa while the school did little to assist me. Then, as now, I was obligated to honor my contract. Yet I couldn't look at this commitment in a vacuum. Looking at the big picture, my quality of life had to take precedence. I was still experiencing burning pain in my upper abdomen. My normal sleeping pattern was topsy-turvy. And I needed dental work. Without concrete changes by KIS, I feared that the diarrhea and the constant stomach reflux would continue, and that the kidney stones would return in full force once the temperature skyrocketed in March. The administrators had made a positive gesture by proposing a new teaching arrangement. While this change was intended to relieve the day-to-day stress, the other issues were unresolved.

Most important, Ira's travel schedule remained in doubt. I had no desire to be separated for another five months. The main reason I interviewed with KIS was to see *more* of my husband, not less. The KIS administration was fully aware of my intentions. It was never a secret.

I charted the pros and cons of the situation, always returning to the same thing—IST's original representations, to which it didn't adhere. Suraj and Vinay's callous and obstinate behavior had been wreaking havoc on both our lives. I became angrier and angrier. The truth was straightforward: I had no recourse against Ira's company. But somehow my outrage had become misdirected toward Ira.

I sat befuddled as I watched the sun setting over the mountaintops. I worried about the future of my marriage. Strolling down memory lane and visualizing all the good times that Ira and I had shared only alleviated part of the negativity. Having several heart-to-heart talks was the key.

We were both reading in bed when I looked in his direction and broke the silence. "Ira, we need to talk."

Ira looked up from his book. "About what?"

I breathed in deeply and started talking. "We're back together, but not really."

"What does that mean?"

"You seem less aloof than in New Delhi, but still different." I hesitated.

Ira's voice became louder when he said, "We've gone over this a million times. I can't explain what happened there. I can apologize until I'm blue in the face. I'm not sure you'll ever accept it."

"I can accept your apology if you listen to me. I needed you in India and I need you now."

Ira shifted and became more upright. "You're not the same, either."

"In what way?" I asked.

"Come on. You know. The person I married wasn't always so indecisive. You can't decide what you want to do and what you want out of life."

"I thought that being apart would strengthen our relationship and redefine my career. Looking back, I realize that my judgment was faulty."

Ira's face became flushed when he yelled, "That's bullshit. If anyone is to blame it's the fuckers at IST."

"Do you remember when I used to share excerpts from a tiny book called *Jacob's Ladder*?"

Ira shrugged his shoulders. "Come on, Sandy. More quotes?"

"Please hear me out. This one is relevant," I begged.

"I'll listen."

"It's about a hypothetical moral compass."

"Huh?"

"Maybe I should read the passage."

Ira rolled his eyes as I reached for the book on my nightstand and found the tabbed page.

Noah ben Shea said,

"Our magnetic north is love, for some of us it is fear, for some of us it is power. If love is our magnetic north, we will embrace our experiences with caring and support. If fear is our magnetic north, then we will be ruled by insecurity and doubt. If power is our magnetic north, then control and worry about who is in charge will fill our life. Whatever is our magnetic north is the veil through which we see the world."

I could tell I was testing Ira's patience when he asked, "Why are you sharing this with me?"

"The point I'm trying to make is that *my* magnetic north has to focus on love. I can't return to India."

Epilogue
January 2012

In the darkness of an early January morning, I drove from my mountain home to the entrance ramp for I-70 and headed west. As I glanced to my left and saw wispy layers of white and gray clouds lingering over frozen Lake Dillon, Led Zeppelin's "Stairway to Heaven" started playing on my satellite radio. Only a few minutes later, I exited the highway onto a snow-packed local road. It was ten degrees outside, but the inside of my SUV was a comfortable seventy degrees. As my car sped toward the mountain pass, I anticipated my first day as a sixth-grade teacher at a rural school high in the Rockies.

"Stairway to Heaven" had ended miles ago, but one line drew me back to the events of the past year. Over and over, I heard the words about changing the road I was on. With a new teaching job about to begin, I was returning to a profession that I adored.

I couldn't help but remember my disappointment after I tendered my resignation to KIS. I had cried the morning that I had planned to return to Bangalore and regretted not saying good-bye to my students. I could only hope that my brief tenure at KIS had left the students and faculty with a new awareness of cultural diversity and the necessity to accept people's differences. My interactions with the students and the faculty had enriched my understanding of Indian culture and also provided an amazing opportunity to embrace a multicultural classroom. In India, a day didn't go by that I didn't learn something from my students.

Much time had passed before I could come to terms with my decision to remain in the United States and not return to India. I put aside my hopes and dreams for the students in 5C and my desire to spend more time with Rachael and Josh, and instead chose a return to normalcy and a place by Ira's side. Writing, reflecting on my life, and spending time with my family became my new vocation.

As an ambulance whizzed by me, I recalled accompanying Josh last spring when he visited a platelet specialist at Johns Hopkins Medical Center in Baltimore. The doctor dismissed all of the diagnoses of cancer. Much of what Josh had been told by the Indian doctors ended up being false. On the one hand, I was grateful that Josh never took any of the high-powered chemotherapy drugs that the Indian doctors had prescribed. On the other hand, I was annoyed that Josh and our entire family had spent months worrying unnecessarily about him.

I glanced at the snow that lined the scenic highway. KIS's icy response to my resignation was finally becoming less of a concern as I looked forward to my new teaching position. It's funny how negative situations lose their intense bleakness when hope is reinjected into life. Twelve months earlier, KIS had swiftly, and without notice, contacted the Standard Chartered Bank in India and removed my January paycheck from my bank account without my authorization. I was never paid my final month's salary, either. I lost one-third of my earned salary— almost $6,000 of tax-free income. Additionally, I was out-of-pocket for all of the medical expenses that I had incurred during my two-day hospitalization—almost $2,000.

E-mails to KIS, the Standard Chartered Bank, the US Embassy, and the Reserve Bank of India provided no recourse. For many months, my naïveté prevented me from coming to grips with the realization that the KIS "family" was a charade. Over time, I grew to understand that some intractable situations have no resolution. I had no choice other than to move on.

Just two years before, Ira and I were on top of the world when Ira was offered an innovative business opportunity. Ira's accident and my six-month sojourn in India initiated a crashing blow to our family's stability.

To improve my quality of life, I chose to give up my teaching position at KIS. Just a few months later, Ira was suddenly asked by Vinay to relocate to India on a full-time basis. He was expected to pick up and leave his American life behind and accept a substantial salary cut, receive no Indian housing package, and forgo his American comprehensive medical-insurance policy. After refusing to live in India full-time, Ira's relationship with his employer deteriorated further. Eventually he was terminated and became immediately unemployed without any severance package. Our economic future became uncertain.

I shook my head as I recalled the 2010 *Wall Street Journal* article that acknowledged IST as India's most admired company. I laughed hysterically when I remembered a hypocritical IST e-mail that read, "I don't care how poor someone is; if one has family, one's rich."

The steep, snow-covered mountains alongside the highway sent my thoughts back decades to my days in Dr. Byron Sherwin's class at Spertus College. Byron had made a fleeting reference to a member of a Jewish mystical movement founded in the eighteenth century, who had compared life to a person wearing a totally white outfit with an open ink bottle on his head. As the person walked across a tightrope suspended over a gully, he ran the risk of soiling his clothing or his body if he made a slight mistake. If, however, he made a major mistake causing him to lose his balance, he could fall and be forever lost. By staying in the States, it was natural to have lapses in judgment. But returning to India without Ira by my side would have caused me to fall into an abyss like the deadly ones I was passing on this scenic highway.

Now, as I drove down the other side of the pass, I ruminated over the lessons I had learned. Finding the courage to step out of my safe world of suburbia and live in India allowed me to explore myself in unexpected ways. Had I never resided in India, I would have missed out on a life-altering experience that ultimately enhanced my resiliency, confidence, and passion for life. "A woman is like a tea bag—you can't tell how strong she is until you put her in hot water." And after my time in India, I could not agree more with Eleanor Roosevelt: The depth of my character could not be fully measured until I was forced to live outside of my comfort zone.

Initially, the mere thought of putting aside my cushy Colorado life made me feel off balance. Without a sense of direction, I floundered in a sea of indecisiveness. My safety net of conforming to what was expected of a middle-aged, married woman provided no assistance when I chose to deviate from the norm. In the process of resetting my compass and locating my true north, I reaffirmed my belief that indecisiveness is a by-product of failing to establish goals. I had to know where I was heading before I could choose my path. I grew as a person when I took ownership of my choices and ranked my priorities.

Years earlier, I gained a new appreciation for my body while I spent an extended period of time recovering from a car accident. Now in the wake of Ira's accident, Josh's medical issues, and my time spent alone in a faraway land, I was once again at a crossroad. This time I was contemplating my marriage and my family's well-being. In both instances, unexpected challenges initiated a time of reflection. My situation reminded me of the award-winning children's book, *It Could Always Be Worse*. In that adaptation of a Yiddish tale, the main character learns to appreciate his life after a rabbi suggests ways to make his life more stressful. Like the character in the book, I realized that I should appreciate my life because it could always be worse.

From the start of my journey until the present, I latched onto my faith for support. My Jewish beliefs had become a core element of my personality since the time I started studying Judaism during my college years. In India, where I was far removed from my Jewish roots, I still relied heavily upon my Jewish beliefs as an anchor. Something indescribable pulled me toward my Jewish heritage whenever my journey became tumultuous. My faith was a source of tremendous comfort. I knew that I belonged somewhere even though I was alienated from my surroundings.

Being able to look toward an intangible, spiritual element of life that was far greater than myself made it possible for me to accept the fact that I might never find answers to all the questions I was facing. Acknowledging my faith and having confidence that I could derive personal satisfaction from my efforts enabled me to find some semblance of internal peace when my outside world seemed chaotic. I gained self-assurance to overcome the obstacles that blocked my path. Without my Judaism, I may have remained off course, perpetually living without an internal compass.

Back in Denver, Ira and I started attending a more welcoming synagogue. We eventually changed our membership, hoping that we would regain a sense of community.

The ups and downs and twists and turns of my adventure left me with a clearer understanding of the word "family" and a new appreciation of my family life. Too frequently, the word "family" was insincerely bandied about by KIS, IST, and others. I learned the hard lesson that, despite their assertions, both institutions failed to understand the basic underpinnings of all relationships—honesty, compassion, and respect. Disregarding these attributes made their words and actions ring hollow. Perhaps Ira and I were both naïve to think that large institutions could adhere to the ethical values that we cherished and passed on to our sons. We jointly decided that our family life wasn't going to be disrupted by work environments that corrupted our value system.

This realization enhanced our desire to strengthen the bonds that held our nuclear family together. Ira's terrifying accident and six months of being on my own led Ira and me to treasure our partnership. The concept of *shalom bayit* was only possible if we spent most of our time together. Both of us had agreed to accept this principle when we stood under the chuppah on our wedding day in 1975. The rain shower on our drive to Congregation Ezras Israel, followed by a double rainbow, was a faint memory, but the hopes and dreams encased in that breathtaking moment couldn't be set aside. I concluded that my marriage and my sons and their families were blessings that should never be taken for granted. My family needed to come first and I derived my purpose in life from that fact.

As I entered the city limits and reduced my speed to twenty-five miles per hour, I hummed the lyrics to the song "Don't Stop Believing." I smiled and took in a puff of arid, high-altitude air and coughed slightly. The inside of my mouth was totally parched. The mountain air made it feel as if I had just skied for hours without taking a drop of water. I licked my chapped lips but it didn't accomplish much. I reached over for my water bottle and took a few sips.

I needed to be optimistic and look forward rather than back. My journey to India had exposed me to a plethora of experiences and provided a fresh perspective on life. When I turned off the engine in the school's parking lot, I was opening a new chapter.

I confidently walked into the school and headed down the corridor to my new classroom. I had spent the previous week hanging various items on the wall, organizing the classroom, meeting with the sixth-grade team, reading classroom materials, and preparing lesson plans. Instead of teaching a self-contained classroom like I did at KIS, I would be teaching my home-room class for science, social studies, and half of literacy, while I would have a mixed group of students for math, writing, and the other half of literacy. I would have only one free period plus lunch each day.

For reasons unknown to me, two of the three previous sixth-grade teachers had abruptly left at the end of the fall semester. I didn't know if they were fired or simply quit, and I wasn't allowed to speak with those teachers who left. It didn't matter to me. I just wanted to teach again. I was eager to meet the twenty-seven students in my homeroom class and the additional students who would attend my other assigned classes.

After the bell rang, I greeted rowdy students as they entered the room. My heart automatically started to race. I asked the class to sit down. Many flatly refused. Clapping my hands, counting down from five, waiting patiently, and flicking the lights did little to control the boisterous preteens who didn't segregate themselves by gender. Much to my dismay, I raised my voice substantially in order to be heard. I cringed whenever I yelled.

Simple activities, such as filling out an information survey or drawing pictures representing individual traits, were met with opposition. Many forms were intentionally left undone or deliberately thrown on the floor. I had wanted to start a new set of classroom pictures. Most of my new students buried their faces in their hands whenever I approached with a camera. I recalled how my Indian students had smiled when their pictures were taken and how eager they were to learn.

All classrooms have a handful of students who present behavior or learning issues, but in this situation the number of students who either refused to listen or were argumentative and outright rude made up more than half the class. I was constantly compared in a less than favorable way with their former teacher. I heard a constant refrain of "We like Mrs. T better." One student said, "You're going to have a hard time earning our respect." Other students snickered and whispered, "Just wait."

Few exhibited self-control. They didn't want to listen to any announcements made over the PA system and refused to wait for dismissal. When it was time to switch classes, they bolted from the room, even if I was in mid sentence or writing something on the board.

In math class, I wrote review problems on the whiteboard. A handful responded. Many didn't come to class with a pencil or a notebook. None had mastered their multiplication tables or could place the numbers 4/5, 11/3, and 37/8 correctly on a number line. *How was I going to teach converting fractions to decimals or equivalent fractions?* The issues with the curriculum weren't limited to math. The textbooks and materials were beyond the grasp of most of the students.

I knew from the abysmal standardized test scores posted online that the school district was struggling, but I attributed these poor state rankings to a high number of second-language learners and the significant number of subsidized lunches. However, I couldn't help but wonder what else was happening. The negative attitude toward adult authority and school in general was shocking.

The other newly hired teacher voiced similar concerns. The oversized stuffed pillows in her reading corner were thrown around her room and the students periodically erased her writing from the board. She had received a comparable welcome. After the students left, she asked for a hug. We embraced.

Driving home, I was overwhelmed and wished that I had brought Tuffy Tiger for support. I had never experienced such a disastrous first day or witnessed such horrendous behavior. The dark shadows formed by the towering mountain peaks intensified my feelings of despair. *Would I have the stamina to put this class back in order? Was it even possible?*

I loved teaching and enjoyed establishing relationships with my students. But now, I was in a position where only some students cared to listen and most ignored me. *How much could they absorb in a classroom where the desire to learn was missing?* These students felt empowered to do whatever they chose and to say whatever they wanted without any reservations. *What type of home life did they have? Would I be able to make any connections with these students or would they remain aloof?*

The administration didn't provide any guidelines for dealing with over-the-top behavior. Somehow I needed to reestablish order in the classroom. I pondered several ways to reward positive behavior and different ways to engage reluctant learners. I started making a mental list of former colleagues and mentors to call.

When I reached my driveway at home, I reminded myself to remain optimistic. No matter what happened with my new career path or Ira's future, we had one another and our family. I smiled when Ira and Chloe greeted me at the door. As long as I had my husband and our children by my side, I knew this could be the best year of my life.

Glossary

Afikomen: During the Passover seder, three matzahs are placed in a stack. The middle matzah is broken in two pieces, and the larger piece of this matzah is called the afikomen. It is saved to be eaten after the meal. Many families traditionally hide the matzah and a prize is awarded to the person who finds it.

Aleph Bet: The first two letters of the Hebrew alphabet and the title to a children's song written by Debbie Friedman, z"l (1951-2011).

Anarkali: A traditional item of clothing worn by Indian women, typically on festive or formal occasions. It is figure hugging on the upper torso and then turns into a flared frock below. It is worn with a churidar.

Aron hakodesh: The cabinet in which the scrolls of the Torah are kept in the synagogue.

BCE: Abbreviation for before the Common Era/Christian Era. Used by authors and publishers who are sensitive to non-Christians because it does not reference time by focusing on the Christian creed that Jesus was the Christ.

Bimah: A stage in the synagogue where the rabbi and/or cantor stand.

B'shert: (Yiddish) Destiny. Meant to be or a divinely ordained spouse.

Chabad: A Hebrew acronym for chochma (wisdom), bina (understanding), and daas (knowledge), that was chosen by its founder, Shneur Zalman of Liadi (1745-1812). Chabad or Lubavitch, is the name of a movement of Orthodox Jews belonging to Hasidic Judaism who follow the teachings and customs taught by their rabbis. The movement is known for its emphasis on religious study, hospitality, technological expertise, and optimism.

Chad Gadya: Translated from Hebrew as "One Little Goat"; a song in the Passover Haggadah.

Chanukah (Hanukkah or Hanukah): (Festival of Lights) The eight day Jewish festival of rededication begins on the 25th day of the Hebrew month of Kislev. (November-December). The holiday commemorates the rededication of the Temple by Judah Maccabee in 165 BCE.

Chanukiah: (menorah) A candelabrum with nine branches used during Chanukah. Technically, a menorah only has seven branches.

Chapati: An unleavened flatbread (also known as roti) from the Indian subcontinent.

Charoset: A mixture of fruits and nuts eaten during Passover. Ashkenazic (Eastern European) Jews use chopped apples, nuts, kosher wine, cinnamon, and honey or sugar. Sephardic (Asian, African, and Mediterranean) Jews will usually use raisins, figs and dates.

Chuppah (Huppah): Hebrew for covering or protection. A Jewish marriage ceremony is conducted under a chuppah. The chuppah is mentioned in the Bible. It consists of a square or rectangular cloth oftentimes made of silk, velvet or a tallit. It is supported by 4 staves. The structure symbolizes the future home of the bride and groom.

Churidar: Tightly fitting trousers worn by both men and women in South Asia and Central Asia. The contours of the leg are revealed and fabric gathers at the bottom of the leg to resemble *churis* or bangles.

Dayenu: Translated from Hebrew as "it would have sufficed" or "we would have been satisfied"; a song in the Passover Haggadah.

Diwali: A festival celebrated between mid-October and mid-December for different reasons. For Hindus, it is celebrated by lighting oil lamps, distributing sweets among family and friends, and performing traditional activities together in their homes. It is also known as the "Festival of Lights."

Dreidel: A spinning top with four sides that is used as part of a game during Chanukah.

Dussehra: From the Sanskrit word, *Dasha-hara,* meaning "remover of bad fate." It is one of the most important Hindu festivals in India that celebrates the victory of good over evil.

Erev: Hebrew for "eve." All Jewish holidays, festivals, and the Sabbath begin on the evening of the preceding day at sundown.

Gelt: (Yiddish) Money. Also used to refer to the chocolate coins eaten during Chanukah.

Grogger: A noisemaker traditionally used during Purim services when the Book of Esther is read. It is whirled to create noise to blot out Haman's name.

Haftarah: The prophetic portion of the Bible read in the synagogue immediately after the weekly Sabbath reading of the Torah; it is also read on festivals and holidays.

Haggadah: The booklet used during the Passover seder.

Hag sameach: Translated from Hebrew as "happy holiday."

Halevai: Translated from Hebrew as "I hope or I wish."

Hamantaschen: (Yiddish) A three-sided, filled cookie that is eaten during Purim.

Hora: A traditional Jewish dance that is performed in a circle, usually at weddings.

Ketubah: A traditional Jewish marriage contract.

Kiddush: Hebrew for "sanctification." A special blessing over a cup of wine.

Kippah (kippot, plural): Skull cap, synonym for yarmulke.

Kosher for Passover (Pesach): Foods prepared specifically for Passover that are certified kosher.

K'riah: Hebrew for "tearing." It is the traditional act of tearing one's clothes or cutting a black ribbon worn on one's clothes. It symbolizes grief and anger at the loss of a loved one.

Kurta: A traditional item of clothing worn in Afghanistan, Pakistan, Nepal, India, Bangladesh, and Sri Lanka. It is a loose fitting shirt that falls above or somewhere below the knees of the wearer. It is worn by both men and women.

Kvell: (Yiddish) To burst with pride.

Kvetch: (Yiddish) A chronic whining complainer.

Latkes: (Yiddish) Potato pancakes oftentimes eaten during Chanukah.

Lekhah Dodi: A Hebrew song that is recited in the synagogue at sundown on Friday night to welcome the Sabbath.

L'shana haba'ah b'y'rushalayim: At the conclusion of the Passover seder, Jews recite these Hebrew words, which mean "Next year in Jerusalem."

Mahzor: High Holiday prayer book.

Maoz Tzur: Hebrew for "O Mighty Stronghold," a traditional song that is sung after the lighting of the Chanukah candles. It is commonly referred to as "Rock of Ages."

Mazel tov: Hebrew/Yiddish for "good luck." The phrase is used to express congratulations on a happy or special occasion.

Mechizah: A partition used in Orthodox synagogues that separates men from women during public prayers.

Megillah: Hebrew for "scroll." The best known is the Book of Esther, which recounts the Purim story.

Mehndi: The word *mehndi* is derived from the Sanskrit word mendhikā. A decorative application of henna is applied to the skin in India, Pakistan, Nepal, and Bangladesh, as well as by expatriate communities from those countries. Intricate patterns of mehndi are typically applied to brides' palms and feet before Indian wedding ceremonies.

Midrash: From the Hebrew root darash meaning to investigate or study. The term refers to the compilation of Jewish teachings that fills many of the gaps in the Biblical narrative and provides a better understanding of Biblical commands and prohibitions.

Minyan: A quorum of ten people. Orthodox Jews only include men in the counting.

Mishaberach prayer: A special prayer said in the synagogue for someone who is acutely ill.

Ner tamid: The eternal light seen hanging above the Holy Ark in every synagogue. It dates back to biblical times.

Passover (Pesach): A spring festival that commemorates the Exodus of the Israelites from Egyptian bondage.

Piyyut: A liturgical poem.

Pooja: A religious ritual performed by Hindus as an offering to various deities, distinguished persons, or special guests. It is done on a variety of occasions and in various settings, from a daily pooja done in the home, to temple ceremonies and large festivals, or to begin a new venture.

Purim: Hebrew for "lots." A spring festival that recalls the Book of Esther.

Queen Esther: The Jewish queen married to King Ahasuerus, who is associated with Xerxes (486-465 BCE).

Rosh Hashanah: Hebrew for the beginning of the year. It ushers in the ten days of awe that conclude with Yom Kippur.

Shabbat: The Jewish Sabbath, beginning at sundown on Friday and concluding at sundown on Saturday.

Shalom Aleichem: Hebrew for "Greeting to You," a traditional Hebrew song recited during Friday night services.

Shalom bayit: Hebrew for "peace of the house," tranquility in a Jewish home.

Sherwani: A long coat-like garment worn in South Asia. It is worn over a Churidar. It is often made from heavier suiting fabrics, often embroidered or embellished, and is usually lined.

Shivah: A week-long mourning period following the funeral of a loved one.

Shpilkes: (Yiddish) Nervous energy

Simcha: Hebrew for gladness or joy. The word is used as a noun to mean a happy occasion—a bar/bat mitzvah, wedding, etc.

Sufganiyah (sufganiyot, plural): A jelly doughnut traditionally eaten during Chanukah.

Tallit: A large four-cornered shawl-like garment with fringes at the corners, traditionally worn by men during morning services, evening services for Yom Kippur, and sometimes by the groom at his wedding. Some women have taken on this obligation.

Tefillin: Hebrew origin is uncertain. (Sometimes called phylacteries.) This word is derived from the Greek word meaning to guard or protect. Cube shaped black leather boxes that are attached to the head and the arm and hand with black leather straps. The boxes contain four biblical passages that are handwritten on parchment by a scribe. These ritual objects are mandated in the Bible to be worn during morning prayers except on Shabbat (Saturday) and some Jewish holidays.

Torah: Hebrew for teaching or guidance; the scroll of the first five books of the Bible; can also be used broadly to include the whole Bible.

Yom Kippur: The most solemn day of the Jewish year; the end of the ten days of awe. An observant Jew spends the day fasting, soul-searching, repenting, and promising to do better the following year.

Author Biography

Sandra Bornstein has taught K-12 and college-level students in both the private and public sectors in the United States and abroad. She is a licensed K-6 Colorado teacher with a K-12 linguistically diverse education endorsement. Bornstein earned a bachelor's degree in history and Jewish Studies at the University of Illinois, a master's in Jewish studies at Spertus College, Chicago, and a second master's in education at the University of Colorado, Boulder. While pursuing her master's in Jewish Studies, she wrote *Rose Haas Alschuler: A Chicago Woman's Life of Service 1887-1979* as well as five biographical essays on American Jewish women for encyclopedias. Married to Ira, a lawyer, she has four adult sons and currently lives in Colorado. In 2010, her husband's international job created a unique opportunity to live in India, where she fulfilled her three passions: a desire to travel, a zeal for writing, and a love of teaching.

www.sandrabornstein.com

CPSIA information can be obtained at www.ICGtesting.com
Printed in the USA
LVOW051705160513

334175LV00001B/150/P